WATCH YOUR DREAMS

About the Author

During her life as a prophet, clairvoyant and teacher, Ann Ree Colton interpreted numerous dreams for her students and others. Ann Ree was noted for her spiritual understanding of dreams, her gift for interpreting the prophetic aspect within certain dreams, and her ability to recover *akasic* or past-life records through dreams.

In her dream research over the years, Ann Ree discovered that there are seven dream levels; three lesser dream levels consisting of the reflected actions of men, and four higher dream veils containing the pure reality of the spiritual dramas.

She also observed that there is a progressive process in one's dreams – a communicable sequence revealing the initiatory action in one's life. Over and over she observed the sequential instructing and correcting aspects of dreams, the difference between lower psychic dreams and higher spiritual dreams, and the drama or myth aspects in dreams.

In addition to helping persons better understand their dreams, Ann Ree opened their awareness of the *Night Ministry*, during which one may aid others, research the higher worlds, learn of past lives, and gain prophetic insight into coming events.

Watch Your Dreams, currently in its ninth printing, is a rich, spiritual archive containing the essence of Ann Ree Colton's rare wisdom and knowledge regarding dreams, symbols and the initiatory process. As such, it is an essential tool and guide for dream initiates who seek to understand their dreams, visions and spiritual experiences.

Painting on cover: *"Dream Veils,"* by Jonathan Murro

WATCH
YOUR
DREAMS

by
ANN REE COLTON

A MASTER KEY AND REFERENCE BOOK FOR

ALL INITIATES OF THE SOUL, THE MIND

AND THE HEART

ANN REE COLTON FOUNDATION
OF NISCIENCE, INC.
Post Office Box 2057
Glendale, California 91209

ISBN: 0-917189-18-3
Third Edition
Library of Congress Catalog Card Number: 96-83735

For information regarding the writings and
teachings of Ann Ree Colton write:

Ann Ree Colton Foundation
336 West Colorado Street
Post Office Box 2057
Glendale, California 91209
Telephone: (818)244-0113
Fax: (818)244-3913

Printed in the United States of America
By Griffin Printing, Glendale, California

Dedicated
to
Knowing Dreamers
Everywhere

CONTENTS

INTRODUCTION

by Jonathan Murro

A dream protected the marriage of the patriarch Abraham and his wife Sarah. A dream saved Jacob from Laban. A dream guided Jacob. A dream caused Joseph, the son of Jacob, to be taken as a slave into the land of Egypt. A dream enabled Joseph to attain a position of prominence in Egypt and, eventually, to save his own people and the Egyptian people from starvation. A dream gave Gideon the courage to deliver his people from their oppressors. A dream proved Solomon worthy to receive understanding and great power. A dream enabled Daniel to protect his people from destruction. A dream told Joseph to take Mary for his wife, and to give his son the name Jesus. A dream told Joseph to leave Bethlehem, thereby saving the life of his infant son. A dream protected the Wise Men from King Herod. A dream told Joseph when he should leave Egypt and return to Israel with his wife and young son.

The Holy Bible records these and other significant dreams which contributed directly toward the survival and developmental rise of a people, from the time of Abraham until the time of Jesus.

What is the strange and mighty power of dreams? One may find his first clues to the mystery of dreams by turning to the Holy Bible. If one researches the dreams recorded in the Bible, he discovers that the majority of Biblical dreams relates either to prophetic dreams or to guidance dreams. However, the Bible also contains dreams of warning, instruction and evaluation.

While the Bible is filled with dreams, visions and revelations, societies which have built their cultures upon the truths and wisdom in the Bible do not provide the individual with the answers to questions about inner or spiritual experiences. Even religious bodies provide little or no instruction regarding such experiences – yet dreams sometimes have deep religious meaning and significance.

This important book by Ann Ree Colton enters the world at a time when helpful scientific discoveries about dreams and sleep are now occurring in certain major hospitals and universities. These discoveries about dreaming do not relate to the spiritual interpretation of dreams. However, they are interesting from a physiological and psychological standpoint, for such investigations are disclosing how the body, emotions and mind are affected by sleep, lack of sleep, dreaming and non-dreaming.

The formal scientific research of dreams and sleep began in 1953 when an alert scientist noticed the eyes of a child moving for extended periods during sleep. 1953 was also the year Ann Ree Colton established a nonprofit Foundation blending religion, philosophy, science and the creative arts. One department of this Foundation is devoted to compiling and interpreting dreams. For many years earlier in her life as a teacher and spiritual counselor, Ann Ree Colton had interpreted thousands of dreams for others. However, her present-day research of dreams is unique in that it concerns the dreams of persons who aspire to live creative, spiritual lives. Thus, the dream knowledge provided through her Foundation dream-research program is of inestimable value. As more persons strive to incorporate ethical principles into their lives, the dream knowledge revealed by Ann Ree Colton will add immeasurably to their spiritual evolvement, understanding, and peace of mind.

It has been discovered by scientists that sleep has four stages. An alpha rhythm, a state of serene relaxation with no thoughts, precedes the first stage of sleep. In the first stage, one awakens easily and might insist that he has not been asleep.

After a few minutes, the sleeper enters Stage II – a deeper level of sleep from which he is not easily awakened. The third stage brings relaxation, a slower heart rate, a decline in temperature, and a drop in blood pressure.

After twenty or thirty minutes of sleep, one reaches the deepest level of sleep – Stage IV, a no-dream stage. However, after approximately twenty minutes in this level the sleeper drifts from Stage IV to other levels. About 90 minutes after falling asleep, one's eyes move jerkily under closed lids as though watching something. He is in a special variety of Stage I, known as REM sleep.

(REM stands for "Rapid Eye Movement.") If awakened while in this stage, he will invariably remember dreaming, probably in full detail. Thus, a person who says, "I never dream" does dream, even though he does not recall the dreams.

After perhaps ten minutes in the REM or dreaming state, the sleeper will probably turn over in bed and begin shifting down the levels of sleep again to the depths, to return in another hour or so for a longer REM dream. Each night the cycle is repeated about four or five times.

Deep restorative sleep, called delta sleep, predominates in the first part of the night. Delta sleep and the REM sleep are of particular interest to researchers.

When a person is deprived of REM sleep (when dreams occur), on each successive night of deprivation he will try more and more often to dream – thereby making up for lost dream time. When one is awakened each time he begins to dream, after a few days he loses his emotional and mental calm, sometimes becoming hysterical. This fact is leading scientific researchers to the realization that dreams are somehow therapeutic, and help one to retain his mental and emotional equilibrium.

Blind persons also experience the rapid-eye-movement periods of sleep, but they do not dream in visual images; they dream in terms of touch and sound.

When an infant is one day old, his REM time is about 50% of his total sleep time. The active movements of his eyeballs during REM sleep are in no way different from those of an adult. Dream researchers find this difficult to understand; they cannot comprehend what the infant can possibly be dreaming about because the infant has had no previous visual experience.

It has also been discovered that a breast-fed baby dreams in unison with its mother, while a baby who is not breast-fed and its mother dream at different times.

It is believed by some that while a baby is in the womb he is experiencing REM sleep, because the body of a child or adult rarely moves during the REM period. Thus, the REM sleep would keep the growing baby quiet within the mother's womb.

While science continues to amass valuable knowledge related to dreams and sleep, Ann Ree Colton continues with her brilliant revelations related to dreams and their symbols. The hundreds of symbols in this book will prove invaluable for many persons who desire to learn what their dreams are trying to teach them.

God's marvelous plan continually unfolds its wonders – and dreams are part of God's plan for man. Ann Colton states, *"Nothing is wasted in God's plan."* Therefore, one should respect his dreams, knowing that they are not unintelligible and valueless projections from subconscious wastelands. One should know that dream symbols are a vital part of a living language – a language used by the soul and heaven to instruct him, warn him, guide him, and prepare him to become a more worthy fulfiller of the glorious Plan of God.

Dreams may be pictorial dramas, or they may be fleeting, quick – darting through the night's sleep as colorful butterflies or as sprightly hummingbirds. Dreams may be projected from the depths of the lower mind and conscience, or from the heights of one's higher or eternal self. Dreams may stir one's lesser emotions, causing unrest and fear, or they may fill one with a blessed peace.

Over the past fifty years, Ann Ree Colton has interpreted numerous dreams for her students and others. She has made them aware of the *Night Ministry,* during which one may aid others, research the higher worlds, learn of past lives, and gain prophetic insight into the coming days and years. She states, *"Symbols are the language of the soul. Dream symbols, especially, are the language of the soul. Poetry is a language of the soul. All poetry is overdirected by the Cherubim Angels – and dreams have a certain poetic essence. Dreams have a voice telling you when you are wrong, or when something very wonderful is coming. Dreams sometimes have a prophetic theme, or they may have a corrective theme. Dreams seek to remind you that there is something which must be done."*

Ingenious ideas have been known to come to men through dreams; fortunately, such men retained and recorded the memory of their revealing dreams. It is said that a famous composer slept with pencil and paper on his chest. From time to time he would awaken and make notations of the beautiful music he heard while dreaming.

A person may be so graced as to dream a dream that gives clear direction and meaningful purpose to his days, understanding and peace to his mind. He may be what Ann Ree Colton calls a "grace-dreamer." This is true today, even as it was in Biblical times: guidance dreams or dreams of instruction may visit all who are receptive to such dreams.

Some of the dreams of great men in history have been recorded. When one reads of these dreams, he is reminded of the prominent role that dreams can play in a person's life. Abraham Lincoln experienced a prophetic dream in which he was shown his approaching death. However, he did not heed the dream warning. A few days later, the assassin's bullet fulfilled the prophecy.

A study of Biblical dreams discloses dreams of prophecy, guidance, warning, instruction and evaluation. Some of these dreams meant the difference between life and death – for one person or for thousands.

The world of dreams has intrigued and puzzled mankind for ages. The ancients recognized dreams to be of great importance – especially the dreams of kings, rulers and holy men. The prophets of old respected dreams as a source of knowledge, wisdom and instruction; they also knew that the ability to interpret dreams is a spiritual gift. It was said of Daniel that he *"had understanding in all visions and dreams." (Daniel 1:17)* This was true of the other great sages in Biblical days and throughout the ages.

In modern times, the world of dreams and sleep is gradually revealing some of its mysteries to certain observing and scientific minds that are scrutinizing the importance of dreams as related to man's well-being. However, higher or *soul* levels of dream knowledge continue to elude a strictly scientific approach to dream research.

Through her revelatory gifts, Ann Ree Colton has researched the various levels of dreams, especially those dreams that express the voice of the soul. She has observed that such dreams are more likely to occur in the lives of persons who are desirous of living according to spiritual principles.

Ann Ree has observed that some dreams are purifying in nature, providing an outlet for suppressed desires, hostile emotions, frustrations, and curiosity. Even as a rhythmic tide washes clean the beaches of the earth, so do dream tides seek to wash away the debris which would otherwise clutter and distort the mind and the emotions. Such dreams are nocturnal cleansers, rendering a service of emotional and mental sanitation and health. This benefic action discloses its rewards during a new day when one awakens refreshed – ready once again to meet the challenges of life.

One who seeks to live according to the Ten Commandments and the Commandment of Love makes every effort to think and feel on the highest levels of purity, love and peace. Therefore, the cleansing action in the dreams of such a person grows less and less necessary, as his waking hours are assigned to the task of purification and elevation of emotions and thoughts. This noticeably affects his dreams, and the cudgel-like action of his dreams trying to hammer home a moral or ethical point is gradually softened.

The sincerity with which one accepts a daytime life of worship of God and love of his fellow man determines his course in the waking world and in the world of sleep. Prayer, meditation, repentance, forgiveness, reverence, dedication, devotion and love cleanse a soiled spirit and give new life and hope to a saddened soul. This is reflected in the nature of one's dreams.

The transition from an amoral life to a life of beauty and righteousness requires that one resolve each dark deed. Certain dreams are part of the resolving process. The march toward creative accomplishments and spiritual fulfillment is accompanied by a cadence of dream dramas. Some of these dreams are unpleasant and disturbing; especially upsetting are the dreams of correction or reproving from the conscience.

Each victory one achieves over outer or inner darkness results in a minor or major ascension toward the immortal light of his soul – the greater the victory, the greater the rise. The revealing power in dreams often contributes to this victory and resurrection. Thus, dreams should not be taken lightly.

In her dream research over the years, Ann Ree Colton has discovered that there are *seven* dream levels; three lesser dream levels consisting of the reflected daytime actions, and four higher dream levels containing the pure reality of the spiritual dramas. Ann Ree is noted for interpreting the prophetic aspect within certain dreams and the recovery of *akasic* or past-life records through dreams. She has observed that there is a progressive process in one's dreams and a communicable sequence in dreams as an initiatory action in one's life. She has seen over and over again the sequential instructing and correcting aspect of dreams, and also the difference between the lower psychic dreams and the higher spiritual dreams, as well as the drama or myth aspects in a dream.

Ann Ree believes that certain dreams contain spiritual gold. To an alert and knowing person, the symbols within dreams are precious nuggets which may be of great value to the one dreaming, to his family, and to the world. Dreams are valuable to the one dreaming because they are seeking to aid him to fulfill his physical and spiritual destiny. Dreams are valuable to his family because some dreams contain warnings, similar to the dreams of Joseph, the father of Jesus; the dreams of Joseph enabled him to preserve his family and to protect them from harm. Dreams are valuable to the world because they sometimes disclose secrets of the soul, or prophecies pertaining to inventions and ideas beneficial to the world.

The more perceptive and honest an individual is, the more likely he is to gauge the depth of a dream and to understand its meaning. But first, he must recognize the dream to be part of a system of timely instruction, supervised by divine intelligences concerned with his welfare as a child of God.

The science of dream symbology includes numerous symbols or combinations of symbols. These symbols may be understood by one who has the gift of dream interpretation. While few persons are endowed with this gift, it is possible for perceptive individuals to derive great benefit from their dreams through a cognitive understanding of the different levels and nuances to be found in their dream symbols. This book will become for them a treasured key toward a better understanding of their dreams, visions, inspirational creativity and spiritual experiences.

The years have proved that Ann Ree Colton has been blessed with the ability to interpret visions and dreams. Her extensive dream research files are filled with the dreams of persons who are seeking to live peaceful, reverent and dedicated lives. In this specialized dream research, she is making an extremely important contribution to the world, for the dreams of dedicated, reverent persons are different from the dreams of callous, irreverent persons. Reverent, spiritually-inclined individuals are ever seeking to unite with the Will of God. While asleep or awake, their ears are open to the voice of their souls, and their hearts are receptive to the protecting and guiding Love of God.

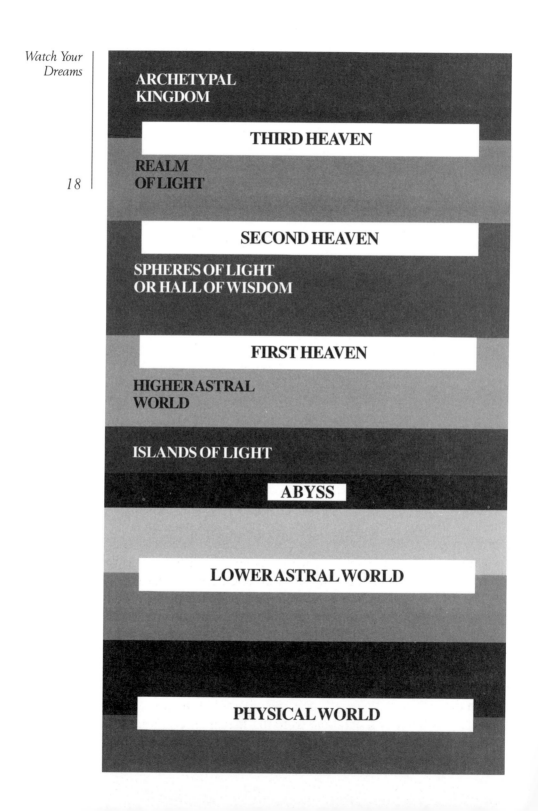

ARCHETYPAL
KINGDOM

THIRD HEAVEN

REALM
OF LIGHT

SECOND HEAVEN

SPHERES OF LIGHT
OR HALL OF WISDOM

FIRST HEAVEN

HIGHER ASTRAL
WORLD

ISLANDS OF LIGHT

ABYSS

LOWER ASTRAL WORLD

PHYSICAL WORLD

Chapter 1

THE SOUL AND DREAMS*

*From across the Milky Way I have come — each starry
body a long lost home. Set in my heart is a reflecting mirror
reminding me that I am a traveler of the spirit, centered in a
soul's dominion.*

Dreaming is a soul power. From other eternity systems the soul
has come. Under the Will of God the soul seeks to expand the
terrains of the spirit. The Will of God rules supreme over the soul's
coming and going – whether in life or death to the body, or life
and death placement in the spiraling destiny of the eternals. The
promise of the soul is eternality – a promise unfailing, unceasing,
manifesting for God.

The soul's sojourn is a joy song. In the music of cosmos the soul
is at home. When consciousness is fixed upon the soul's eternality,
an inner cosmos peace begins. To envision with a cosmos peace is
to master the tumults of the alternates, or the duality action in this
eternity system. The third attribute of the soul – vision, seeing
through and into the cosmos peace – enables the initiate to walk
upon the waters of chaos with an untroubled spirit. This is the
promise of the soul: man is a vessel for God in all worlds. As an
envisioning creator, the abysses of the deep become as bridges of
light over which he may leap with the holy abandonment of the
soul and the spirit.

Through mastery of dream codes and symbolic initiation man
comes closer to God. Dream codes and archetypal symbols origi-
nate in the sphere of the soul's action. Long before men spoke or
used the written word, symbols were the means of communication. Languages may come and go in the world of man; the power

At the conclusion of this book may be found a glossary defining unfamiliar terminology and words.

within symbols remains the same from age to age. Each age leaves to man a record of its symbology.

All symbols correlate to the greater archetypes and are of etheric origin. All symbols are energized vortices containing a life ether and a light ether. The life energy and ether mold and shape the form of the symbol, and the light ether is responsible for sustaining the intelligence speaking within the symbol.

Symbols are a necessary part of spiritual instruction; they are the *logos vocabulary* in dream experience and in meditative experience. Many persons experience dreams of rare and unusual nature, but due to their unfamiliarity with the etheric symbolic codes contained within their dreams, they cannot perceive what the dreams are seeking to say. To interpret the etheric symbolic code without spiritual training is to gather a psychical or psychological interpretation of dreams rather than a spiritual interpretation.

The etheric codes concealed within dreams and visions are a verbal and tangible asset. One who masters the science of heavenly symbols will become a responsible server for God. He will have no difficulty in expressing and creating; for his logos will become a mighty and dexterous instrument touching the hearts and minds of those who know – and also, in certain instances, even the unknowing will hear and come to know.

The art of *seeing* in symbols is acquired throughout many lives of spiritual dedication and application. The science of symbolic speaking is given to only a few. Symbolic speaking expressed in parabolic form is a mighty healer, dispelling the pain of abuse through wrong vowing and affirming.

The culture of symbols through the inner music and the inner hearing is a mighty peace-giver to the emotions and a soother to the organs of the body.

Were it not for the symbols men leave behind them, the history and memory of tribes, races, and society would be erased. All symbols are in reality deathless, immortal, living nuclei. Centered within each symbol is an etheric, intelligible code. In each eternity, symbols play their part to make known to all conscious beings the archetypal blueprints and intent of God.

Regardless of what language is spoken, the cosmic symbols in this eternity enable men to retain something of an inner, intelligible communication. The hidden meaning within symbols holds the key to the inner understanding between men.

All human events contain symbolic clues. Through the hidden symbols in history the historian may unveil the moral purpose and spiritual age of a people. If the historian is highly evolved, he may touch the deeper layers of sensitivities in symbolic interpretation, and thus render to humanity a spiritual service rather than a patriot's service.

The research of symbology through archeology may literally set free the grace or karma of a former people of ancient times. In the case of geology, the dedicated geologist, if highly evolved, may perceive and also reveal the hidden and little-understood creative powers of an epoch or age.

When archeologists unearth ancient sites or cities, symbols long dormant in human consciousness awaken and overflow into receptive, ready minds. Ancient cities of the past come to life to teach men of the present, that they may return to certain myth and symbolic powers used in former lives.

In fairly recent history when modern archeologists opened the tombs of the Egyptian kings, the Western world became heir to a virile symbology needed in a new era of civilizations.

All throughout the earth it may be seen that men of the Western world are being exposed interiorly and exteriorly to symbols of the ancient worlds. England's dominance in India opened the door in the Western world to the great Rishi and Upanishad myth streams of consciousness. This was timed to man of the Western world so that he might draw upon the essential virility of myth consciousness gathered or garnered from the ancient techniques for salvation.

The Western-world ego, so dependent upon external materialistic expression, for centuries sealed away the subconscious or quelle flow of symbolic memory. Thus, the Western world became materialistically dependent upon the outer or external aspect of the senses.

Everywhere there is evidence that certain men are responding to the true and basic myths of the past and also that mankind as a whole is being prepared to develop a new or virginal myth symbology for the future.

HOW SYMBOLS BEGAN

In the first four great intervals of this eternity system, our Father – working with the Elohim-Hierarchy and the archangelic presences – imaged, formed and shaped all things. The Father established the original blueprints or archetypes for each thing imaged. Within each archetype He implanted a *master image* containing multitudinous symbols.

After the four great intervals or the *forming* period for this eternity or earth system had concluded, the Father gave the earth and its contents over to the creative faculties of man. Thus began the *informing* stage, which will last for the three remaining great intervals of the world. In the informing stage man is informed or instructed.

Though one may be continually the recipient of creative archetypal formats and symbols, he must earn the right, through certain initiatory trials, to interpret and to ethically use them.

THE GENESES SYMBOLS

In the beginning of this earth system and of man's evolutionary progress, in the period of *tribal-genesis* tribal priests understood symbology through atavistic, psychic powers. They transmitted these powers to their tribal dependents through the use of certain images on clay. They also used stones and metals for certain protective amulets, using atavistic symbolic ritual to sustain the primitive energy and ether contained within the amulet. The talisman-amulets of ancient times were known by the priests and chiefs of tribes to hold potent magical power. Present-day amulet beliefs stem from tribal memories of primitive symbolic initiation passed down from one generation to another.

As men of the earth formed a self-identity in *human-genesis* or *family-genesis,* priests in religious cults working with a higher level of symbology established the religious symbology and rituals known even in the present time, thus keeping alive the worship resurgence within their flock or congregation.

In human-genesis and *lower self-genesis,* dream symbols may be experienced from three levels: (1) atavistic, animistic; (2) religious; and (3) the soul and ego-shadowed record dwelling upon the vibratory hum of the soul's medallion, and in some instances of grace, the grace-record reflected upon the soul's medallion.

In *higher self-genesis,* symbols are received from the grace level of the soul's record, from the record of the higher self, and also from the true records of the archetypal worlds. The soul-logos symbology speaks to the highly evolved person through contemplation, meditation, and through higher dream levels.

When higher self-genesis comes to full expression, symbology will instruct and also reveal. With spiritual sensitivity one may eventually attain one of the greater symbolic or spiritual arts – the power of the parable. Such persons, having used the symbolic arts through many lives of spiritual sensitivity, can induce upon the thought power of an attentive listener the actual and living image within the spoken word. The Lord Jesus used this power of image-parable. His words will never die because they were directly empowered by the master images within the greater archetypes dwelling within the third heaven or the kingdom of God. *"Heaven and earth shall pass away, but my words shall not pass away." (St. Matthew 24:35)*

In the third heaven there are master images which work directly with the greater archetypes. These master images reside in the center or heart of the greater archetypes. Through progressive stages in spiritual evolvement one may open and have a continuing access to the master images residing within the greater archetypes. Through contact with the master images an initiate may produce a unique and immortal thing. The understanding and use of reflected archetypal symbology is the first step toward the master image.

HOW ONE IS INITIATED THROUGH SYMBOLS

One must undergo seven degrees of initiation to attain the use of the master image and, therefore, the power of image-manifestation. The seven steps of dream and meditation symbology initiation are:

1. One is first initiated through the animal symbol to learn sentient and emotional correspondences. In this he is assisted by the Cherubim Angelic revelation, and he opens his awareness to the Cherubim helps. The Cherubim Angels are master craftsmen overdirecting formalistic and ritualistic arts in the world. In such symbols one contacts the lower and higher astral planes in dreams. The lower astral dream correlates to Freudian interpretation; the higher astral, to the soul memory.

2. Secondly, one is initiated through the twelve zodiacal prototypal symbols, relating him to the temperament and form of man. He learns of dualities, polarities, placement, and the humanities. He becomes at one with the Terrestrial Angels. He opens the Book of Laws or the Ten Commandments. He unites

with the Angels of Mercy and with the Recording Angels of the humanities.

3. He is next initiated through the atavistic competitve symbols residing within the subconscious or quelle memory. From these initiations he learns to rise above the emotional astral tumults, and he balances his mind strengths, mind control and will.

4. He is next initiated through planetary kinetic psychic power and energies. He unites with the minerals, ores and jewels of the earth. He is initiated as to the timing in symbols and also as to time. He becomes prophetic. He is also initiated into the symbols within the drama of creation. He unites with the Sanat Kumara, or the Ancient of Days; he learns of timing through symbology.

5. He is initiated through rhythm and the symbology in music. He learns of the great archetones or the Holy Ghost action within the archetypes, and of the atavistic origins of music affecting generation and propagation. He is taught to sensitize his reception to music. He overcomes the astral discordant sounds and provides himself with insulation against discord. He unites with Cherubim Angelic helps through Cherubim music. He unites with the music of the seven reflected planetary spheres around the earth and learns of cosmic order in the universe.

6. He is initiated through the symbols of the soul which reveal to him the records and activities of his former lives; he learns his purpose, and how to use his ethic. He also receives the reproving and warning from his Guardian Angel through symbols. He is initiated through the Saints and Flora Angels. He becomes a prophetic pray-er for God; his prayers are answered mightily. The sustaining atoms within the plant kingdom are revealed to him. The Flora Angels of the plants use symbols to open the voice of his soul.

7. He next opens the informing or *Buddhi* principle of spiritual divination and is initiated through the Bodhisattva symbology. He unites with the higher self, the audible hum of the life current, the eternal telepathy through the master images correlating to the greater archetypes. Thus, he is open to the Christ, to the Father, and to God.

Through dedication, mantramic speaking, contemplation, listening and meditation, one unites himself with a cosmos vocabulary.

THE ARCHETYPAL SYMBOLS

All telepathic initiates are in alignment with one or more master images. These master images are sustained within the hum of a cosmos archetype. In this eternity system there are thirteen basic cosmos archetypes. Within the thirteen basic archetypes a master image remains for ages or even for aeons. The master image sends forth billions of symbolic codes or etheric forms. These eventually fall into the receptive minds of those who creatively interpret and activate them.

As long as there is concern solely for physical or sensual expression, dream symbols are experienced on an astral level; they are presented or clothed in earthlike garments or symbols. These earth influenced symbols are reproduced in dreams and sometimes in daytime flashes of intuitive omens and instinct.

Cosmos archetypal symbols fall into the various levels of the soul's medallion where they are first experienced in the higher dream states, in pure meditation, and in lucid telepathic insight during daytime activities. These symbols are received intuitively in parabolic abstractions.

When one has the grace to aspire to spiritual instruction in meditation and in dreams, he must clear away the childish concepts clouding his mind and obstructing his higher will. His instruction begins in the Cherubim Angelic levels of symbology. He comes under the direction of the Cherubim helps. The Cherubim Angels are the perfect master builders for God. It is perfect grace when one comes under the guidance of the Cherubim builders.

Dream symbols received from the Cherubim evaluate, reveal, and instruct. Animal dream symbols most frequently used by the Cherubim angels are of the higher characteristics of the animal kingdom. If the animal symbol portrays a negative or lower order of correspondence, one should search out the hidden flaw delaying or deterring his spiritual evolvement.

WHY WE MUST DREAM

God took Eden away from man and gave him a heaven. Man experiences this heaven in sleep and in death. How he experiences heaven is determined by his belief in God and in his own eternality.

Physical self-consciousness in its exploring and in its external-ity is not enough to express what the soul of man truly is. The soul is the sun of the ego, having its rising and its descending. Day-time, physical consciousness is the night of the soul. Night or sleep-ing consciousness is the daytime of the soul. In the daytime man must depend upon his senses to determine what he experiences and what he knows through experiencing. In the nighttime con-sciousness, one is unhindered by the superimposed consciousness of daytime collective thinking and conceptual thought processes.

In the world of sleep one does not gauge his learning by the standard of what other men teach or tell him, nor is his conduct weighed by what men in the world suppose or think. One is ex-posed in the night to what he *really* is, and he is inducted into the receptive suggestibles of the night that he may bear and support the limited daytime action of his external world.

WHAT IS SLEEP?

Sleep to some persons is a form of anesthesia or a means of escape and forgetfulness, but to others it is a recovery and awak-ening to a greater sphere of consciousness. Sleep may become a creative labor within the night in which one may unite with the blueprint of God's intent for him.

The soul works without weariness to enable all persons to ex-tend and expand their states of consciousness during the hours of the day and the hours of sleep. The vocabulary or language of the soul is symbology. This language of symbology is more frequently experienced in the dream world during the night's sleep. When the senses are stilled during sleep, the soul seeks to mirror pure, mediative instruction. However, when one is worried, anxious, or frustrated, the senses are astrally magnified in the dream world – and the higher mediative instruction of the soul is sealed away.

SPIRITUAL SIGNIFICANCE OF DREAMS

Spiritual instruction emphasizes the spiritual significance of dreams and the importance of the soul's action within the dream world. Such instruction points to the way one may penetrate the seven dream veils, and thereby interpret the etheric code within dream symbology. All dreams are of vital importance to persons who desire to evolve spiritually. In time, one comes to hold each dream experience as a sacred action overdirected by the work of the soul. His understanding of the initiatory phases within dreams, and comprehension of the etheric code within dream symbology and dream experience, will enable him to better understand his physical, emotional, and mental impulses and also the hidden cause directing and stimulating his attitudes and actions in the world.

When a person is deeply engrossed with physical concerns, he rarely understands the true significance of dreams and the part dreams play as related to the soul. The average person is yet to fully recognize the soul's action in dreams, and either ignores his dreams or leans in the direction of the Freudian or psychological interpretation of dreams. The superstitious person fears his dreams. Few in the world relate themselves intelligently and constructively to that which the soul is seeking to reveal through dreams. Even those who intuit that dreams are spiritually significant are seldom qualified to fully interpret the etheric codes concealed within dream symbology. Reverent dedication, earnest and repeated prayer, pure alignment in meditation, selfless contemplation, the speaking of mantrams, and certain periods of dedicated fasting will extend and sustain the time spent in the higher realms of the dream world. Such practices assure the retention of memory of dream dramas, disclose the meaning within the dream dramas, and enable one, in time, to coordinate his soul's action of the night with his physical labors and creative works of the day. To achieve a closer intimacy with the higher reaches of the soul's action, while either asleep or awake, requires a rhythmic and uninterrupted training and also an inner perception which may be gained only through purification and dedication to God.

DREAMS IN THE BIBLE

There are a number of Biblical references to dreams and the life which man experiences while he is in the state of sleep. The story of Joseph in the Old Testament is the story of one whose life course was determined by dreams. Joseph's dreams increased his brothers' envy and hatred of him, and thus were directly responsible for his being sold by them to merchantmen, who took him to Egypt. Egypt proved to be the land of his greatest achievements and triumphs, for Joseph's ability to interpret dreams eventually made it possible for him to have great authority and to preserve the lives of many people.

Joseph dreamed a dream, and he told it his brethren: and they hated him yet the more.   *–Genesis 37:5*

And Pharaoh said unto Joseph, I have dreamed a dream and there is none that can interpret it: and I have heard say of thee, that thou canst understand a dream to interpret it.
    –Genesis 41:15

And Pharaoh said unto Joseph, Forasmuch as God hath shewed thee all this, there is none so discreet and wise as thou art: Thou shalt be over my house, and according unto thy word shall all my people be ruled.   *–Genesis 41:39,40*

Daniel, having the power to penetrate the seven dream veils, had access to the prophetic or sixth dream veil. When Nebuchadnezzar demanded that his dream and its interpretation be made known to him, Daniel was able to tell the king what he had dreamed and also the interpretation of the dream.

Daniel had understanding in all visions and dreams.
    –David 1:17

Then was the secret revealed unto Daniel in a night vision. Then Daniel blessed the God of heaven.   *–Daniel 2:19*

The king answered and said to Daniel, whose name was Belteshazzar, Art thou able to make known unto me the dream which I have seen, and the interpretation thereof? Daniel answered in the presence of the king, and said, The secret which the king hath demanded cannot the wise men, the astrologers, the magicians, the soothsayers, shew unto the king; But there is a God in heaven that revealeth secrets, and maketh known to the king Nebuchadnezzar what shall be in the latter days. Thy dream, and the visions of thy head upon thy bed, are these...
    –Daniel 2:26-28

When Jesus was an infant, His life was saved because the three wise men and his father were warned in dreams.

And being warned of God in a dream that they should not return to Herod, they departed into their own country another way. And when they were departed, behold, the angel of the Lord appeareth to Joseph in a dream, saying, Arise, and take the young child and his mother, and flee into Egypt, and be thou there until I bring thee word: for Herod will seek the young child to destroy him.   *–St. Matthew 2:12,13*

Jesus was returned to the land of Israel after His father experienced another dream.

But when Herod was dead, behold, an angel of the Lord appeareth in a dream to Joseph in Egypt, Saying, Arise, and take the young child and his mother, and go into the land of Israel: for they are dead which sought the young child's life.
         –St. Matthew 2:19,20

Such dreams pertaining to the Saviour of the world, the Lord Jesus, were experienced by the wise men and His father, Joseph, within the seventh dream veil, where all spiritually imminent events may be perceived. In each age the wise or highly evolved personages, through their dreams and visions, are in uninterrupted proximity to the higher worlds, and thus know all forthcoming spiritual events of the earth.

THE SILVER CORD AND SLEEP

The etheric body has both a higher aspect and a lesser aspect. The higher aspect is called the *higher etheric body;* the lesser aspect is called the *lesser etheric body.* When a person is asleep, the lesser etheric body remains with the physical body, sustaining the life-restorative functions of the physical body. During sleep the lesser etheric body acts as the ballast for the higher etheric body. The energy etheric, magnetic, electric and vapor-like cord linking the higher etheric body with the lesser etheric body is called the *silver cord.* During the day the silver cord is connected to the etheric counterparts of the spleen, the liver, the heart, the larynx, and the crown of the head. When a person dies, the silver cord is totally loosed or severed from the lesser etheric body and the physical body, and after death he lives in his higher etheric body or everlasting body. However, in sleep the silver cord is but partially loosed from its etheric moorings, remaining attached to the lesser etheric body and the physical body, thus enabling the higher etheric body to travel and experience the dream veils. Due to gravity's effect upon the silver cord's action, a magnetic pull draws the silver cord back to the physical body after dreams and sleep. When one's interest during sleep is focused too intently upon certain inverted figments within the lesser dream veils, the vitality of the silver cord is devitalized and depleted and the one sleeping may be snapped back to his physical body, shocking his nervous and muscular system. This accounts for a person sometimes awakening with a violent start or with the feeling that he is falling or being catapulted into waking consciousness.

The following Biblical verses in the book of Ecclesiastes, chapter 12, relate to man's death experience and the silver cord.

> *Because man goeth to his long home, and the mourners go about the streets: Or ever the silver cord be loosed....Then shall the dust return to the earth as it was: and the spirit shall return unto God who gave it.* —Ecclesiastes 12:5-7

THE DREAM VEILS (see chart page 18)

In the three higher dream veils, or in the first and second heavens, one assumes his spiritual responsibility as a son of the heavenly Father, exploring the higher dream veils with emotional and mental maturity. The higher dream veils are penetrated only by one with clean hands and a pure heart, and with uttermost reverence toward what the soul is seeking to say. The higher dream-veil experience is not always remembered as a dream, but may be manifested in the daytime as intuition, impression, apprehension, inspiration, guidance, or a vision.

A person who lives only through material and sensuous concepts cannot completely release his higher etheric body to the higher dream veils. His higher etheric body, being charged with gravity and subtle vibrations, is limited to the lesser dream veils.

In the low undertow of the grotesque and fantasy dream veils, night action is experienced in a womblike state of inverted retrospection. One relates himself to primitive memories and to unresolved ancestral compulsions.

In the wish level of dreams one has exaggerated or inverted introspection. He pictures his immature wishes to obtain without earning.

In the lower aspect of the fourth dream veil one reenacts physical and external compulsions, magnifying his individuality and self-importance.

DREAMS AND THE HIGHER ETHERIC BODY

The higher etheric body does not have pinions or wings; nightflight is experienced as a form of spiraling flight. Thus, experiences in the higher dream veils are often spoken of by the initiated as *night-flight.* Any moving vehicle in a dream is a symbol of the higher etheric body's movement and action. If an antique car or a jalopy is seen in a dream, this indicates that the higher etheric body as a vehicle is detained in the lesser dream veils, similar to an elevator being caught in its shaft; it also indicates that one is yet to understand the techniques of night travel.

To dream of a bus with many people indicates that one is with a group of other persons who are also rising in the night with him. If he is in a faster vehicle, such as an airplane, it means that he is using his higher etheric body in the rarefied etheric atmosphere of the higher dream veils. If he is in the driver's seat of any vehicle, it is indicative of his using his own will to arrive at his particular destination for the night's action. If he dreams that another person is driving the vehicle, it signifies that he has yet to earn the power and use of his will to ascend alone into the higher dream veils.

BANKED RECORDINGS

In sleep the physical-brain radiations are slowed down; the ordinary thought processes are partially quiescent. The mental higher-mind triad atoms, working with the higher etheric sheaths of the brain at night, register the thoughts within the dream veils. Thus, a highly-evolved person thinks with his mental triad atoms in the night's sleep. All night's sleep thoughts are telepathically imprinted and photographed upon etheric banked-recording orbs within the brain. The mystery of dream recollection may be best explained by the *banked recordings* centered within the sensitive, etheric orbs of the brain. These banked recordings may be compared with the indented grooves of phonograph records, in that they remain inactive until some outer action, interest, or stimulus sets up a chain reaction within the memory cells of the brain. Thus, a dream is not always remembered upon rising, but may be recalled in odd moments of the day, or even days, weeks, or months after the dream experience. This is due to the fact that a person may for a moment align his memory with his etheric, banked-recording orbs and his mental triad atoms. The soul sometimes uses the flashback of dream recollection at a needed time or in a desperate circumstance. For example, such banked recordings of dreams may be recalled to warn of danger or accident when the person is approaching a scene or place as formerly seen or experienced in a dream.

There are three etheric, banked-recording orbs within the brain. One is located at the base of the skull; one is in the center of the forehead; and another is at the exact top of the head. The three etheric, banked-recording orbs determine what sort of dream is remembered and also determine whether a dream is remembered with clarity or in part. When the three etheric, banked-recording orbs are in alignment with one another and are at one with the three mental triad atoms, the result is a perfect dream remembrance and a full cognition of the spiritual action in the higher dream veils of the night. However, when but one of the three etheric banked-recording orbs is active, a person who has had a higher dream-veil experience would recall it only in part. When all three etheric, banked-recording orbs are inactive, dreams within the higher dream veils are not recalled. This explains why some people who experience the higher dream veils do not always recall their dreams.

When dreams are recorded solely by the etheric orb in the center of the forehead, a person would record only the wish dream veil, where the imagination has total command. Thus, his dreams are imaginative and chimera-like; there is a magnification of the emotions and exaggeration as to wishes. In some instances he may see mirages and chimeras played out as dramas of his hopes and wishes. Hence, in his dreams he may find gold or money, or may consummate his hidden, amorous desires, or may contact glamorous persons.

When only the etheric, banked-recording orb over the head is active, dreams are recalled as doing or participating, for the will of the individual is involved in such dream experience. In action dreams, one dreams that he is playing a piano, driving a car, climbing a mountain, swimming, chopping wood, performing feats of strength, or doing other activities in which the will is involved.

When only the etheric, banked-recording orb at the base of the skull is active, the grotesque and fantasy levels of dreams are remembered. In such dreams, persons sometimes turn back the clock of the ages and recall prehistoric animals and events or primitive conditions, for in the lesser dream veils one draws upon the *world subconscious*. Such dreams may be atavistic, primitive, hallucinatory, or relate to inverted or negative memories.

HARMFUL DREAM DISTORTION

Certain mechanical recordings, when played while one is asleep, hinder the soul's freedom of action in the night. Sleep is a sacred function. One should make his environment of sleep as peaceful as possible. The room should be orderly, sweet, clean, and properly ventilated. Disorder, odors, poor ventilation, noises, or any sounds that intrude upon the sleeping state keep the senses engaged, thereby preventing the rise into the higher dream veils and interfering with the soul's action at night. Anyone who listens to suggestive mechanical recordings during sleep builds an involuntary dependence upon the wills of others. Such sleep-teaching annuls the soul's mediative action of mirroring God's instruction to man.

> *For God speaketh once, yea twice, yet man perceiveth it not. In a dream, in a vision of the night, when deep sleep falleth upon men, in slumberings upon the bed; Then he openeth the ears of men, and sealeth their instruction.* —Job 33:14-16

PRACTICAL DREAM TECHNIQUES

Through the use of prayer, contemplation, meditation and the speaking of before-sleep mantrams, one may begin to set up a rhythmic alignment between his three mental triad atoms and the three etheric, banked-recording orbs of his brain. Thus, he will come to know and observe more prominent and substantial testimonies of the dream world. In time, the study of dream symbols and interpretations will knit together the meaning of dreams. If one will keep a *dream diary* regularly, he will be benefited beyond his expectations. It is recommended that he look back over his dreams at the end of each month. He will acquire the gift of cognizance or mentation. From this, he will begin to intuit and observe what his soul is saying to him.

HOW TO IDENTIFY YOUR DREAM EXPERIENCE

I GROTESQUE	II FANTASY	III WISH	IV AKASIC RECORDS	V INITIATORY	VI PROPHETIC	VII SPIRITUAL
	UNDISCIPLINED EMOTIONAL	PUBERTY DREAMS OF CHILDREN	TRIBAL SYMBOLOGY OF SELF	EVALUATION OF SELF, FAMILY, OTHERS	APPREHENSION	PROTECTION
					WARNING	HEALING
		UNDEVELOPED EMOTIONAL	FAMILY-GENESIS SYMBOLOGY	CORRECTION	GUIDANCE	UNIVERSAL
			KARMIC	INSTRUCTION		COSMIC
	ATAVISTIC		WORLD-MEMORY			
			PAST-LIFE RECORDS	CONSCIENCE		

NIGHT MINISTRY AND RESEARCH can be on all levels

Chapter 2

NIGHT INSTRUCTION

The ministry of night serving supports my going in and coming out. May I gather the knowledge gained from the night. May l be inspired for my serving in the coming day.

The desire to learn in the greater dimensions of sleep is first inspired by the universities of heaven. These universities are called the *Halls of Learning.* All initiates are enrolled here by the great gurus or Masters that they may render a greater service to the world.

Night instruction is a vivid, vitalizing, rejuvenating experience for the mind. The soul is free at night to beam its searchlight into the mind with full freedom and the use of a memory, and of an awareness of the overdwelling cause; also, the creative aspect of man's being in the world can be revealed in night instruction.

Procedure in night instruction is orderly, reasonable, its purpose being to equalize and synchronize the soul and mind potential of man that he may be a creator in the world of men.

One aspect of research in the great universities of the night is research into the physical, etheric, emotional and mental bodies. Anyone preparing to render a healing service in the world must become an initiate of the four bodies: the physical body and its organisms, its purpose, and its functions; the lesser etheric body and its velocities and psychical currents; the emotional body, the glands and the astral planetary forces working with the emotions; one must also learn of the nervous system, of its power and influence upon the thinking processes of man. To gain this knowledge he must have developed in former lives an intuitive faculty as related to these bodies and their functions. Such intuition prepares him to enter into a specific instruction, that he may render to the world a more meaningful service in the ministering to human needs.

Whatever the specific talent of a person, when ripe it will be re-enforced by inward instruction when one spiritually desires to serve or to give.

No matter how perfected a person may be as to spiritual gifts, he must come under supervision and training continually in the Halls of Learning, and he must also keep his instruction current with the karmic processes of the earth.

Spiritual research in the universities of the night is not compulsory. However, all who have mentation and sustained cognition – that is, dream intuition – are aware that it is necessary to keep current the night and the day learning and earning. Anyone engaged in the healing arts who does not keep equal his night's instruction with his daytime actions eventually loses the power to give off the magnetic effluvia overflow accompanying all spiritual instruction and healing.

Superconsciousness and super-energizing powers are received through inner-plane instruction in the Halls of Learning at night. Memory of an unusual kind is added to earth conscious memory when one is engaged in research in the night.

The lunar light in dreams contains a special plasma of indentation which imprints itself upon the mental processes of the initiate and healer. The mind expands in a unique way in the lunar light of dreaming.

Universal diagnostic helps and healing techniques are received during the instruction of the night. Cause and origins of a disease are identified to the dream initiate. Karmic influence upon germ life and bacteria is discerned and understood. The study of septic antipathies are discovered through which the psychic aspect of a virus is pinpointed, weighed and understood.

It is the work of the initiate of the night to soften, mitigate, and eventually to eliminate something of the misery in the world. Spiritually dedicated healers of the human body must learn of their bodies. They begin this by first understanding their own inner-plane bodies. Thus, every healer's laboratory lies first within the etheric and psychic precincts of his bodily functions.

In the etheric healing processes one does not dwell upon the weaknesses in the structure of his various bodies. In his research of the night he learns, and knows, by seeing in his *own bodies* the potential for diseases and for weaknesses.

To learn how to command the psychic wavelength of disease,

and to change the currents of suffering into health, thus producing for himself a body of service unto God, one must enter into a special form of instruction in the Hall of Learning or university of the night – and that is, the laboratory of the mind. Such instruction comes to the one who finds his personal self to be inadequate physically as to the source of total healing.

KARMA AND SLEEP

The veil between dreaming and waking consciousness is extremely thin in all persons having receptive and suggestible natures. Travail in dreams and sleep, struggle and assertion of the ego, are experienced in the dream state by persons fearing confrontation with their karma.

In the waking state one lives in a form of anesthesia, mesmerized by the theory that the outer waking state is the only state of consciousness. However, time and time again one is made aware that there is an extension of mind and feeling in the state of sleeping.

Persons overladen with unfulfilled desires in a past life encounter these desires during the dream state. They are exposed to these old festering desires and must assess them alongside the desires of the present life. To such egos comes bewilderment concerning dreams.

If one has died in a previous life with selfish or base desires unmanifested, and though he has sought to live in the present life a chaste and good life, he is horrified to encounter in dreams these powerful reflexes of emotions as expressed in a former life.

In each life there is some progression and advancement. Yet, there must be a way to make the thrust of evolvement more rapid and more decisive in each life so that the soul may be given its full reach of expression.

No matter how much one may desire to shut away the repressed and inhibited emotions of a former life, he cannot refuse or deny their reality in the world of dreams. It is also true that little-understood good and beauty in one's own nature often withheld through timidity and false modesty in the outer life must be encountered in the inner planes at night.

Even as there are born and talented pray-ers in the world, some persons are born dreamers. A born dreamer is one who knows the world of dreams to be a natural, adjacent attribute of his physical life consciousness. He knows this because he has for many lives practiced the art of the continuity flow between waking and dreaming. Yet, few of these think it important or necessary to research or to find out how the gift of dreaming has been obtained. On meeting a teacher having the gift of dream interpretation and initiation, they learn that they are initiates of dream unfoldment. Whereas many persons are only concerned with life on the physical planes, their gift of dream unfoldment is a rare and priceless gift.

In initiatory schools, vortices or environments where certain egos are drawn together to render spiritual service in the earth, there may be found many who have mastered the art of dream unfoldment. Some of these may understand their dreams intuitively; others may yet be reticent to use this power, feeling themselves to be on uncertain ground.

To be born in a dogmatic age with limited spiritual culture is painful to the sensitive soul. Many in the world having spiritual gifts camouflage them so as to appear as others in the world. Sooner or later, their spiritual potential must come to the surface and be utilized by the transcendental powers in meditation and in dreaming.

All persons having spiritual gifts are as jewels faceted and cut by works of light in former lives. The light of God sooner or later will fall upon them and reveal the splendor of their souls to those needing the light in the world.

Night dreamers travel into corridors and heavenly plateaus to which karmically-laden persons cannot freely rise. Karmically-laden persons, however, can witness the glorious dream pageants; they can also be aware of the heavenly corridors and the presences of those dwelling therein. They can travel to many planes so as to be enlightened, comforted and instructed. Yet, they can only enter into these planes as observing witnesses, not participants. To be a participant in the initiatory dream dramas of the night, one must have earned this soul power in former lives.

It is stated in the higher echelons of learning that "what a mind knows, to there it can go."

THE ANGEL GUARDIANS OF SLEEP

The dream keepers of the night and the overlords of dreaming are the angels. One's own Guardian Angel watches over his night-flight and accompanies him over the fearful abysses of the night. If one has the grace to be united with his own radiant Master, he is aware of the Master's influence upon his night-flights. The Master's aura protects his protégé in the day; and in the night his radiant form shields him from the terrors of psychic intrusion.

In night dreaming, when a man encounters an angel, he sees and contacts the feminine polarity of the angel. As a male consciousness of the earth, a man contacts and attracts the opposite polarity of woman for polarity balance; so does the male ego in the night attract his opposite polarity – the feminine side of the angel. By contrast, a woman of the earth attracts the masculine polarity of the angel during dream or sleep.

In dreams one may encounter many angels as in a company of angels. This is often the case when one is witnessing certain dramas, such as seeing a person being released to death, a child dying, or a person suffering an accident. In a dream one may behold companies of angels clustered around a soul in the state of transition or fear during death or near death. Companies of angels can also be seen when in critical accidents in the world some persons suffer suspension between death and life. In dreams one sees the combined succoring angels pouring their angelic atom-vitalities into a soul caught between life and death.

In dreams one can be a witness to souls taking form and shape into ego-consciousness in birth matrices. They can see the angels looking into these pools of birth, and also see that the angels are assisting the one to be born to incorporate the soul powers into the mind he is to use in the world, thus giving freedom to his past-life ego identity imprints. They can also witness how the ego will accept or not accept the ancestral memory stream into which he will be born.

Dream initiates learn in the night that many persons are born to the earth to lift other men. They also become aware in the night that one's own Guardian Angel stands always as a mediator between the soul of man and the many other angels who serve mankind.

There is no justice of men to be compared with the justice of God's equation. His order, His rightness and His mercy exist in the dream state of consciousness, and it is manifested during sleep as it is also manifested in the day.

Man goes into his sleep willingly, relaxing to sleep. He knows from many ages and aeons of time that sleep is a necessity and a natural process, and that dreaming is a vital joy of communicableness and a revival of soul energy giving to him a providence and acceptable view in the waking state.

Dreaming is an essential and vital function given of God to proportion His world with reasonableness, with accepting. To those who do not believe in the extension of consciousness through dreams, life is but a particle of consciousness encapsulated into exterior fumblings of perplexity. Persons dying to the physical world, not understanding consciousness extending in dreams, must encounter after death this vacuum state caused by their own shortsightedness.

THE SHARP ANGEL

When a disciple or initiate prepares for the journey toward the light, he must move over racial barriers or the encasements of race controls. He must encounter the *racial dweller* or shadowed body from whence he has come over many lives. This dweller action exposes the initiate to the Sharp Angel or the angel who is the retributive representative of the race from whence he has come. The Sharp Angel's work for the race intensifies the taboos in the race controlling the heavier guilt aspects of the race. The taboos are held ever before the minds of all prophets, priests and leaders of a race. The protective angels of the four bodies of the initiate in this time move aside, permitting the Sharp Angel entry into the subconscious or quelle action of the initiate's mind and conscience.

It is the work of the Sharp Angel to cut away the instinctual mental and emotional footholds of reliance upon race by challenging the strength and the weakness of all human ties. When the last vestige of racial possessivism and of personality possessiveness is cut away, the Sharp Angel moves out of the auric sphere of the initiate, leaving him under the protection of his own dear angels who have stood temporarily inactive, that the clearing and cleansing work might be done. During this period the initiate evaluates through his dreams his feelings and thoughts regarding family, relatives, children, mate. All have memory of security through tribe, race and family. All initiates must release their dependence upon these inbred instinctual clingings so that they may truly live within the thought mold of Jesus, who was a World Avatar for all – that all might become one in God.

THE READING OF AKASIC RECORDS IN DREAMS

The Western world has repressed knowledge, research, and testimony of the truth concerning reincarnation. Therefore, the soul records or akasic records relating to previous existences on earth must be more often read or found in dreams.

Carl Jung, the great psychoanalytical scientist, came very close to the clue to reincarnation through his work and research into the dream life of man. In one statement in his memoirs he admits having come close to a concealed dream code speaking of past incarnations in the dream life of one of his subjects.

All persons believing in the laws of reincarnation and karma are more inclined to see the total picture of life as it is. Such persons, as a rule, keep a dream diary so that they may be in proximity to all waking and sleeping situations.

The Western ego is very often filled with guilt or a sin-concept regarding belief in reincarnation. It is very interesting that such persons – on contacting or being accepted by a Master, guru or teacher who understands the higher ability of the psyche in dreams – experience in their dreams powerful and infallible confirming proofs of past lives. The akasic-record dream dramas speaking out of such egos are as ripe plums waiting to move into the outer consciousness. There exists a coinciding principle working in their souls and lives preparing them for better understanding and a more relaxed identification of their true being.

To meet one who truly understands and interprets dream-code symbols is grace. Few persons of this nature exist in the world who can open the archetypal symbols and free men into the full-energy mental and emotional capacities of their souls.

The lowest aspect of the subconscious and the sovereign aspect of the higher unconscious give to each person of the earth the power to remember and the power to forget. The censoring lower aspect of quelle gives the power to remember. The higher monitoring aspect of quelle, or the higher unconscious, gives the power to erase or forget. The higher unconscious monitors all phases of memory and determines what man *consciously* remembers from past lives.

The monitoring aspect of the higher unconscious determines how much a person can bear as to his past-life emotions and thoughts. The monitor of the higher unconscious is also the mediator between the objective mind and the quelle subconscious mind.

In dreams past lives desire to flow into the outer consciousness during sleep. Persons not having been initiated into night-flight sift down their dreams into the outer consciousness through an intense emotional action of the night. Persons not understanding the power-charged reincarnation symbols in dreams believe such dreams to be some peculiar and unknown factor in man's complex nature. Such egos receive their reincarnation symbolic recordings in a stepped-down or transposed action.

Dreams of a past life to one uninitiated sometimes appear in the symbol of a house furnished as in a previous period and time. Clothing worn by the dreamer in the dream is often unfamiliar to him as compared with the style and fashion of the present time.

Reincarnation dreams differ from dreams related to present-life correction and instruction. In dreams reaching beyond the lower astral currents affecting the lower emotions, one does not dream that he is of any sex, male or female. In reincarnation dreams one can identify a life of an ancient time as to whether he was male or female in that life. By his clothing, by his attitudes, and by his actions in the dreams he recognizes – with the help of the quelle pictograph factor in dreams – his polarity weaknesses or his strengths.

Reincarnation dreams come to the initiate in timing to his need to incorporate with the life of the present the mental and the emotional images and attitudes of one or more lives that he has lived in the past.

When a person reaches his thirty-fifth year, he begins to relate his present consciousness to the consciousness used in previous existences. Reincarnation-dreaming absorption is initiatory, affecting the outer and present life.

Every seven years after one reaches the thirty-fifth year, he must absorb into his objective or outer consciousness something of the consciousness he has used in previous existences. This is one way God keeps a balance between the karma of past lives and the karma of the present.

From the thirty-fifth year to the forty-second year, one must absorb past-life religious and spiritual attitudes. In dream life he undergoes three phases of experience: (1) if he has any atheistic beliefs, he may be pulled back into the undertow of his atheistic unbelieving; (2) he may be picked up on the crest of a karmic wave to experience wider dimensions of reality as to his personal motives; (3) he is shaken and sifted as to what he really knows about his inward self.

The forty-second year is a crucial year in the outward life. It is a time in which one is comforted by his accomplishments or plagued by his failures. The quelle reminders, called *samskaras,* at the base of his skull press upward, flowing over the protective higher unconscious plateau into his outer mind. When karma is heavy, the forty-second year is a turgid time for the subconscious. These years are the meeting time between the motivation and the aptitudes of the present life and the former-life drives fermenting within the subconscious side of one's nature.

On the physical plane, during such dream initiations one experiences much outer restlessness, self-analysis and discontent in these years, for he is being inwardly and outwardly weighed against past-life abilities, talents and desires.

During the period of the forty-second year to the forty-ninth year, in dream experience one may retrogress childishly to desires unfulfilled during childhood in this life. He is in danger of opening primitive psychic desires in his emotional nature. If karma from his past life contains lechery, lust, violence or hatred, this will outpicture itself in the physical consciousness. Very often a person loses touch with his basic protective instincts supporting character, making new karma and further sorrow in this life.

Dreams of such persons are weird, active, fearful, reproachful and suggestible. In some instances, if the spiritual life has not been expressed in this life, the person can outwardly become totally another identity, being overshadowed by a dominant ego-memory of a former life. A dominant characterization of a former-life compulsion can temporarily set aside the true and good aspects which until now have been the ordinary and acceptable motivation of the present life.

Men are just now coming to understand the importance of a compelling continuity in the dream flow as related to the outer consciousness. What psychiatry and psychology must yet learn is that dream life absent from consciousness would produce no consciousness. Also it is necessary that the vital theme of rationality in dream sequence and progression be understood, and especially that its activity during the state of sleep should be reproduced automatically after each night's dreaming into the outer-life consciousness and action.

As men become more complex on the consciousness plane through pressure, amorality and selfishness, more indifferent to each other in the self-genesis age, it is necessary that all cultivate and understand the science of dreaming. Without understanding of the reincarnation signals, signs, symbols and vocabularies through dream interpretation, no one can obtain an honest clue or formula process for utilizing his dreams.

As long as one seeks to interpret dreams from the outer consciousness inward, rather than the inward consciousness outward, he will remain cynical and fatally materialistic.

Dream symbols are treasures etched by the eternal consciousness overdwelling all phases of consciousness in man. To have access to a vocabulary of dream symbols related to man's eternal origin, his primitive origin, and his natural origin, plus a recognition of his consciousness symbols, is to keep free the progressive states of dreaming.

Spasmodic recollection of dreams, while not wholly satisfactory, can produce temporary soporific therapies to give the conscience certain easement and relaxation.

The method science presently is using to artificially produce dreams will prove to be harmful. In the study of dreams certain drugs given to produce dream data and statistics will prove to be misleading and harmful to the essential ego balance.

The only true and right way to produce ego-balanced, progressive sequence in dreams is through the use of pre-sleep mantrams, prayer and meditation. The etheric membranes surrounding the karmically energized contents of quelle can be ruptured and opened prematurely by any form of manipulative research while under the influence of drugs or external inducement in dreaming.

THE HIGHER SUGGESTIBLES

The lesser aspect of quelle, or the lower subconscious functioning, acts as a repository for latent karma. The initiate is sometimes caught off guard when quelle unleashes the sediments of old sin or karmic action into his unprepared outer consciousness action. High suggestible action can be taken in right timing to clear the karmic sediment residing in lower quelle. Fortunate is the seeker who knows the techniques of transposing and utilizing karmic sediment.

One should use the high suggestibles in right mantramic speaking, right visualization, right tonal sounds (such as the OM) to dissolve and to clear the bronze lake of passion seeking to sully the desired passionless detached state of the mind and feeling.

The purifying crystal lake of transcendence is centered in the higher unconscious. The higher unconscious receives, monitors, and transcends the overcharged overflow, using a correcting aspect of the undertow of karma in the lower subconscious or lower quelle.

The bronze lake in lower quelle, seated at the base of the skull, contains all past-life negative feelings and thoughts. During meditation the bronze lake becomes clear amber liquid, clear in color until the sediment in the bottom is stirred due to present-life and former-life faulty desiring. When one overactivates the bronze lake of quelle, it is similar to a liquid pranic fire burning sometimes as a mental acid, sometimes as a dry heat, affecting the passions and the desires. Overabundance of karmic sediments sent up to the higher unconscious without consent from the higher unconscious can result in shock to the total integrating principle supporting the outer consciousness. When the higher unconscious cannot organize instantly or adjust to the karmic overflow from lower quelle, the result can produce more than the ego can handle.

Every seven years after the thirty-fifth year, all spiritually sensitized persons undergo the major initiations. Major initiations invoke old karmic states. One must prepare the higher unconscious to anticipate karmic overflow from lower quelle by making positive the rhythmic flow in meditation, and he must also come to union with the higher imagery process of the new action centered in the forefront of the brain. This can be done by use of mantrams or the higher suggestibles; also by the exercise of concentration.

All of the old or primitive processes of various brain phases in evolvement are under command of lower quelle. All of the new processes of the brain are working with the higher unconscious through the fore lobes or frontal lobes of the brain. When one meditates, he must expect to set up the higher octaves of mind action. Through meditation one uses what men are calling today the alpha tone in the mind. This is the mind in Christ. Since Jesus, all men are moving to give the new or most recent development of the brain the most prominent place in thought or thinking.

The higher unconscious can be made a more powerful asset to this new mind through the use of pre-sleep mantrams and through mediative healing processes. The budding point of the new mind is between the eyebrows. Thus, in meditation one begins to receptively visualize love in the heart and to raise the light to the point of the starry portal between the eyebrows. This enables him to make contact with *the third eye.*

DREAMS AND THE SEVEN LAYERS OF ETHER IN THE EYE

Recent observations into the world of dreams and man's physical reaction to his dreaming set into motion by scientists have shown that during a certain period of sleep a moving of the eye may be observed. All spiritual scientists understand and use the vision processes of the eye with a full knowing. The physical eye is the center of self-consciousness. The iris of the eye induces the will to see or to vision. The soul working with the will to see enables the one seeing to become a witness to his inner world.

Physical-eye seeing is yet to be fully developed in the world. Spiritual-eye seeing has been a perfected instrument since man entered the earth. To use the power of seeing through vision in the waking state or the sleeping state is given to those who have retained the memory of cosmos sight.

Vision in the day and vision in the night can be recovered through processes of initiation. The third eye, enabling man to see inwardly and to speak of visions outwardly, seeks to use the physical eye in the day and in the night.

Mind and sight are interconnected. An initiate of the light, or solar psychic, stays in contact with his third eye at all times.

The iris of the physical eye has seven layers of ether: (1) the ring of ether affected by the planets; (2) an opaque ring affected by the moon; (3) an inner ring affected by chlorophyll and the plant life; (4) a layer of ether affected by akasia and akasic fluid; (5) a layer of ether which acts as a photographic lens, recording what is seen and what has been seen in the physical world; (6) a layer of ether correlating to the illumination of the soul; (7) a layer of ether which records everything seen within the inner planes and in earth, and seals away the memory of what has been seen until the mind and the heart are ready to receive what has been observed through vision and sight.

When the first layer of ether in the iris of the eye is activated in a dream, one sees in vision the planetary action affecting his lesser etheric body. During sleep or dreams he becomes more aware of the effect of the constellations of the zodiacal system upon the lesser etheric body. If there is a negative planetary action of the night, he will awaken on the morning with an apprehension, as he will have seen in the dream the negative aspects of the planets affecting his actions for the day. As one advances in his initiations in the higher worlds, through the first layer of ether in his eye he will discern the beneficent effects of the planets upon his higher etheric body. On awakening, one may sometimes remember having been trained or instructed in the night concerning the planets, the stars, and the universe. When one has the grace to be trained in this manner, he becomes a dreaming-astronomer, beholding God's universe.

When one opens the second layer of ether in the iris of the eye during sleep, he observes the moon's reflected sphere. He researches his emotions and desires. He beholds the silvery phantomlike forms of angelic beings inhabiting the *reflected sphere* of the moon situated on the outer edge of the magnetic belt of the earth. When the moon-layer of ether in the eye is active, one sees all things in the waking world mystically through his emotions, and he communes with other men through his emotions.

In dream experience the third layer of ether in the eye enables one to literally will to rejuvenate his lesser etheric body and physical body through the healing potencies of Nature. He wills, sees, and draws upon the chlorophyll fire within the plant kingdom and takes into his body living essences. He awakens with vigor; he is refreshed and healed.

If one is being initiated through the fourth layer of ether in the eye, he travels in the night to see or read the soul-memory records of the archives. He opens his vision to his own life-record and to the record of the earth and its action. If he is highly evolved, he can also see and research the life-memory records of others.

When the fifth layer of ether in the eye is quickened or activated, one aligns himself with the memory of things of the past. He weighs and balances them with events of the present. If he has grace, this enlargement of sight or vision will enable him to act with discernment. A sense of justice will enter his being in his outer works. He will seek to live within the law of God's equation.

When the sixth layer of ether in the eye is unrestrained, one will see and look down upon all things in the physical world with a fourth-dimensional objectivity. He will behold the rarefied heavenly planes, and will see them in their infinitesimal dimensions. When the sixth layer of ether in the eye is quickened, one acts as a seer, a prophet, an Illuminati.

When the vision of the dreamer expresses the seventh layer of ether in the eye, the one dreaming unites his vision with the combined vision of the presences of heaven; and he unites with the rhythms of revelation. He conjoins his own wisdom with the archetone, silent logos or sound current of the Archetypal Kingdom. While his inner mind will record what he has seen, he will be unable to speak of what he has seen – until he is given the sign by the Holy Ghost to speak of and reveal what he has seen.

Men not seeing inwardly are dependent upon what is seen in the physical world. Such men are as blind men. Beyond physical sight, beyond physical knowing, there are worlds open to him who has throughout the ages developed the inner seeing and knowing.

When the gravity pressures of the day are taken over by the moon's action at night, the vital ethers supporting sight or vision in the brain are free. No matter how much one may depend upon the physical sense of sight in the light of the day, with the sun's going down he has a certain sense of sight in the night. All men see in their dreams visions never contemplated in the day. From seeing dreams of the night, one is gradually initiated into an extended world of truth and reality. In the higher dream levels, one is made aware that he is a significant part of an eternal world. No matter what state his physical life may be in, through the dream state he learns that he is important in the whole of life.

INITIATORY DREAMS AND THE MOON

The ego is the centralization of the individuality. When the moonrise begins at dusk, the personality-will is lessened, and the individuality becomes predominant in the mentality and within the soul. This occurs at dusk with the receding of the sun's rays from the earth.

During the night's sleep, when the moon is in the *sign of Aries,* one is initiated and tested by warring and hostile impulses. He is shown the face of his adversary; and if he has earned the grace, he is insulated from the irritating and challenging events of the coming day. During the daytime, when the moon is in Aries, one is weighed as to his competency to lead. If there is any remaining shadow of cupidity in him, or any desire to force his will upon another, this will be expressed by him. He should be alerted at this time to avoid any form of forcing or pressure. He should refrain from forcing issues, and he should not submit to force and pressure from any outside source or person. At all times he should seek to retain his equilibrium, his emotional and mental poise.

When the *moon is in Taurus,* one may search his record of stewardship over possessions and persons during night-flight or sleep. He is shown by his Guardian Angel whether he has envy of other people's possessions or whether he has a balanced attitude as to earning and giving. Following such initiations he outpictures in the daytime hours hidden covetous and envious attitudes as to objects, possessions, things, money, spending, lending, saving, giving. He is also alerted as to his karmic dependence on persons and their possessions.

When the *moon is in Gemini,* during the night's sleep the analytical side of one's thoughts is extended; and one is weighed as to his worldly nature and his spiritual nature. His Guardian Angel shows him how he may fuse or blend these two qualities within him. In the daytime actions he should be alerted, for he will be presented with certain trials concerning double-speaking, criticism of others, discontent, mental unrest. In this period he has the danger to be one who divides or separates. He should be alerted that he become a mediator rather than a separator. He should also see the good rather than the negative.

When the *moon is in Cancer,* one sinks deeply into his subconscious memory during sleep. He touches the world matrix, or world womb of birth; he draws upon the memory of the birth of humanities. In the night he activates the birth stream of ancestral memory within himself. He touches the feminine influence upon mankind. He sometimes researches the records of wrongs enacted against him. In the daytime, when the moon is in the sign of Cancer, he should refuse to yield to any form of self-pity. In this period he should refuse to blame others for his circumstance. He should give praise to God for his grace, his good, and for the grace of all souls. In the daytime hours he should make a covenant to pray for the healing of men who delude themselves. He should pray that he may use the higher aspect of his service and sympathy. He should also pray that the magnetism exuding from his emotions be undefiled.

When the moon is in the *sign of Leo,* one who has the grace will unite with the soul power of the self and of the great souls in the inner life. Thus, he will extend the power of magnanimity and illumination. He may also read the record of his own intent, whether it be colored by self-pride of personal achievement or of the glory of attainment for God. The moon-in-Leo initiation during sleep will enable him to widen his spiritual periphery, to extend the reach of his silver cord's action. During the daytime actions, if there be any false pride or any shading of ethic, he will be reprimanded through some outer source or event. He will receive a humility lesson, demoting him from self-appointed authority. If he has grace manifesting in this period, he will receive additional responsibilities. How he accepts these responsibilities will determine the amount of authority he will be given by the greater authorities of heaven. In this period he should seek to be honest with himself, to admit that he is a frail vessel dependent wholly upon the Father in him and the Will of God.

When the moon is in the *sign of Virgo,* sleep can be fitful, restless, as there are daytime tensions weighing upon the mental action of the night. In the night hours of this period one comes face to face with his thought world, with his pure or impure sexual impulses. If there be grace, he is taken by his Guardian Angel to behold God's storehouse or God's wealth of abundance. He learns the difference between sowing and reaping. He also perceives the necessity for discrimination in thought and in act. If he is undergoing a special initiatory action in this period, he will evaluate his sentiment-tinged thinking, and he will learn that attachments colored by man-tradition produce pain. Thus, in this time he will gain the lesson to use his mentality in a chaste manner. He will cut the Gordian knot of former vague thinking. In the daytime action he will begin to appreciate truth for truth's sake. If he is a father, he will seek to be loving, tender, just, wise and discriminating for his child. He will be used by God to render right justice in right timing. If the initiate is a mother, she will be more considerate of the soul-worth of her child, rather than the trivial irritants which stand between her and the love she seeks to give.

During sleep, when the *moon is in Libra,* there is pronounced activity in the ego. One undergoes a research of motive, often becoming a judge of his own actions.

Should the moon fall into Libra on a Friday night, a special Venus initiation is experienced. The one sleeping and dreaming is faced with the length and breadth and height and depth of his love.

If he is highly evolved, he will receive healing and anointing from the saintly cloisters. If he is an unruly personality, he will be exposed to the records of his errors, and awaken on the morning weighted down by the burden of self-guilt. However, if he has a sense of justice, he will respond in the day to what his Guardian Angel has said to him in the night.

When the moon places her lunar light in the zodiacal *sign of Scorpio,* the one dreaming is challenged as to propagation or sex. If he has used the lower side of his temperament in his daytime action – such as retaliation, dominance and revenge – on this night he will be exposed to strident forces of the subtle world. He will war with these unruly representatives of his lower nature. But if one has an innately forgiving nature, an admiration for righteous works, he will be strengthened on this night. His avocation will be clarified to him, and some of the barriers of the daytime will be relaxed. He will awaken on the morning with clarified purpose, and his dedication will be without deviation.

In the *Sagittarian* lunar action of dreaming, when the moon falls into Sagittarius, the night's instruction reveals to the dreamer his dependencies upon others. He is made aware that he is not alone, but is dependent upon those who stand with him in his pattern of destiny. If he has grace, he will discern in these night hours that he should adhere to loyalty, fidelity, ethic. His dream imagery will also reveal to him certain ritual formulas in religion; and he will unite with the powers of the Cherubim Angels through poetry and music. His dream will be portrayed to him through musical sounds, poetic words. He will awaken determined to put his symbolic instruction into daytime daring and reality.

When the moon is in the *sign of Capricorn,* the Guardian Angel of one having grace discloses to the dreamer the Lord's table with a white cloth, and also shows him the basin and the towel which Jesus used to wash and to wipe the feet of His disciples. On this night the dreamer will be shown the very kernel and heart of humility. If he has any particle of arrogance or forceful thrusting of his will, he will awaken with irritability and self-reproach. If he has a true devotion to selfless labors, rather than desire for executive powers, he will awaken with renewed dedication to spiritualize his serving as a humble masterbuilder for God.

When the *moon is in Aquarius,* the one dreaming is faced with his Guardian Angel who shows him the other side of frenzy, fantasy and unreality. He is warned to use his daytime zeal with practicality, ethic and devotion. If he has been overzealous at the expense of some other person, the Guardian Angel will warn him to return to ethic, consideration. When the moon is in Aquarius, during sleep one may also encounter the magnetic, energized electrical currents of the astral stratosphere. If this occurs, his lesser etheric body will be psychically overcharged on the following day. He should be alerted to falls or accidents on the day after these fretful and exhausting challenges. Should he have the grace to move beyond the astral stratosphere energy currents, he will behold the etheric-braille imprints of things to come. He will commune with the Higher Guardians or Illuminati who are entrusted with the unknown or inventive treasures waiting to come to the world. If one has reverently used telepathic knowledge from the higher worlds, on awakening he will have recollection of the night hours, and he will utilize and put into formulas the instruction received while dreaming or sleeping.

When the *moon is in Pisces,* one dreaming may recall, upon awakening, the subconscious chaotic regions he has visited during the night; for when the moon is in the sign of Pisces, the initiate-dreamer is exposed to the subconscious matrix of humanity's memory. On these nights the dreamer comes close to the hidden side of man's unlawful emotions and desiring. He sees the dark side of duality; the subtle side of his own personality is revealed to him. If he has earned night-ministry powers, he will etherically visit penal institutions, hospitals. He will look into the darkened side of the souls' records of those who have maliciously harmed him. He will look into the darkened side of his own soul's record. In such dreaming he is accompanied by his Recording Angel and Guardian Angel, who assist him in this experience, and also protect him from being consumed by despondency, or being permanently impressed and influenced by what his night vision has seen and recalled. In the daytime action the initiate-dreamer finds himself seeing men with the eye of mercy and compassion. He determines to help men to overcome, to rise above the soiled and sordid side of desiring and sensuality. Healing consummated on these nights, when the moon is in Pisces, is a mighty healing of mercy and grace.

HEALING AND THE HIGHER ENERGIES AT NIGHT

The solar energies feed and nourish the higher energies of the lesser etheric body. When the spiritual initiate breathes through the higher solar energies, he draws upon a *third vitality.* The in-and-out currents of his breath come under the command of the higher etheric body. This third vitality works in a circular clockwise motion upon the organs of the body, particularly the heart. The high solar energy within the third-vitality breathing enables the initiate to catapult his higher etheric body from the physical body at night. Should he have conscious command of this solar high vitality, he spirals out of his body, entering into the night ministry with awareness and cognition.

All great adepts use the higher solar breath to slow down the heartbeat during sickness, that they may partake of the regeneration reflexes within the lesser etheric body. The adept knows that during sickness the solar restoring vitality heals and sensitizes; the lunar vitality relieves, regenerates and purifies.

When one is aware of the spiritual use of the higher solar energies, he becomes a healer under Christ. He heals with the spiritual sun. All of his luminal-lunar qualities, his higher subliminal-subconscious qualities and his illuminative spiritual qualities become an incandescent, authoritative healing body for the Christ. The daytime healing ministry and the night healing ministry become equal when one attains the third-vitality breath.

Through dreams, an initiate is taught how to "go in and out" – that is, to experience night-flight with full consciousness and return to the physical body with a clear memory of the night's experience. An initiate also has access to his akasic record. In the night while dreaming, an initiate is taught in the inner planes how to regenerate his physical body to withstand the daytime trials, and how to restore the higher etheric body through returning to the source of the white fires of the higher solar light each night in sleep.

All cells and organs of the body are in motion. This unceasing motion correlates to the movement of the cosmic system supporting all organic life, and to the rhythm of the cosmos system supporting the spiritual life.

To become an illumined avatar for God, one must think and live in the light vitalities in the day and in the night. Where physical darkness is, his light will be preeminent; where ignorance is, the light in his mind will be an omniscient vessel emanating light.

All sicknesses are caused by disarrangement of energies; all healings are manifested through rearrangement of the pattern of energy distortion causing sickness. This is made possible through the use of prayer, meditation and mediation within the light.

Health begets coordination, symmetry, harmony. When fear of sickness persists in one's thoughts during the night's sleep, he absents himself from the light. When health is reinstated during the night, the body is revitalized on the morning, and one returns to the day with new vigors, new vitalities.

To reinstate health, or to reverse sickness, the night-ministry initiate is initiated into the higher solar vitalities supporting his everlasting body. The light received in the night for health becomes a holy magnetism in the day. This magnetism, when sustained by pure solar energies, heals.

DREAM LEVELS: INITIATORY
PROCESSES IN THE NIGHT

Archetypal Kingdom (Spiritual)
The Christ.
Archangels. Logos Angels.
Spirit of Truth.
The Greater Archetypes (or the unmanifested Word).

Realm of Light (Spiritual)
The Lord Jesus and His Disciples. The Celestial Angels. Dream initiation in the Realm of Light is extremely rare, and is experienced only by a perfected telepathic disciple or a cosmos disciple.

Spheres of Light (Spiritual)
The Great Immortals or Masters. The Terrestrial, Seraphim and Planetary Angels. Hall of Wisdom. Dream initiation in the Spheres of Light may be experienced only by perfected Night Servers, or by those who have commanded the lesser astral planes and the 8th sphere or greater abyss trials set up by Satan.

7th Astral Plane (Sacred level)
Devas or Shining Ones.
Buddha.
Bodhisattvas.
Sacred men.
The Illuminati.

6th Astral Plane (Prophetic Level)
Prophetic certainties.
Communion with the Saints.
Hall of Learning.
The White Brothers.
The Risen Dead.
Cherubim Angels.

5th Astral Plane (Initiatory level)

Initiation into the abstract plane of the astral world. Contains the reflected formulas correlated to the Greater Archetypes in the Archetypal Kingdom. A threshold plane in preparation for going into the higher levels. The Labyrinths or Pavilion of Light.

4th Astral Plane
(Archive Memories and Embodiment Records level)

To make alignment with the Seraphim and Cherubim Angelic Kingdom, Maha Chohan, Melchizedec, Ancient of Days and the Great Rishis, the disciple must master the three lesser astral planes. In this, he is given the power to research the Archive Memories and Akasic Records or Reincarnation Records. The beginning of the greater abyss trials.

3rd Astral Plane (Wish, Bliss and Paradise level)

To master the wish, bliss and paradise level, one must deglamorize desire; his desire must correlate to his true need seen by "Our Father which art in heaven." The Transitory Dead are on this level. Phenomena and illusion. Predictive possibles. On the first three astral planes, one undergoes the lesser abyss trials.

2nd Astral Plane (Fantasy and Purgatory level)

To master the Fantasy and Purgatory level in dreams, there must be organization of thought, and the ability to rationalize the Plan of God.
The Unrisen Dead are on this level.

1st Astral Plane (Grotesque level)

Discarnate shells. Subtle entities. Sub-elementals. To master the Grotesque level in dreams, one must have perfect faith in the Father and His image for man.

Chapter 3

SOUND AND SYMBOLS IN DREAMS

Each life is a pure stone set upon a temple structure for my soul. Each day fresh mortar is added to the building for my soul. Let me be not empty handed at the end of my day.

FOUR SYMBOLIC KEYS TO DREAM DRAMA

In the present stage of man's evolvement, there are four basic symbolic keys to drama in dreams: the primitive; the domestic; the individualistic; the soul and the spiritual.

Primitive. Primitive symbols in dreams and in meditation portray the will to survive. All primitive symbols stem from unresolved tribal-genesis association and memory. Some of the primitive symbols are experienced as fire, avalanche, snow, iceberg, tumultuous water, drowning, earthquakes. Also among the primitive symbols are animals and reptiles, such as serpents, crocodiles, alligators, tigers, gorillas.

Domestic. Domestic symbols portray the competitive alternates of winning and losing. In domestic symbolic dream dramas, the integrity and honor are researched. One's desire to be approved by his family is magnified and gauged through domestic dream symbols. Sex, love, health, birth, and death are symbolically pictured in dreams on the level of domestic symbology. The family-atom dweller or conscience of the family action is also researched in dreams through domestic symbologies.

Individualistic or Lesser Self-Genesis. Symbols in individualistic dream dramas are activated by the immature mentality, by frustrations caused by egotism, and by a mentality charged with ego power-drives. In individualistic dream dramas, one receives reproving from his personal conscience; he magnifies and estimates his faults.

Higher Self-Genesis or Soul and Spiritual. These initiatory dream symbols appear when one has overcome the lesser levels of geneses evolvement. Soul and spiritual symbols in dream dramas portray heavenly attributes and mediative associations, keeping the balance between the physical and spiritual worlds. In soul and spiritual symbology, one experiences his dreams as instruction rather than apprehension. The one dreaming beholds the beauty of the higher worlds, and remembers the manner, voices, and intonations of his instructors of the night. He moves into wavelengths of revelation observing without fear the visions of the dark. He is given ritualistic power through certain dream-code understanding, that he may be protected from the dark. His spiritual powers in the day expand into creative action of the day.

All initiates having entry into the rarefied atmospheres of the spirit use their knowledge through the true rituals of the spirit, beginning always in the inner planes during dreams.

SPACE, TIME AND SYMBOLS

Space is the expanding canvas upon which God extends and perfects His design. Time is the means through which His design and plan proceed. Space and time are as yet little understood by the factual or materialistic mind. The ultimates of God are unchangeable; however, the results and effects of creation stemming from God are ever-changing.

Symbols are the cosmic communicable keys bridging space and time, enabling the intuitive and illuminative faculties of the soul to take command of the mind, that one may unite with the design of God.

The uninitiated have yet to earn the capacity to receive directly the greater ideas upholding the framework of creation. They must depend upon the language of earthlike symbols as an intermediary communion with God.

While man has never been an animal, he has certain corresponding traits that relate him, symbolically, to the animal kingdom. Therefore, the first initiation into symbology is through animal symbols.

Through dream symbols reflected in etheric-imprint paintings, and symbols seen during contemplation and meditation, one can determine what degree of initiation he is undergoing. There are symbols suitable to every degree of initiation. The greater the dedication and the purer the disciple, the more beautiful and positively creative is the symbol.

MUSIC

The most deep desire of all initiates is to contact the audible life stream, or the archetones upholding all life. The audible life stream is the life current, the sound current, the spiritual current of logos flowing forth from the greater archetypes. Christ has command over the archetypes supporting the Mind of God.

The *Word* spoken of in the Bible is the vibrationless vibration or the soundless sound. To unite with the soundless sound or the sound current in its vibrationless state is to unite with the unconditioned Supreme One, or God. *To hear* the audible life stream is to unite with the conditioned God, or our Father which art in heaven. In both waking and in dreams one unites to some degree with the sound current of the celestial. *The Being called the Holy Ghost frees the sound current of the great archetones.*

The sound current experienced in dreams is a celestial music having a centrifugal flow – that is, outward to man. It also has a centripetal flow, a music rising upward to God through the prayers of the saints, the works of the angels, and the supplications of the souls on earth. In the night in dreams these two flows interfuse and touch one another, pressing upon the inner ear of the one dreaming. In dreams one may hear his own prayers amplified, and the answers to his prayers may be enlarged by a saint's responding through words, or by the Master's voice speaking into his inward right ear.

Many are the compositions composed in the higher exalted state of mind-hearing during sleep. Many are the directives, the guidances and blueprint instructions received through the sound current or the celestial musics of the night.

In dreams the inward third eye is the instrument of vision. The sight of the day is partially limited or tied to the ego-consciousness seeing and recording. The inward ear is also free in the night as a soul instrument. Whatever the ego believes, knows, trusts, or has faith in, he can receive, confirm, enlarge and hear in his inward ear. The ear is a receptive instrument. Its range of hearing covers the total etheric body, the physical body, the skeletal-bony system and the aura surrounding the etheric body.

The ear as a receiver and recorder draws upon the four senses of touching, smelling, tasting and seeing, to express itself as a whole and receptive vehicle. The ear is also a vehicle of feeling. What one hears in the night or the day is dependent upon an intensely concentrated desire to know, to learn, to experience.

Outer physical deafness does not influence night inner hearing. One can be in contact with the inner ear in the waking state or in the sleeping state, regardless of his physical hearing. In meditation, one unites with the audible sound or celestial music.

In dream initiation, unison with the sound current begins with the release of the silver cord from the body. In undisturbed night-flight, sound becomes a floating, billowing ocean or a vibrational loftiness. Sound takes the higher etheric body up into its transcendental flight. In night initiation, the sound current enables one to penetrate higher and higher states of transition in flight.

Celestial music in the night is healing to the sleeping body. It is also the vehicle for the voice of God to speak into the ear of man in the night. The voice of God is differentiated into many voices – helping, instructing, evaluating and correcting.

In the lower astral world, the great sound current is toned down by the gravity reaches of the earth and of the lower vibrational rates or subelectromagnetisms. One expressing the lower side of his ego can undergo a frightening experience in the lower astral world.

When one is unable to relax his sense faculties of the day, these faculties remain in the proximity of the chakra-vortex of the throat, close to the thyroid center. To be wholly free in the night, the speed of sense action and cares of the day must be slowed down in sleep within the lesser etheric body. When a person is worried before sleep, his senses are churned and stirred by subelectronic gravity tensions, and he is unable to totally release himself etherically to the night's action. Thus, he experiences the raucous, atavistic, mesmeric inductive sounds of the night, as he can reach no farther in night-flight than the lower astral world. Such dreaming yields only interpretations on the Freudian levels.

True night-flight is the release of the higher etheric body, the higher emotional body and the higher mental body to the world of dreams. In the first training for night-flight, the initiate is assisted by three angels, that he may slow down his senses and relax in true sleep. One must anesthetize the lesser etheric body, the lesser emotional body and the lesser mind, that he may rise in the night. If he has the grace, his three angels – the Luminosity Angel, his

Guardian Angel and his Recording Angel – assist him to move over the gravity astral tumults of raucous, perverted sound.

The initiate in his training for night-flight action, uses certain mantrams before sleep, that he may assist himself in night-flight and thus avoid the turbulence of astral shock.

Many persons on awakening in the morning, not having angelic protection, are jolted back into their physical bodies too quickly. Such persons sometimes have the sensation of falling. In reality, they have failed to unite with the positive sound current in their silver cord's action assuring their flow or fluidic return into their bodies.

When one fails to make union with the positive sound current acting with the silver cord in the night, he cannot completely leave his lesser etheric body. When this occurs, the lesser etheric body, the lower emotional body and the lower mind are suspended hammock-like between the physical, the etheric and astral worlds. Through the positive sound or audible current in the night, one freely leaves his physical body, keeping intact his higher mentality, emotions and ego consciousness.

In free night-flight, one literally travels to places in the regions, planes, spheres and realms of the spiritual worlds. In such dream states, the soul is free when one relieves his consciousness of his karmic burdens, his doubts, his fears, to travel to places of spiritual reality, to research them and to record them, and to use his knowledge on the coming day.

Distracting outer noises during sleep, such as traffic noises intruding upon quiet and rest, clocks ticking too loudly, dogs barking, radios left on, mechanical sleep-teaching techniques – all prevent the etheric body from being totally released. Dreams become fragmented and one experiences magnified, intrusive astral sounds. Such dreams are exhausting, leaving one with dissatisfaction. Hallucinatory and chimera dreams can be caused by uncomfortable mattresses, faulty body hygiene, offensive odors, wrong posture of the body during sleep, too much food before sleep, defeatist attitudes before sleep and fear of burglary intrusion. All of these external conditions prevent true and clear dreaming.

Persons having overstimulating mental and emotional pressures before sleep are unable to rise into the pure sound levels of sleep, and thus experience their dreams in the lower raucous sound of the astral world.

In dreams, pure and true sound is encountered by the inner ear in the upper or higher astral world, called the First Heaven. When one contacts the true audible sound in sleep, he will thereafter understand that vibration holds together all life. Were it not for the sound current supporting all life, all things of the physical plane would dissolve into nothingness. God as the *Vibrationless* extends Himself into soul life, mental life, emotional life, animal life, plant life and the life of the sea *as vibration.* The Word or the audible sound unites all life, from the very least into the highest. He who unites himself with the audible sound current with knowing and awareness becomes a consciousness channel for the Will of God and the power of the audible sound, or the Holy Ghost.

Every word spoken in this world is made possible due to the supporting audible sound current. The mantram and the mantra used by all sages and saints are the vehicles for the audible sound in action.

The mantram when used with awareness and consciousness produces the power to free one from the erosions of sin and negation. One with awareness of power in a mantra or mantram may literally be freed from karma and sin. All initiates know the power of the Great Vibration through the use of mantrams.

In meditation one enters through the door of the audible sound or vibration by speaking a mantram or sounding the sacred OM. One's intent should be to move into the Supreme One or the vibrationless, and thus remain in a continued state of union and alignment with God.

Pre-sleep mantrams move one out of the boundaries of fears and discord of the day, giving him winged powers to rise in the night upward in consciousness. Night instruction comes to him who prepares his heart and mind to receive.

In the night one sometimes is shown the musical scale. He unites himself with the seven key tones of the inner ear's tuning fork. The musical note of "A" represents creation, wonder, reverence, awe, self-denial, renunciation. The note of "B" represents, "Lord, I believe; heal Thou me." The note of "C" releases the discovery power and the seeing-consciousness. The sounding of "D" frees true desiring, effort, sacredness, devotion, discipline. "E" frees the will to relate to the power of God and the Will of God. "F" attunes one to the Father, to healing of the impossibles, to adoration of the Supreme One. "G" unites one with the Christ.

All minor notes enable one to unite with the Seraphim Angels. The sharps and flats producing dissonant sounds unite one with the subconscious realm influenced by the audible sound. There are zodiacal musics, celestial musics and angelic musics. The viola, the violin and the cello are overdirected by the Cherubim Angels.

All brass instruments, influenced by the planetary rays of Mars, relate to power, force and levitation. Drums, influenced by the rays of Saturn, are related to the heartbeat of the body, and are telepathic instruments for primal memory and for primitive communication.

The harp is an illuminative instrument and relates to the Wind Devas of the angelic stream. The harpsichord relates to the emotions; the sound of the harpsichord can heal emotional traumatic conditions.

The organ is a power instrument. Mastery of the organ by an initiate unites him with the great Masters. The piano is a will instrument, freeing the will of the player and healing procrastination tendencies in the hearer.

All wind instruments are related to the Lunar Deva Angels residing in the astral world. Wind-instrument music gives penetration into the glandular system of man, creating certain moods and desires. To hear the lute or flute of Krishna in the night in a dream is to learn that one is being prepared for initiation into higher strata of evolvement; he is researching the parallel between Krishna and the Christ.

All music in the physical world on the classic level has been given to master composers that they might be freeing agents for mass karma. To hear a symphony or to participate in symphonic music is to free mass karma of peoples, countries or nations.

Singing of great music in dramatic form, such as opera, dissolves certain karmic molds of human conduct. Folk music and folk dancing unite one with the generation archetypes and the memory ancestral streams expressed in families and locales.

All music expressing emotional pathos is induced by the Divine Mother principle. All music such as the music of Beethoven, Grieg, Handel, Sibelius, is induced by the Father principle.

Present-day music, jazz, ragtime, rock and roll, correlate to lesser self-genesis birth in the Western world. Such music is emotionally-charged ego music. It is sent from the Cherubim Angels that men may break free from crystallized patterns of former geneses laggardness. Too much of this music heard in the physical ear can give offense to the nadis points in the etheric body and also can damage the physical ear with loss of hearing.

When the waking ear constantly hears the beat of ego-charged music, this overstimulates the glandular system and produces amorality. It is important that one accompany the hearing of such music with movement in his body or else he will be surcharged with over-concentration of the physical and psychical aspects of the lower audible sounds.

The audible sound in heaven falls into the inner ear and into the mind of the night in a different manner from the way it falls into the outer ear used in the day, as the lower senses used in daytime action are limited as recording instruments of the audible sound.

Celestial music or music of the spheres is in reality the higher planetary tones made audible to the true inner ear of the spiritual body. The fourth plane of the astral world is the beginning of the First Heaven. In the higher regions of the fourth plane of the astral world may be heard the divine cosmic music. It is on this plane that celestial harmonies are heard by great musicians – and through their creation, these harmonies later fall into the outer ear of man.

Condensed etheric music resounds into the expanded vibrational hearing of the initiate who has attunement with universal or cosmic music. All persons of the earth producing music affecting the soul impulses of men, such as the great hymns and the mantramic chanting tones, have known the cadence, the beat, the rhythm and the harmony of celestial or cosmic music.

The celestial music produces movement, elevation, expression. In the night, mind and soul contact with the audible sound currents through music enables one to rise into the higher spheres and realms of light, making contact with the spiritual arteries of instruction.

To experience dancing in the night, as one often does after he enters the Path, is to set up extended wavelengths of receptivity in the time clock of the etheric body. Such persons, while awake on earth, can identify the audible sound in a tree, in a piece of sculpture, in a waterfall, in a butterfly, in a rainbow, or in any living thing produced by God. Music can be heard and lifted into sounds, harmonies and melodies, and passed on into the living action of civilizations, nations and persons.

It has been noted by many that persons having inner hearing

sometimes become physically deaf, as in the case of Beethoven. Had Beethoven been able to unite himself with the vibrational music in the plant, mineral, animal and human world, he could have produced music even beyond the majestic music he gave to man.

The center or chakra of hearing coincides with the hollow of the throat directly above the breast bone. A creator of music transposing the audible sound to the world must have this chakra in his throat continually united with the *Hum* of the universe.

Beethoven retained the celestial music he heard and gave to mankind healing of mass karma through his great symphonic music.

In the era now facing men having higher degrees of evolvement, the tones of the earth, Nature and mankind will be registered on physical instruments. However, to reproduce the true cosmic music the inner ear will prove to be the only infallible instrument of receptivity and transmission.

Music received from the lower astral world playing upon the senses is given to man that he might express himself through movement of the body.

The Eastern world having understood and used the rhythmic laws through the practice of yoga has had no need of the charismatic music of jazz, ragtime and rock and roll as experienced in the lesser self-genesis age now occurring in the Western world.

Persons of the West using yoga practices or the asanas and the sounding of the vibrational OM to channel audible current in the etheric and physical bodies unite in the night dream experience with a higher order of celestial hearing. From such egos in the world will come a new music to draw men upward spiritually and mediatively.

Wind instruments which have in recent years been less conspicuous in music expression will return as being the major supporting tones in orchestration.

Jesus during the Last Supper sang hymns with His disciples. He understood the necessity for channeling the audible sound current. Hymns sung together, mantrams spoken together, holy chanting, keep alive the communicableness between souls reverently seeking to serve God, the Supreme One.

TOUCH IN THE NIGHT

In dream experience in which jewels are used to give instruction, one may be led to touch a jewel stone; on touching the jewel one will find that it is warm and alive and vibrant. Jewels, cloth, brocade, wool, fur, stone, water, flowers are all used in night instruction to train one's sensitivity as to texture in touch.

One takes this vibrancy into his body and is healed of karmic diseases, and changes the magnetic depletion in his body and emotions. To touch a sapphire stone in the night is to recharge the mind and to become one with the Christ Mind.

To feel that one is clothed in fur while dreaming, touching a furry animal, or that he is covered by fur indicates that he is being instructed as to the etheric-intensity energy and degrees or primal origins in the viable structures of life supports. If the fur is dry or scant, he is being warned of devitalization of his etheric vitality.

Fur in dream symbols is especially used to describe one's etheric state of health. The etheric fiery energy-weave and nadis flow of the lesser etheric body and of the aura is fur-like when magnified infinitely through touch in the night. One can gauge the health of his etheric body and of his aura through the touch of fur.

To touch metal or smooth objects in a dream indicates that one is being taught how to transmit energy and how to draw forth magnetism from dense or solid objects.

To dream that one is touching human flesh in the night is to gauge one's own sensual feelings as to physical persons or those whom he contacts in the physical world.

To touch an angel while dreaming in the night and to feel the vibrational atom charge of an angel's touch upon one's own body, hand or head is to be healed and charged with a mighty vibration lasting for days to come.

Sometimes in dream instruction a true and devoted disciple of a Master receives the touch of the Master's hand upon the command portal between the eyebrows, the master audible sound center. This indicates that one has been assisted by the Master to open the third eye and should apply himself more consistently to meditation, that he may know the joy of spiritual fulfillment.

To touch the feet of one's Master in the night is to be pledging obedience, or an acceptance of a right discipline.

Chapter 4

MYTH ASSOCIATION
AND PREHISTORIC
SYMBOLOGY IN DREAMS

*If it be my grace, may my going into the light tonight reveal
to me some of the true forms supporting form, the true ideas
supporting creation.*

The symbol of half-man and half-beast as portrayed by the centaur signifies that all men are initiated emotionally through correspondences to the four-footed animals. The centaur is a mythological key to man's correspondence to the animal kingdom, in that each man has one distinct animal characteristic which identifies the predominant quality in his character and temperament. The centaur is an etheric hybrid elemental dwelling in the interior regions of the astral world. Hybrid elementals work directly with some of the initiatory processes of man. The centaurs are guardians of wooded places where men meet in Nature initiatory conclaves, such as in witchcraft rites or rituals. The centaurs are in command of all lesser creatures of Pan. Elementals do not incarnate as men. Elementals have intelligence of *neh-man,* that is, "not-man" intelligence.

Mythological forms or figures with wings and with human and animal characteristics are hybrid elementals and have triple functions. Those having triple functions or attributes are the intermediaries between all Nature forces, Nature elementals, Nature Spirits and the angelic kingdoms. Such hybrid elementals are etheric protectors and guardians working directly with man, the angelic worlds and the astral world. When hybrid elementals have human heads, they work with man. When they have wings, they work with the Deva Angels. And when they are four-footed, they work with the animal kingdom and the astral world. The etheric hybrid guardians, being a link between the lesser elemental kingdom and the Deva Angels, protect certain communities, environments and nations. When they withdraw their protective helps, the lesser elemental kingdoms take possession of communities and environments. Thus the forces of darkness take command, and people channel their beliefs through magical powers rather than spiritual worships. When the etheric hybrid guardians withdraw their help from a nation or country's archetype, the lesser elemental kingdom takes command and such a nation becomes decadent, attracting only laggard and straggler souls. Immediately after Socrates, Plato and Aristotle, Greece fell. Immediately after Ikhnaton, Egypt fell.

The unicorn, once living as a creature of the earth, now withdrawn into the etheric twilight, works in the higher regions of the lesser astral planes. The unicorn works to inspire and assist one to sustain and maintain the higher degree of alignment with the higher astral planes, and thus bring forth the pineal gland or third eye, so as to perceive with truth rather than with fantasy.

The Egyptian sphinx, having the combined attributes of man and beast, when encountered on the etheric planes, signifies a dual rather than a triple function. The Egyptian sphinx is the elemental symbolic protector of initiatory areas. The Greek sphinx, having wings, the body of a lion and the head and breasts of a woman, represents a matriarchal initiation, initiation within the astral world and initiation for telepathy and communicableness through angelic helps.

Since the coming of Jesus, the elemental kingdoms have become subordinate to the Deva angelic beings. One may experience the etheric hybrid elementals in initiatory dreams, in mediative symbols and – when one is not wholly insulated in Light – in certain *dweller* experiences. A Western ego having no guru, using psychical powers, and not having entered through the "Door" of Jesus, is subjected to chimeras of dream fantasy produced by the lesser dual Pan etheric creatures working with the darker side rather than the higher side of the centaur powers. Such a person will be subjected to astral and psychical obsessions and delusions.

The story of Noah has caused much controversy and confusion because its allegorical meaning has been degraded into fable. There

have been numerous cataclysms in the earth and inspired surviv-
als overdirected by angelic helps, particularly in the earlier days
of humanity when men were more aware of their etheric relating
to God. The physical life of Noah correlated to a great cataclysm
and the withdrawal of an inverted type of humanity into a twilight
state. Noah, one of the Elect or advanced beings of his time, was
made the custodian of a new animal life-wave and a new humanity life-wave. The "ark" described in the Bible represents a spiritual "*arch*etype." Noah, being the pure, prototypal representative
of a new life-wave of humanity and a coming rise in genesis, sustained the thread of life-survival for animal and man of the earth.
In all new beginnings or new life-waves of the earth, the animal
species archetypes and the zodiacal prototypal and human generation archetypes work with a cleansing and extracting action. In the
ancient times these withdrawals always coincided with great tidal
waves or cataclysms.

Every 10,000 years masses of laggard souls are withdrawn into
a twilight state and certain of the obsolete species of the animal
kingdom are also withdrawn. Prehistoric animals such as the dinosaur, etc., were withdrawn in the ancient cataclysmic times.
When a withdrawn species of the animal kingdom is seen by one
in the dream world or in meditation, he is observing and researching these ancient periods. By the animal or creature seen he may
determine the period he is observing and researching.

Animals as symbols in dreams, allegories, parables and meditative experience correlate to the emotions and thoughts of man,
identifying his character and temperament. Thus, if a person sees
a hog, swine or pig as a main figure in his dream symbology, it
would indicate that he has a nature of greed or that he is to be
exposed to one who has a nature of greed, depending upon the
correlated symbols in the drama of the dream. Animals are used in
the Bible in both allegorical symbols and parable form because
the greater prophets and leaders of men understood the law of
correspondences between animal and man.

Men use the symbols of animals such as oxen, crocodiles, eagles,
doves, calves, etc. because they intuit the etheric correspondences
between animal species and man's temperament and character. In
ancient times the sphinx, griffin, unicorn, and creatures of Pan
were placed at the entrances of temples, tombs and treasures because men knew that the species elemental guardians, the etheric

regents over animals, worked through the animal sculptured shapes or forms and protected the treasures or cherished things. A sphinx with the face of a human, the wings of an eagle, and the body of a lion signifies that the elemental presence guarding the sculptured form has power in the physical world (human face), power in the airy realm of the winged creature (wings), and power in the astral world (lion). Those who used these symbols knew that such elemental portrayals in stone were vibrational vessels for elemental habitation. Thus the physical possessions within a tomb were guarded and protected by etheric elemental presences working through the vibration tones in sculptured forms. The Egyptian Sphinx, having a lion's body and a man's head, was a vessel for a tremendous elemental force to manifest within the polarity of Egypt, and thus Egypt was both a protected community and a polarity power. With the decaying of the purer Egyptian dynasties, these elemental powers changed to an inverted elemental action.

Each animal species archetype has its Species Guardian Angels. For example, the feline species has the Species Guardian Angels to control and time the mating seasons and to protect the animal in birth and death. When an animal dies, it is taken into the Species Guardian Angels' etheric anesthesia, and thus does not suffer pain in death as compared to man. In the case of one animal destroying another animal, the captured creature is anesthetized by the Species Guardian Angels, and the death pain is nullified. When man kills or destroys an animal, he has violated the Commandment, *"Thou shalt not kill."* The animal suffers pain because of this violation and is not protected by the Species Guardian Angels. When man kills for lust, for the sport of killing, or domesticates an animal – thereby imposing his karma upon the animal – the animal is isolated from the help of the Species Guardian Angels. The Species Guardian Angels are not the same as the species elemental guardians.

Bird life of a higher order is a corresponding species to the angel kingdom. Carnivorous birds correspond to the inverted astral elementals.

Animal species archetypes are etherically ballasted in the second region of the fourth astral plane where they are overdwelt by the Species Guardian Angels. The animal Species Guardian Angels work directly with the Cherubim Angels, producing all animal symbols in meditation and dreams. Man's moods and temperament, which so closely relate to the astral regions and planes, correlate directly to many animal correspondences. In this, man may be seen to express attributes in his character which are similar to particular animals. These similar correspondences between animal and man may be seen especially in the habits of man, in that a man be selfish as a hog, stubborn as a donkey, cunning as a fox, timid as a hare.

When a man has a cat in his home, he has a contact with the feline Species Guardian Angels. Should this animal be altered, it will be devoid of the Species Guardian Angels' help. If a man has a dog in his home, he has alignment with the wolf Species Guardian Angels, and with that which works through the dog. It may be seen that men who own dogs are inclined to prefer to hunt in packs, or that is, to associate in close working relationship to other men in the world rather than to be self-dependent. If a man has a bird of higher order in his home, the angelic kingdom may work more directly with his home.

The soul uses the animal species correspondence symbols in the dream world. If a person should see an animal in a dream, he may best interpret his dream by first determining the species of the animal, its habits and temperament in its primitive state rather than its domestic origin. Animal symbols in dreams may be used in a prophetic manner to predict the outcome of events. For example, in the dream world one may dream of attack from a boar and on the coming day contact an insensitive, forceful person with an unreasonable and belligerent attitude.

The habitat of an animal seen in a dream or in meditation describes the degree of genesis being expressed by the person meditating or dreaming. For instance, a tropical animal, such as the hippopotamus found in Africa, describes a thick-hided, stubborn, tribal-genesis trait. The behavior and temperament of an animal, bird or reptile seen in dream or meditation describes certain inclinations or tendencies of a person. For example, a bird symbol, such as a crow, an inverted bird species – seen destroying the crops in a field – would indicate one who has intellectual avidity, plagiarizing the thoughts of another person. If one sees a deadly snake, brown in color, and if it is in a state of attack, this would indicate lust and harmfulness from a material level (brown), disturbing to the emotions and thoughts. One should always alert himself as to the natural habitat or locale of the animal seen in a dream.

If certain parts of an animal, as an etheric symbol, are magnified, such as a small rabbit with oversized ears, this would denote to the person that he is timid in the use of his telepathic power, as the rabbit indicates harmlessness, sensitivity and timidity as to the physical and outer world, and oversized ears would represent extended hearing or clairaudience.

In waking or sleep, a person is attracted to that animal which is yet the most untamed within himself. He is more likely to see this animal in his dream world, meditation, or attract it in the physical world as part of his domestic environment.

Man and animal are often closer in their sentient penetrableness to one another than man is to man. Thus many in the world feel more at home with the animal than with man.

The bull of Osiris was worshipped in Egypt because it was the symbol for the zodiacal Age of Taurus. The ram was used as a sacred symbol in the zodiacal Age of Aries during the time of Moses. The zodiacal symbol of the two fishes was used in the time of Jesus in the Piscean Age or age of fishes because this was the age of the great division between tribal-genesis and family-genesis.

In the symbol of Pisces, the fish swimming to the left represents those who prefer to remain laggard or to be held in the lower genesis state. The fish swimming to the right in the sign of Pisces indicates those who are swimming toward the higher rise of genesis or self-genesis. To dream of either one of these signs is to be in a state of research into one's own placement as to the rise in genesis.

To see the skeleton framework of a fish indicates that one has only a skeletal or dogmatic structure upholding his faith. The meat of his faith is yet to be earned.

Daniel was a fire initiate; he knew how to use the akasic fire contained in his kundalini or spinal canal. When Daniel was thrown to the lions, he was protected by the feline Species Angel who anesthetized the lions and closed their mouths and sealed away the saliva stimulating the hungers of the lions. King Darius, being a co-atom soul to Daniel, was highly evolved and cognizant of spiritual powers; he fasted and prayed and remained awake all night so that he might work with Daniel to overcome the ferocity of the lions. Daniel's akasic power correlating to the feline species of angels and to the power of the Leo Hierarchy enabled him to remain in the lions' den without harm.

In modern times, when a man prefers the cat as a domestic animal it denotes that he has a close relating to Regulus, where the Leo Hierarchy dwells.

PRIMITIVE SYMBOLOGY IN DREAMS

When one dreams repeatedly of primitive or untamed animals, he is researching the primitive memory residing within the lower side of Center Q (quelle). This primitive portion of the memory, located at the base of the skull, is the fearful threshold feared by all who have retained any latent, unresolved hostility, guilt or fear.

When one begins to seek the spiritual life through the process of meditation, the primitive symbols are magnified and reflected in dreams and in visions.

The soul, using the primitive symbology, impresses upon the mind of the one dreaming the necessity to correct any remaining or hidden aggressive traits.

The Guardian Angels work during sleep, sending forth the harmless-animal symbologies into the mind of the sleeper. Such symbologies fall into the receptive mind, instructing, rectifying.

Primitive symbologies may often be used in dreams to warn or to caution. In case of warning, this usually means danger from hostile persons other than oneself. In case of caution, this is a corrective dream reminding the dreamer to lessen his aggressive desires.

Prayer and mantramic speaking before sleep will enable one to view and research the primitive symbologies with detachment as an observer rather than a participant. One will awaken from dream-observing refreshed, while one who participates in primitive symbology will awaken depleted and apprehensive.

TWO DREAM ACTIVITIES: OBSERVING AND PARTICIPATING

When one dreams of an animal, fish, or feathered creature – and is aware of a sense of smelling, tasting, seeing, hearing or touching the animal or creature – this is indicative that he is at work upon *sentience absorption*; or, in some manner, he is exploring his degree of mastery over his senses.

To dream of combat with an animal pertains to an initiatory trial. For example, to dream of being charged by a lion indicates that one is to be challenged by a fellow initiate. To dream of a fish of a harmless variety would mean that one has entered into a Christian way of life. If the fish is swimming left, it is negative; if right, it is a higher elevation. If one is repelled in dreams by an alligator, snake or any slithering creature, he is being warned that a sex trial is imminent, or his distorted attitudes toward sex are being researched.

Fear or apprehension during dream-experience should be carefully recorded, as recoil from certain symbols seen during dreams will enervate the lesser etheric body and depress the daytime emotional and mental action. One should record all apprehensive and fearful dreams so as to trace and find the hidden symbol of his secret fear seeking to speak through night-initiation.

The revealing aspect of the soul seeks to free the conscience attribute of the soul. Dream symbols are the major instrument used by the soul to discipline, to direct and to instruct.

One thing to be remembered at all times concerning dream symbology is that dreams are divided into *two activities:* (1) observing, (2) participating. All *observing dreams* are instructive; all *participating dreams* are initiatory.

The symbology within all dreams flows or is fluidic. In dreams there are seven levels of observing and participating. The seven observing and participating dream levels are: (1) the disclosure as to the degree of one's evolvement; (2) the particular phase of evolvement and its purpose; (3) the underlying theme or thread of instruction, discipline, guidance; (4) a fourth-dimensional attribute whereby the former-life records may be observed and sealed into the memory through the symbolic dynamics of the soul's action; (5) an observation and also direct instruction from night-servers or greater Presences; an occasional contact with the risen dead or the quickened dead; (6) a prophetic or foretelling help in the night to prepare one to accept certain coming events for oneself and for the world; (7) a spiritual functioning of the higher attributes of the soul's cognition, whereby one is initiated into the higher atmosphere of heavenly association. In such dream experiences, one becomes initiated into the night-serving ministry. The master images of the greater archetypes are sealed into the will, the imagination and the memory. Also, certain spiritual gifts are quickened, enabling the one being initiated to serve in the outer world with recognition, protection, guidance, peace.

SYMBOLS AND THE SKY DRAMAS

From the harvest moon in the month of August into the latter part of the autumnal equinox, approximately November 11th, the atmosphere of the sky becomes a screen for angelic symbolic work. Upon the fleecy cloud formations may be seen from day to day a symbolic panorama of the animal kingdom.

The Species Angels, working with the Cherubim Angels, shape and form upon the screen of the sky the animals corresponding to the evolvement of the beholder.

One who looks into the cloud formations of the sky may behold animals of varying species. If one has yielded to facetiousness in thoughts and emotions, he may see his own corresponding mental and emotional state outpictured in a form of humorous pageantry. For example, if one has a stubborn tendency, he will see a goat or a donkey; or if precocious, a poodle; if timid, a hare or rabbit.

If one be more highly evolved, he will also note that the sky dramas sometimes portray the akasic record of the animal kingdom; he may trace the records of evolution and origin of the animals of the earth through sky scrying.

The shepherd initiates of old understood the sky pageantries, and reverently awaited their seasonal helps and direction – knowing them to be of angelic origin. The initiates of today know and understand the universal meaning of symbology as enacted through etheric impregnation. The ether in the atmosphere of the sky, the plant and the water is an intelligible mirror upon which the angels seek to symbolically imprint their telepathy to man.

THE ANGELIC GUARDIANS OF SYMBOLOGY

All symbols portraying Nature are sacred. All symbols representing sentient or animal life are reverent. All symbols portraying a higher consciousness life are holy.

Every symbol is under an angelic wavelength, affording an angelic protection. All animal symbols are under the guardianship of the Fauna Species Angels and the Cherubim Guardian Angels.

The Cherubim Angels, working with the soul during sleep and during meditation, use and project, telepathically, familiar animal symbols. The Cherubim Angels build a living vocabulary of correspondences. This symbolic language is imprinted upon one's thoughts and emotions. When one begins his first dream and meditative initiations, animal symbols are opened to his mind. After one has mastered the animal symbols, he moves on to a greater range of symbologies.

When an animal is happy and rollicking in a dream-vision, it is always indicative that the Cherubim Angels are happily at work in the affairs of the one dreaming.

If one with a sensuous heart or an unethical mind tries to open the seals of symbology, his efforts will be futile; the result will be defeat. Only the pure in heart may cross the thresholds of symbology interpretation. The good intuit the language of the symbol, yet know not the sacred combining of ritual, sound and imaging. The pure, being devoid of the expectancy of magic, step by step open the portals of symbology interpretation.

The first symbols disclosed to the pure in heart are the animal symbols. The next symbols to open are the symbols of plants, trees, seeds, grains. The third symbols to be revealed are the symbols of mountains, water, rivers, oceans, air, earth, fire. When one is spiritually ready, the consciousness symbols or prototypal symbols will be sent forth from the four Archangels and Hierarchy. When one is ready to unite his serving with the spiritual worlds, the spiritual symbols containing the initiatory nuances are sent forth from the Seraphim Angels, the Bodhisattva Saints, the Masters, the risen dead and the Illuminati. When one has reached the degree of evolvement in which he may work with world-grace, the archetypal master symbols are sent forth from the Kingdom of God by the Celestial Angels, the Saturn Angels, the Recording Angels and the Archetypal Guardian Angels.

The Fauna Species Angels and the Cherubim Guardian Angels overdwell and protect the inner meaning of each sentient or animal symbol.

The Flora Angels, working with the Cherubim Guardian Angels, protect the symbols concealed in the plants, trees, grains, seeds. These angels withhold the inner meaning of animal symbology from the unethical and the profane.

The Deva Angels and the Cherubim Guardian Angels place their mantle of protection over the symbols concealed in the mountains, the rivers, the waters, the air, the fire, the earth, the ores, the jewels in the earth.

Four of the Great Archangels – Gabriel, Michael, Uriel and Raphael – are the protective Guardian Angels of the prototypal symbols as sent forth from Hierarchy.

The Seraphim Guardian Angels and the personal Guardian Angels protect the initiatory symbols sent forth during meditation and contemplation. The Masters, the Illuminati and the risen dead work with the Seraphim Angels to prevent disclosure of knowledge out of timing.

The archetypal master symbols in the Kingdom of God are protected by the Recording Angels, the Archetypal Guardian Angels, the Celestial Angels and the Archetypal Recording Angels.

The science of symbology is a sacred science given only to those who are at one with the angels. Only the pure in heart may unravel the thread of symbology and earn the power to use symbols through ritual-formulas, and thus gain the power of manifestation and de-manifestation.

Symbols proceeding from the greater archetypes are spiritual vibrationless symbols and are beyond defining as to their degree of light.

All sentient symbols stem from the lower astral world, the higher astral world and the reflected archetypes, and are contacted through an etheric braille. All initiatory symbols stem from the Spheres of Light. All superconsciousness symbols stem from the greater archetypes.

As long as man has a possessive desire of any kind, his symbols will be colored with something of the sentient. When he is wholly selfless, he will receive the true superconsciousness symbols, and thus become at one with the Christ Mind. The true and pure consciousness symbols may be received only when one is in direct alignment with the master symbols of the greater archetypes. *A perfect consciousness symbol is an archetypal idea which overcomes the barriers of time and space; heaven and earth are one in a perfect consciousness symbol.*

THE EGO MIND IN SLEEP

In giving death and sleep, God has given a respite to the tumultuous lesser will and mind. All sleep, all dream, so as to experience a consciousness unhindered or bound by the gravity action of the senses. Dreaming is a necessity and a natural requirement providing and expressing the full or spherical ranges of consciousness.

The more one understands his dreams, the more he achieves the total fulfillment of consciousness. The greater the genius, the more unique and creative the dream. All persons having soul-liberty speak and hear with awareness the dream logos of the spirit. The soul at dusk prepares the lesser etheric body and the physical body for the task of sleeping and dreaming. As the sun's light decreases, the light of the soul increases, taking precedence over gravity sense thinking and feeling.

The ego mind in the world of sleep can be given uninhibited freedom within the subconscious and the higher unconscious. The soul can expand into the ego mind, if it is unhampered by the lesser aspects of the senses. In sleep the ego mind opens as a petaled flower to grow and develop within the lunar fires of dreaming until 3 a.m. of each night.

During sleep, the instincts protecting and alerting man in daytime action are drawn inward into the solar plexus atavistic brain centered in the region of the navel. The ancestral and individualistic psychical will-vitality of the senses is drawn into the etheric chambers of the heart and in the area of the throat, there to remain until dawn. Thus, during sleep the higher and sensitive vitalities of the senses become dream extrasensory powers.

The lesser etheric body energy during night-travel sleep is slowed down and transposed into a third or psychic action. The energy is transposed into the higher vortices of the brain. The higher etheric body then takes possession of these psychic energies, giving freedom to the three minds active in sleep: the subconscious mind, the higher unconscious mind and the superconscious mind.

Sleep is not a benign event as many think. Sleep is a state of creative action. The interior symbols encountered in dream sleep are coagulated molecular molds precluding all exterior thinking and acting. Symbols experienced in dreams are detonators for ideas, igniting the thinking processes of the outer consciousness. Were it not for the parent symbols or master symbols presiding over the thought cluster of the mind, there would be no cognizance in thought.

In sleep man is exposed to morality, to conscience, to self-awareness, to guidance, to instruction, and more, he obtains stabilizing supernatural resources through which he maintains and contains the life of his outer and objective mind.

In certain ancient philosophies those who sat at the feet of instruction were taught that to look upon sleep as an antidote or escape from life was a sin of indolence. The wise, the prudent and the initiated knew that to expect escape from life through sleep was to invite an increase of karma or burdens in the action of the day.

Teachers disclosing the inner way gave wisdom guides of sleep to those who sought the full answers to the riddle of life in earth, in mind, in soul, in spirit. Their instruction stressed the necessity to utilize *all aspects* of consciousness, their concern being for the unconscious and for the conscious. These seers or Rishis likened the body of man to a tree of life containing seven blossoms growing and flowering from the base of the spine upward. The lower blossoms or chakras existing at the base of the spine were awake in the day and the blossoms on the highest peak of the tree or spine were blooming in the night.

Sleep to the hierophant in Egypt meant travel through the aid of the *Ka* body. Initiates of Egypt knew sleep to be an interdependent process through which man was initiated into secrets profane and also divine.

Dreams, visions and sleep to the heirs retaining the Atlantis knowledge of the angels – the Hebrews – were sacredly accepted as a prophetic way of direction and also as a participating way of extending worship and communion with Jaweh, or the living God.

INCUBATION AND SLEEP

In the ancient times when men lived close to the etheric mists, they understood the method of incubation, or psychic induction. They entered into their temples and remained there in a state of semi-sleep until they received the answer needed as a solution and sometimes a therapy in their affairs. Today, many who subconsciously remember the etheric communicableness, while not going into physical temples or buildings, use the ancient practices of incubation techniques during sleep. One aspect of etheric incubation still exists today – and that is, that one, while in full consciousness just previous to falling into deep sleep, can release himself partially from his body, and thus travel in astral consciousness. Such periods are made possible by certain planetary reinforcement. More often this occurs when the moon is full; or this may also occur during the time of a lunar eclipse.

Some persons use the practice of incubation during meditation. This is a form of semi-trance in which one drains off the sense and sensual functionings of the body from the nine openings of the body, and draws his consciousness to the higher extrasensory portal between the eyebrows. In this state of quiet, spiritual consciousness or superconsciousness becomes active.

In olden temple incubation, men relied upon the unseen and etheric presences inhabiting the temple to instruct them and to guide them, entering into a self-suggestible sleep through certain initiatory mystic incantations. This sleep consisted of a magnified clairsentient slumber wherein the etheric voices were enlarged and magnified in the ears of the one in incubated sleep.

Sometimes this sleep lasted for a period of three days. The etheric consciousness experienced in the temple was limited according to the capacity of the one in the psychic state of incubation. On awakening, such persons were given by the temple priest an elixir to drink to enable them to remember the protective potencies received during incubation. Oracle receiving as practiced in the Delphic temples in Greece was a form of incubation. Induced by self-hypnotic suggestion, a person entered the closed confines of the Delphic oracle chambers, where he heard in magnified clairaudience the answers given through the prophetess of the temple.

In present-day dreaming these incubating rites and temple procedures are sometimes recapitulated into dream consciousness at night.

Due to sleep need or desire, dream pictographs can return a present-day ego in his research of the night to olden mysterious incubation rites stemming from the memory aspect of the subconscious.

Certain dreams, even though seeming trivial when outwardly remembered, carry with them an awesome milieu or atmosphere. Such dreaming is highly impressionable, lingering in the mind long afterwards.

Euphoric dreams leave the dreamer in a state of lingering joy, hope or happiness for days or weeks. Pessimistic dreams impregnated with a sense of futility and weightedness impair the health. Such dreams are subtle, parasitical drainers of a vital energy which can be regained only through sleeping. It is sleep's providence to benefit the sleeper. The lower etheric body, when the mind and the emotions are at rest, should ordinarily be mended and strengthened in the night.

In dream research one is constantly reminded that the ego is dependent upon the mind for its expression and that happiness, harmony and peace in both sleeping and waking are dependent upon the state of the mind.

Chapter 5

THE COLOR VOCABULARY IN DREAMS

At sunset time I turn my face to soul horizons. My soul knoweth where I go on this night, and I know that I shall fare well with my soul.

There is great significance in seeing color in a dream or in an illuminative or meditative experience.

Some persons are telepathically recipients of warnings or guidance through color. For example, when in danger they may see a reddish-brown, or when some thought of malice is directed toward them they may receive, through inverted telepathy, the color bilious green. One learns on receiving such warnings to immediately build a shield of light in his aura so as to insulate and protect himself. To do this he floods his aura with his own major tone and color. Those who have the gift of receiving telepathically in color have earned this grace through their works of Light for many ages.

One may be assured of a protective Presence by seeing violet, indigo-blue, white, or any of the higher etheric colors.

It is rare that color alone is seen in a dream. Colors, in the majority of dreams, invariably are accompanied by symbols. Color is one of the greater keys to the vocabulary of the dream world. To see a colorless form or object as a symbol in a dream demotes its full meaning, as color is the life within the symbol. Hence, to understand symbology of any nature one should first know the meaning of color. For instance, if a book is seen in a dream, it could mean an embodiment record, or a former-life record. However, if a *gold book* is seen, it would mean that one is being prepared to receive his soul-record of grace from some former life.

As one evolves he will discern that color becomes more and more a part of his world, both waking and sleeping. To better un-

derstand color in dream vocabulary and illuminative or meditative experience, one should familiarize himself with the following
color identifications.

AMBER – Relates to the pranic flow of the life current. One sees
the color of amber when he is researching the pranic life and
light. To see a symbol diffused with amber indicates that it is a
life symbol. The eye, either in dreaming or waking, when beholding the pranic color of amber, unites with the healing energies obtained from the life force.

ASTRAL COLOR – All lower astral colors are muddy, repelling, giving off to the person who beholds them a sickening
dread. The astral palette, or color range in the lower astral world,
is the reflection of man's soiled and unclarified emotions. All
evil potencies are seen in the lower astral planes. During sleep
one may have a grotesque experience in dreams during which
he is warned of impending danger in action, feeling and thinking. Color is a kindly, beneficent source of communication to
the initiate of the night.

The symbolic language to be pure and true must be clothed in a
garment of more than one color. Colors on the inner planes are
energized by cosmic rays rather than by the sun or lunar rays. To
understand the greater cosmic rays energizing this earth, one first
meets and masters them in the night in his dreams. Dreams without color pertain to the physical planes of life in which emotion is
yet to be understood. Black and white dreams are devoid of emotion. It is therefore necessary to be emotionally involved in dreaming to perceive the colors holding the etheric code to dreams.

BEIGE – A neutral color of non-involvement. On the outer planes
when one continually expresses himself in beige environments
or in neutral tone colorings, he is a person desiring retreat from
life involvement. Beige vibrations of color are seen in dream
experience only on the lesser etheric and lesser mental planes.
To encounter this color during sleep or meditation reveals that
one has entered into a neutral field and is using the indecisive
mind, and thus needs will-rejuvenation. Beige is a borderline
color. Beige personalities offer nothing and give nothing. They
are in danger of becoming parasitical.

BLACK, CHARCOAL – Black with tones of gray when seen in

mass indicates obstructions unintelligible, unfathomable. Charcoal black seen in a dream or meditation indicates that one is standing upon unsympathetic ground. This color denotes mass indifference, mass unawareness, mass obstruction. Reaction from this after dreaming or meditating is frustration and futility. One should remember to pray earnestly to receive strength, patience and spiritual understanding after seeing this color in dream or meditation. Persons who feel at home with black coloring or clothing are usually adamant persons who desire to make powerful the negative aspects in their lives.

In symbology black may be used as a contrast to reveal brightness in a vision as is sometimes the case of an artist's desiring perspective. In the inner planes at night when one is being initiated into the sciences of night-flight and instruction, he must learn to cross the black caverns or abysses. One does this by calling upon the Christ, his angels, and the Master. The effulgent light of a protective Being will enable the initiate to cross over the black caverns of the inner planes. In time the initiate, on becoming an adept, will become a protector of other persons being so initiated.

BLACK – Imponderable. Unknowing. Ominous. The color black is a vibrational projection of the negative force. It is the low octave of the color white, which represents supreme light or Deity. Black is not evil as a color to accentuate light. Black as a mass with no light is of negation. Negative black is seen to warn of secrecy, death, danger. Black has a negative dissonance action upon the mind when too abundant. Too much black obliterates will. Black and brown seen together in a vision or in a dream represent a karmic penalty to be exacted. Black and gray represent depression and negation.

In meditation or dreams, to see or to be confronted with the darkened opening to a cave or a portal indicates that one is being challenged as to whether his fears are greater than his desires to make union with the Supreme One.

If one in this experience will affirm with confidence that he is not afraid or that he knows his angels and the Christ are with him, the darkness will be immediately transposed into light, and one will find himself in the light at the feet of his Master, who will instruct him in the laws of transubstantiation.

The power to transcend or to change substances through the gift of transubstantiation must be mastered by all initiates and adepts of the path. To do this one meets the Master in the inner archives and comes under his instruction. If there is sickness, he is taught how to transpose it to health; if there is poverty, how to translate to plenty. If there is ignorance, he must learn how to transcend it into wisdom. One by one the major negatives are transcended by an initiate. The day's action is a time of struggle and service. The night's action is a time to sift the service of the day and its intent, that one may add to each day a freedom of the soul's action in both sleep and waking consciousness.

If one sees in vision or in dreaming a darkened, man-made cave such as a tunnel or a mine entrance, this pertains to physical karma and indicates a temporary research into some karmic interception, that is, the one dreaming is being shown that he must search out a physical concept and assess its limitation.

A black tunnel indicates that one must move forward with his karma, accepting it, that he may break through or go forward toward the light to obtain his liberation from karma.

Black water is the sign of stagnant water and the refusal to face one's own karma; it is the symbol of guilt, of grief and sorrow, due to one's own refusal to move with the flow of life.

A black tree symbolizes death to a member of the family or to a family-atom relationship.

BLUE – Represents emotional, mental and spiritual peace.

BLUE, CERULEAN – Relates to the higher etheric, the higher mental and the higher emotional planes. Cerulean blue is the color used by the Cherubim Angels to announce their presence or their contacting love. To see cerulean blue in a dream indicates that one is aligning himself with the pure spheres of the cosmic music. Cerulean blue can only be experienced in dreams when one has stilled his sentient atoms. The angels use the color blue to give hope and divine assurance to one who aspires to use his higher mind.

BLUE, INDIGO – The color of akasia, the highest aspect of prana. The akasic flame is used by the great Masters to cleanse the auras of their disciples. As one increases in meditative powers, he gives off more of the akasia blue light. During meditation when one has opened the akasic fire, he often sees a blue flame centered within his own aura in the proximity of his head or over the command center between his eyebrows. To see the blue flame in the aura of another person in the waking state is to know that he is approved of or accepted by the Master or the Greater Presences. To see this light while sitting in semi-contemplation is a confirming that the Master is near. Also, to see this light as a form of a penciled blue line beneath the words or sentences in any book speaking of spiritual ideas is proof that one is reading a magnetized book blessed by the Holy Presences and the angels.

BLUE, JUPITER (ROYAL) – A slightly darker shade than indigo, royal blue is a sign of a blessing and a promise of substance and expansion. This color can only be seen when one is in alignment with higher etheric and higher mental aspects of the light. Every person has his distinct vibrational ray or tone of color. Persons having the Jupiter blue light in the center of their souls' medallion are powerful manifestors for God. They are builders under cosmic law. Wherever they serve, creation follows.

BLUE, MADONNA – A blue between Jupiter blue and pale blue. It is often used by painters coloring the garment of Mary, the mother of Jesus. It is a higher emotional and etheric color relating to the mother-principle of human mothers who work with the Divine Mother, or Mother of the World. Madonna blue is an inoffensive healing color, inducing feelings of impartiality. It is a passionless color devoid of possessivism or subverted attachments. This color in dreams indicates a healing of possessive tensions and the healing of infatuation.

BLUE, MIDNIGHT – Ruled by the planet Saturn. Pertains to discipline of thoughts.

BLUE, PALE – Indicates neutralized emotions; willingness to arbitrate. Also indicates that one is preparing to move in an impersonal attitude toward things karmic. All borderline pale colors seen in the inner planes indicate that one is slowed down in sentient action, preparing for a new experience.

BLUE, SAPPHIRE – The color of the sapphire jewel or stone. To see the white akasia light within the center of a sapphire stone indicates that one has united with his higher mind. One who has entered into Christ consciousness or superconsciousness has mastered the Ten Commandments. His emotions have budded into love instruments. His mind becomes a lucid field through which the Christ may speak.

BLUE, TURQUOISE – The color related to the higher astral world or First Heaven. Persons dreaming of this color stone or jewel symbology are remembering an Atlantean life. A turquoise bracelet indicates protection earned during an Atlantean existence. A turquoise pendant or necklace indicates one has earned protection due to old initiate powers in Atlantis. A turquoise ring indicates one is remembering and recalling these ancient powers into the physical action of the present time.

BRONZE – Relates to condensed pranic fire in the lower quelle or subconscious, where karmic sediment is immobilized, awaiting the timing to flow upward into the higher unconscious and into the outer consciousness. This bronze pranic sediment is fiery, and within quelle makes a hissing sound, which may be heard by one who is clairaudient. When one is ready to outpicture the karmic sediment retained in the bronze fire of quelle, the immobilized bundles of karma come into fiery action, flowing into the outer mind as anger, hatred, violence. When one does not have the action of the higher unconscious to restrain this forceful thrust of pranic-propelled karma, he suffers disintegration of the outer personality. If one has grace through dreams to assimilate and evaluate his karma, he avoids the overflow from the bronze lake of quelle. Each night's dreaming will take care of the bronze lake of unresolved karma when one unites himself in all actions with God as the One. The bronze lake of quelle, or the lower subconscious, is Pandora's box. All true initiates understand the law of moderation in the physical world and the law of rhythm in their inner worlds. To come under a Master or a saint, to be aware of the angels, keeps quiescent the combustions of lower quelle's action. One should identify himself continually with the mediative flow of interconnected soul-light, that he may clarify life's meaning and its fulfillment.

BROWN – Indicates that one is to make a physical sacrifice or to render a physical service. Also indicates the need for practicality and industry. Brown is a color of physical satisfaction or receiving physical recognition for one's physical services.

BROWN, EARTHY – One unites himself with the sense of smelling when he sees earth brown colors or earth colored in brown tones. He is making alignment with the Nature forces through the sense of smell and gathering the mineral healing fires into his breath.

BROWN, CHOCOLATE – Materialistic pressures, materiality, material expectations, material ambitions.

GOLD – Soul-power, soul-grace, soul-memory, enlightenment. To unite with gold as a metal indicates the power of manifestation. To see the earth as golden is to unite with the Lemurian memories in which all of the soil of the earth was tinted in a goldlike mist. To unite with the golden nimbus of a person or of a saint indicates that one is receiving a soul-gift due to the blessing of the saint.

GRAY, BLUE – Symbolic of deliberation and analysis.

GRAY, DARK – Discipline of the will.

GRAY, PALE – Detachment and aloofness.

GRAY, YELLOW – Depression, weariness, parasitical, doubtful.

GREEN, BILIOUS – Astral hate, hatred, envy, malice, a lie.

GREEN, CHLOROPHYLL – Vitality, health, generosity and abundance.

GREEN, FOREST – Peace and healing. Key to Nature. First instruction from a guru.

GREEN, MUSTARD – Astral deception. Self-deception.

GREEN, NEPTUNIAN (scintillating, delicate green) – A pure healing flame of greenish fire seen in the aura of a Neptune initiate. This color may also be seen in dreams when one is preparing to be initiated under the planet Neptune. When Neptune is in a fire sign, as in Leo, Aries, Sagittarius, the colors experienced in initiation are lettuce-green and magenta. Neptune in Sagittarius produces initiations purifying and overcoming the fantasy and restlessness of the mind. Neptune in the earth sign Capricorn produces organization of a rare and unique order. All planets give off prismatic vibrational tones of color. When these are activated in one's chart, he expresses color in unusual and striking ways. Cosmic color operating in the dream world produces emotions in the waking state. The Neptune green under the cosmic prism rays of the night produces moods and desires in the daytime that can be defined only with the aid of a true interpreter – a teacher, a guru, or a Master. As an animal or a serpent is irresistibly drawn to music, so is the organ of light, the eye of man, drawn to color. The true inner eye responds to cosmic light, cosmic vibration and cosmic color. All Masters understand the science of color and its effect upon the etheric body. All spiritual healing and instruction is reinforced by the cosmic colors. When one enters the Hall of Learning for instruction, he becomes receptive to his instruction through the color rays of the night. His etheric body and his higher emotions become receptacles of cosmic light, vibration and color. From this he becomes a daytime channel and presence of healing love.

The thoughts of an initiate having perfected induction powers are filled with nuances of penetrableness. Any service rendered by a receptive initiate of the night is a creative, masterful work in the physical worlds.

GREEN, PALE – Depleted vitality. Also timidity; sensitivity of a mystical nature. Thoughts are meandering.

LAVENDER – Accentuated mother consciousness; mother partiality; a lover of tradition.

MAGENTA – A higher etheric, spiritual power.

MUDDY COLORS – Astral; stagnation; error in seeing and perceiving; foggy outlook; refusing to face one's mixed emotions; astral-soil coloring in an aura. Sicknesses giving off muddy emotions project their coloring as fearful and feverish atmospheres.

ORANGE – Personal pride. Family pride. Lust. Ancestral clinging. Possessiveness. A surfeit of orange is offensive to refined persons.

ORANGE, DEEP – Indicates fixed will and stubborn pride; inflexible; sarcastic; cynical; unapproachableness; flattery; infatuation; delusion.

ORANGE, GOLDEN – Life force vitality or healthy life current.

ORANGE, VERMILION – Uncontrolled passion; pride of possessions; impregnable ether.

PINK – Love and devotion; tenderness; sensitivity; chastity; reverence.

PINK, VIOLET – Healing; life-giving; restoring; faith; wisdom; humor; non-intrusiveness; understanding.

PRANA (peach-gold) – Pranic health; pure pranic life-current; healthy etheric body; harmlessness; restoring; rejuvenation; emanating finest of ether; inoffensiveness.

PURPLE – Raw electric telepathy; delusions of superiority; pompousness; egocentric; karmic voltage; arrogance.

RED – Power charged with cosmic dynamism.

RED, BROWNISH – Blood guilt held over from past-life violence; jealousy; physical danger; obstructive; covetousness.

RED, CRIMSON – Healthy life force; pure bloodstream; honesty; ego-command.

RED, PURPLISH – Karmic suffering caused by past-life physical offenses; lower astral gravity vibrations.

RED, ROSE – Personal love; communication with a saint; blessing from a Most-High Saint; selfless healing; highest personal love expression; healing of fevers of the emotions.

RED, RUBY – Integrity; respect; authority earned; a sign of approval from the Master; a protective talisman against forces of evil; healing of fevers of the blood. When transparent, it is the symbol of being chosen for spiritual honors.

RED, SCARLET – Distemper; temper; agitator; disturber; accuser; irresponsible, without conscience.

RED, VERMILION – Race pride.

ROSE – Mystical love; responsive affections; empathy; sympathy.

SILVER – Cool emotions; expanding moods; mystical powers affecting lower psychic nature; initiation into the moon's elixir; understanding of its indwelling illuminative power. The moon's elixir is located beneath the nostril cavity in a sacred hammock called the sacred lake. It gives off a silver-white light to the inner eye. The elixir is fluidic or moist. To open this elixir and to receive its healing, cleansing and purifying fire, one presses his tongue upward with gentle firmness against the center of the palate in a brief exercise. *Silver* seen in a vision in ornaments or metals indicates that one is manifesting actual moon power or vitality. Silver is a reflective color acting as a mirror or a mediator when one is not totally prepared to receive the more direct solar initiatory light. All initiates undergo the silver or moon initiation before they can experience the direct, divine, prismatic cosmic rays stepped down through seeing. This occurs in the solar plexus. To make union through the silver door of initiation, one must understand the laws of magnetism and their physical as well as etheric emanations.

TAN – Hypersensitivity, uncertainty and retreatism.

VIOLET – Tenderness and selfless love. The color of the spiritual life.

VIOLET, VENUS – The Jesus garment of healing love, protection. To be sealed-in in the violet light is to be free from the lower sentient charge of sensuality.

WHITE – Spirit, perfection, purity, chastity, virginal, the transcending power of Spirit, union with the Supreme Being, the vibrationless state of light.

BLUE-WHITE LIGHT – Correlates to the eternals and the Father.

GOLD-WHITE LIGHT – Correlates to the greater archetypes and the Christ.

IVORY-WHITE LIGHT – Correlates to the Lord of Love, Jesus.

VIOLET-WHITE LIGHT – Correlates to the Spirit of Truth.

YELLOW – Intellect.

YELLOW, CANARY (with a tinge of green) – Inquisitiveness, curiosity.

YELLOW, CHARTREUSE – Neurosis tension, zeal, self-importance.

YELLOW, CLEAR – Lucid thoughts, honesty, integrity, pure intellect.

YELLOW, GOLD – Pure reverence, humility, soul-power.

The colors of the rainbow as seen by the eye of man relate to the plane of Nature and the vibrational life existing in Nature. All colors seen etherically relating to the etheric body and to the planes of life supporting the etheric body existing in astral life and etheric life are influenced by the rays of the moon. In the physical world the key color is green. The key color of a plane keeps intact all companion colors; that is, the green leaf of the plant in the physical world determines what man sees as color in the physical world. In the astral world the key color is black. All colors in the lower astral world begin with darkness, gradually merging into light. The emerging color seen in astral sight is pranic amber. As one extends his spiritual sight on the inner planes the range of color is fixed and determined by indigo blue. The more refined and sensitive the sight used in spiritual research, the finer and more delicate the color.

As one advances spiritually, he gradually comes to incorporate the cosmic-ray palette of color into his vision and sight. Through color he can experience in a more spiritually sensitive environment absorption and healing containing no excitement. Cosmic-ray color can fall only upon the sensitive open buds of illumination. The finer or more delicate a color seen in vision determines the plane on which one is undergoing spiritual experience.

As the iris of the eye on the physical plane is seeking to unite itself with chlorophyll green, that it may unite itself with the harmony within Nature and the health vitalities received in vibration in color, so does the spiritual eye or third eye seek to eventually rest in the total white light of the supreme Lord over all.

Vibration and color on the physical plane are heavier, moving in a more solid or dense action into the eye of man. Astral color as an impact on man's emotions stirs in a repelling and attracting manner, influencing his moods and his temperament. Astral mesmeric colors affect one sensually inclined, attracting to him situations unpleasant, distorted, fanciful, unrealistic.

Astral colors are always accompanied by discordant sounds affecting the atavistic side of the nature. Persons heavily charged with psychic sensuality are disturbers in the emotional lives of other men. Overabundant astral colors collected and condensed in the aura act as alien energy forces in peaceful environments.

Etheric color is basically supported by the higher pranic light. The etheric palette is stimulated by the vibrational or energy tones from the planets. The etheric colors are more distinct, less diffused than astral colors. Thus, geometrical designs and patterns formed by the coagulating aspect of ether may be seen by the seer.

These designs are beautiful and inspiring at times. As one gradually moves into the finer levels of etheric consciousness, the akasic
light in ether, using the finer essences of pranic light, produces
scenes and designs of beauty and divinity. One begins to experience these divine visions in the First Heaven.

All things seen in the lower astral in color are turgid, dark, nebu-
lous. Astral color especially affects the saliva content in the mouth
during dreams. An experience at night with astral color and turgid
movement caused by astral dreams induces dryness in the mouth;
one awakens with a bad taste in the mouth.

Astral color experienced in dreams is sometimes accompanied
by odors. The sense of smell is active in the state of dreaming. The
respiratory function of the body is maintained in the night by the
subconscious, working in a unique way with the medulla oblongata. Tasting, smelling and touching in the astral state of dream
life are especially influenced by an overly charged karmic
sensuality.

The eye of the night on the astral plane has a different function
from that of the eye on the etheric, mental and spiritual planes of
dream action. One sees in part in a dream in the astral grotesque,
fantasy and wish levels of dreams. In astral consciousness the
mesmeric side of dream action under the moon's influence produces intense emotional reaction and involvement. One awakens
from such dreams with a feeling that he has been exposed to an
unresolvable puzzle.

Mesmeric, astral dreams occurring over long periods are exhausting. Such dreams, being unsupported by the higher aspect of the
mind, cause daytime irritability. All persons having mesmeric
dreams with accentuation upon astral color and exaggerated use
of the senses can be protected by use of pre-sleep mantrams and
higher suggestibility techniques. Persons seeking a spiritual life
should prepare themselves unfailingly to move over the undertow
of astral dreaming.

Dreams are progressive. Through night instruction in the Hall of
Learning, one learns to extend the time limit of dreaming. Through
spiritual understanding in evolvement, he learns how to use the
releasing projectile, or the *silver cord*, within his etheric body so
that he may remain longer in the tutelage precincts of the night
university.

In the first phases of night travel under the tutelage of the divine companions, angels, Presences and the Masters, one first experiences clairsentience. All dream instruction is sealed into his mind through his emotions and feelings. This is reproduced in the waking state as a deep longing, yearning and desire.

Such persons in the first phase of night instruction become extremely intuitive. They rarely are able to make coherent their dream experience; yet they know – not knowing how they know – that they have received something unique in the night, and therefore have gained revitalization of faith and vitality from the night.

There is more, however, in dream experience than feeling. As one continues in night instruction, he begins to extend the use of the third-eye functioning in dreams. He is no longer dependent upon the subconscious pressures upon the medulla oblongata.

Certain aspects of the third-eye observation in dreams produce in the physical eye a dilation, movement or the rolling of the physical eye due to that perceived inwardly during sleep. However, one must have total freedom of the third eye while dreaming in order to have full and complete dream cognition. The Masters work to lead one to this state, that he may keep regulated the three states of consciousness: consciousness, subconsciousness and superconsciousness.

The cosmic rays vibrate into the third eye in cognition dreaming with clarity, impressing into the mind the vision, the meaning, the statement, the direction and the instruction. In cognition dreaming one experiences actual life forces in the dream picture so that he never forgets a dream impregnated with life force produced by cosmic ray vibration.

Life force dreams give to the one dreaming transubstantiation power to reenact his dreams and to reproduce their pictured forms as a reality into his outer life. Only initiates experience such dreams.

In the Hall of Learning the initiate comes under the instruction of the planetary Overlords so that he may understand the uniqueness of planetary action influencing sleep, dreams and night travel.

In the Hall of Learning one is shown how during certain periods, when the planets influencing his own natal chart are favorable, he will have entry into a certain kind of instruction correlating to the auspicious aspects of his chart. He learns in this instruction to evaluate the multiplicity action of the cosmic universe working through the galaxies and the stars.

In the Hall of Learning he is taken into vast observatories that reproduce galaxy action and planetary action as related to each individual unit of sentient life, consciousness life and cosmic life.

To come under the master seers of astronomy in the inner planes is to unite with one's own zodiacal power, that he may free cosmic life into his individualized zodiacal expression. In night instruction the initiate, over and over, views his cosmic unity with all life through the limitless and infinite strata of comprehension.

The Overlords or Hierarchy working with each eternity system in the universe may be contacted in certain periods of a solar year. The Hierarchs over each zodiacal sign are especially known to the initiate in the night during the times of solar and lunar eclipses, during the times of the equinox and solstice periods of a solar year, and also during the new and full moons. To be born with an open zodiacal communication with Hierarchy, one must have a highly organized mind, a sensitized intuition and a soul awareness.

Every person reflects the zodiac in his aura. The spiritual initiate undergoing especial enlargement of his instruction and wisdom during Hierarchal periods must communicate cosmic regenerating action to the world. It is his responsibility to keep his covenant ever alive as a channel of mediation. Man is not aware of this in the self side of his nature. Yet even the trees bow down in response to constellation Hierarchy influences for life on earth.

The zodiac of man in his aura may be seen, gauged and measured during sleep. Very often a person who has initiatory Hierarchy understanding will read and interpret a chart portraying universal attributes.

Persons astrologically inclined sometimes during sleep enter the Hall of Archives or akasic records in the Hall of Learning, and there they may read not only the inner-mystic chart of a person who is destined to bring something to the earth, but they may also go back in time and see the accumulative charts or records of past lives. Looking into the twelfth, the tenth, the eighth and the fourth houses of the chart, they are able to see the projected destiny of the one who is to render a service in the world.

Each zodiacal sign contains infinite vibrations. The degree in each sign affecting the counteracting energies in a chart produces a unique vibration and color spectrum that each soul wears for a lifetime. As the planets relate themselves to one another in transit, the colors may vary slightly, but the major and basic color for each zodiacal sign remains the same. The various aspects in the chart become diffused colors stemming from the basic zodiacal color in each sign. Thus a person born with major emphasis upon the sun and moon in the sign of Leo would emanate a vibrational diffusion of the color gold tinged with rosy and silver ether.

A person born in the zodiacal sign of Cancer and having the moon in Cancer would emanate diffusions of silver and pale green throughout his chart. Vibrations of these two color tones would color all interrelated aspects in his chart. Some persons thus enter the world with hot, energizing and forceful color diffusions in their charts. Regardless of the placement of planets, there is always the major influence of the zodiacal color influencing the personality as seen by other men in the world.

ARIES – The color of fiery orange.
TAURUS – Emerald green.
GEMINI – Indigo blue.
LEO – Golden, peachy ether.
VIRGO – Canary yellow.
LIBRA – Opalescent.
SCORPIO – Crimson orange.
SAGITTARIUS – Turquoise blue.
CAPRICORN – Ruby crimson.
AQUARIUS – Aquamarine blue.
PISCES – Violet.

The zodiacal palette begins its positive formation wherever the natal sun is placed. In dreams one goes to the solar color to find the key to the mystic zodiacal chart of the one he would heal. If he reads with the lunar eye or astral consciousness, he will see in part. If he reads the chart with the third eye, he will not only communicate with the soul divine in the ego, but he will know the ego as a brother and become his fellow server in the walk in light.

Chapter 6

JEWELS

*There is a star watching over my destiny, counting out
the time of timelessness.*

Some hidden instinct within men recognizes that jewels are indeed impregnated with a first or virginal touch of God. To dream of uncut jewels is to be seeking to unite with the energized precious metals and ores of the earth, and also to be initiated into the first processes of creation of the earth. Cut jewels seen in a dream or experienced in meditation signify that one has earned grace and the use of spiritual power.

There are jewels yet hidden in the recesses of earth which have never been seen by the eye of man. Men will recover and find such jewels when they enter the aprons or plateau strata adjacent to the core of the earth.

When the moon was ejected from the earth in the fiery moulding formation period of this eternity system, there were many jeweled particles formed in the earth due to the tremendous pressure and heat seething and fermenting within the core of the earth.

As each planet was ejected from the earth, certain jewels were formed correlating to the planet being ejected. These jeweled masses which were formed during planetary ejection pressures began their action as lines of force or energy points between the moon and the earth, the planets, the sun and the earth. When the sun ejected the earth mass which was to form the matrix for the chain of planets around the earth, the metal gold was formulated in the earth's coagulated heated mass.

Stones precious to men are used symbolically in dream experience. They energize his remembrance of ancient times and unite him with the remembrance of God the Creator. Jeweled stones are not only precious as a decorative supplement to costume or apparel, but they are literal, dynamically charged receiving stations for planetary energies.

The belief that jewels contain amulet or protective powers is not a fallacy. Jeweled talisman power is a true science. The jewel correlating to one's birth or zodiacal sign is a powerful amulet protector against negation, physical and etheric.

The earth has her own necklace of jewels or precious stones, though uncut and awaiting the eye and hand of man. Cosmic jewels of the earth are balancers for cosmic energy. When man wears them, he is insulated magnetically and etherically against the raw forces functioning cosmically, sentiently, etherically.

The soul-light is enhanced by the right jewel worn by a person. The ancient Rishis understood these laws and also knew the value of a jewel talisman worn suitable to the time of birth. The Rishis also understood the need to give with each talisman jewel a sacred mantra correlating to an action of the soul-light within the jewel.

Though there are seven known chakras as taught in the outer schools of mysticism and yoga, there are in reality twelve chakras in man's etheric body. Each of these chakras correlates to one of the jewel stones relating to a birth sign.

Jewels or sacred ores most frequently seen in a dream are as follows:

AMBER – Relates to electromagnetism, pranic, etheric power. Light golden amber relates to purity of prana in the etheric body. Bronze amber relates to condensed pranic fire residing in the lower subconscious or lower quelle.

AMETHYST – Sacrifice, inoffensiveness, the healing of the impossibles, overcoming of karma.

DIAMOND – Correlates to spiritual initiation; represents the higher self. To communicate with the diamond, one directs all of his soul-power through the center between the eyebrows. Here he first encounters the diamond body of his radiant Master who leads him to the eternal treasure of superconsciousness. One is more likely to experience this in the vernal equinox when the Archangel Raphael works to free the diamond of the higher self.

EMERALD – The great initiate Hippocrates, the master of medicine, used the emerald fire in his healing. When persons see the emerald in a dream, it indicates that they are contacting the healing element of the chlorophyll fire in the blood. Persons wearing the emerald are channeling a unique healing fire. To observe the emerald in a dream is to be prepared for initiation into extended healing powers.

JADE – A Lemurian stone. In dreams and in meditation one can, through contemplating jade, draw higher pranic etheric powers into his consciousness. Also, through the seeing of jade in meditation or dreams, one can unite himself with powerful resources and strengths from past incarnations in Oriental lives or lands.

JADE, PINK – To see pink jade ornaments on a woman in a dream or a vision denotes that the person seen has lived a life devoted to the Divine Mother in India and that such persons have retained a cosmic generosity of initiatory wisdom and enlightenment. Pink jade represents the Mother principle; green jade represents the Father principle.

OPAL – Opal is a protective stone outpicturing more than one star or planetary energy. It is a galaxy stone, galaxy formed, containing unique solar, lunar, Jupiter, Venus and Mercury fire. An opal provides protection, justice, harmony and depth to the emotions.

OPAL, BLACK – Unites one with the planet Pluto. To come under the influence of the black opal in the dream life means one is being shown that he is to undergo a subterranean research in the lower astral planes and will thereby learn of the unrisen dead, and the cause of premature death. He will also research the karma of the dead. He will learn of the rituals for the dead, and he will also accept through these initiations that death is a balancer and a necessity in this earth or eternity system.

PEARL – The pearl, having an affinity with the center between the eyebrows, is used as a contemplative symbol by an initiate during contemplation to open his soul's record. To visualize a pearl centered between the eyebrows while speaking sacred words or mantrams will open the sacred canal flow of this master nadis point connected with the pineal gland. One will thus have access to a perspective gained beyond his own knowing.

The pearl is a jewel made through irritation between water and sand playing upon the life mass in an oyster. In human life the pearl represents victory over self-made tribulation. It also represents the surrendering or renunciation aspect of the soul. To sell all to gain the pearl, is seen sometimes in dreams. In such dreams one is usually buying something in a store. His attitude toward the price of the purchase indicates how much he is willing to pay for earning the pearl and thereby to make union with God.

PEARL, BLACK – To see a black pearl indicates that the consciousness is moving downward into one's own karmic history; the mind is being drawn downward into the bronze pranic lake of the lower subconscious so that one may free himself from accumulative karma of many lives. The black pearl also indicates a karmic agent or one who is setting off a karmic action. To be physically attracted to a stone representing blackness indicates that one is in some manner fascinated by the fearful aspects of death, or has in some former life used dark occult powers or magic.

RUBY – What effluvia is to prana, color is to vibration and sound. Color is not just an aftereffect of sound or vibration. Color contains the most high vibrational sensitivity in the light or vision spectrum. Color is healing, peace-giving, health-giving. Color has the power to penetrate non-intrusively where vibration would fall too harshly into the mind and the emotions. Color penetrates consciousness inoffensively, lifting, soothing, exalting. The more sensitive one is to spiritual life, the more he is the recipient of the spiritual emanations existing in color.

The ruby is the arch-stone supporting all jewels. While the diamond is the crown of spirit, the ruby is the crown of the Son-of-man power in earth. One perfect ruby condensed as a perfected jewel contains a velocity of ether equal to millions of heartbeats or blood particles of consciousness life.

The ruby is a healing jewel for the blood. It was formed in earth simultaneously with man's receiving a coat of skin, a bloodstream, and a glandular system.

To see in a dream a ruby pendant similar to a tear drop indicates that one has access to miraculous powers of healing for the humanities.

To meditate on the ruby shaped like a teardrop as dwelling in the heart is to open the akasic fire in the heart and to unite one with the human spirit.

To use mantrams with meditation each day visualizing the ruby in the heart moves one into selflessness.

The omnipotent power of self-knowledge becomes selflessness through two powerful heart contemplative meditations. One is to contemplate the red rose or the ruby stone in the heart. In contemplating the red rose one should feel a diffusion of its fragrance moving into the receptive hearts of men. Secondly, in contemplating the ruby in the heart one should see it as liquid, communicable life fire, healing, touching, communicating, flowing into the closed and unknowing hearts in the world.

The ruby is the stone of physical honor and action. To wear it as a ring on the hand indicates that one is an initiate of the life force, the life current.

SAPPHIRE – Represents the higher mind. To see a sapphire in a dream indicates that one is being initiated into the sapphire-blue tablets given first by Moses and then recalled due to the lack of preparation of his people.

The sapphire-blue tablet of the higher mind relates to one's having power to stand for the law and yet to be non-judging.

To earn the sapphire initiation one must live in constant union with the archetypal light. The light he emanates becomes the law in the life of those he contacts. Such initiates do not force their knowledge upon the uninitiated. They dwell in a constant state of alignment with the superconsciousness or the Christ Mind.

In the Rishi teachings a sapphire initiate is called a Jnana initiate. He lives in a state of transcendental consciousness or oneness with divine mind.

One never sees a sapphire worn as a pendant around the neck in a dream because it does not express the devotional aspect of the soul. A necklace or a pendant in a dream always indicates a devotee. A person in attaining the higher-mind alignment uses both the devotional and mental nature, expressing them as a total fulfillment. One may see in a dream the sapphire stone in a ring on the marriage finger of his right hand. Such initiates remember this ring talisman in their dreams and call upon it for sustaining strength in the expansion and use of their mental light.

The tone of the Supreme consciousness sounds in the sapphire stone more than in any other stone. He who wears it represents mind creation in God.

TURQUOISE – The turquoise stone appeared in the earth during the period of transition between Lemuria and Atlantis. The volcanic action of the continent of Lemuria produced the turquoise. The turquoise came full form to the world needing no cutting. It appeared in the time of Atlantis in vast moulded fragments. It was used in the Atlantean temples as an obeisance stone and a sacred touching stone. In this period of the formation of the early Atlantean continents, the turquoise gave off a condensed etheric fire which was used in communication ceremonials, that the high priests of the temples might make contact with the higher Elect in the inner planes.

Turquoise as a jewel was used in early and latter Egypt after the sinking of Atlantis. The memory of the power of this stone was used to extend the telepathic etheric powers. In the priest and Pharaoh dynasties, this stone was used as a forefront or forehead stone assuring the wearers of extended telepathic powers. The American Indians used this stone in North and South America, knowing it to be a vital talisman and a source of etheric protective rejuvenation.

To see a turquoise in a dream is to unite oneself with the mineral etheric fires of Lemuria and Atlantis.

To see a turquoise in a dream means that one is being initiated into world akasic records and into the records of submerged continents beneath the sea. These records lead the dreamer into ancient dynasty powers and ritual memory. There is a certain twilight state of memory in the archives of the Hall of Learning to which an initiate may go to relive this initiatory drama memory of ancient lives. The turquoise stone seen in a dream is seeking to lead him there, that he may add to his consciousness a memory necessary for his perspective in his present state of evolvement.

All other stones or jewels not mentioned herein are rarely seen in a dream due to the fact that they have no planetary function in the dream life of man. Such stones may be termed incidental against the prominent jewels playing their part in the symbolic language of dreams.

There will be, however, a discovery of stones far more precious than any known to man on earth when men open up the mineral depository resources in the magnetic points and regions in the Arctic and the Antarctic. Such stones will contain far more energizing power than any used in the earth until now.

Sometimes in dreams initiates come in contact with these mysterious layers of the earth, for in dreams one having the power of right research in night-flight may enter into corridors of life-creation impossible to reach in the physical waking state. Initiates having such contacts are eventually the ones who stimulate the pioneer impulses which operate in the waking state. These are the true pioneers. Their pioneer operations on the soul level cannot be estimated save on the weighing scales of the Recording Angels.

Chapter 7

EMOTIONAL INITIATION THROUGH ANIMAL SYMBOLS IN DREAMS

*O wonder of my heartbeat, O splendor of God's Spirit
sounding the hum within all universes, all worlds.*

One experiences emotional initiatory trials in his dreams through animal symbols. Through contact and union with animal symbols in dreams, through visions of animals in meditation, he evaluates his aggressive instincts and hostilities. In observing and absorbing the energy in an animal symbol in a dream one is absorbing a lesson as to some inherent trait within his nature.

In dreams of animals one may also have revealed to him, if the animal is peaceful, that the trait of the animal is a symbol of potential strength to be used as a preparation for an initiate to gain spiritual power.

Initiates, while dreaming, sometimes portray through an animal the next step in evolvement, and thus are prepared for certain transitions in their attitudes toward religion, family, sex, and responsibility.

Should one dream of fleeing from an animal, he is being shown his penetrable point of fear, weakness and insecurity. If one is fighting or contesting an animal, or seeking to trap an animal, he is being told in his dream that his initiatory action is now enabling him to overcome certain corresponding negative animal traits in his nature.

To hunt an animal in a dream indicates that one is tracking down and conquering his own traits corresponding to the animal. Thus, if one dreams of hunting a lion – a lion being the symbol of the initiate's will – this reveals to him that he is tracking down and seeking to overcome his untrained sentient nature. If he is hunting a tiger, he is being alerted that something in his nature is ruthless and tiger-like. Should he be hunted by a tiger, this indicates that he is associated with a person who has a ruthless and cruel, tiger-like nature. In the dream he is being warned to fortify himself against cruel persons. Should he dream of an elephant, he is being shown that his will will be the chief aspect in the dramas of his initiations. When the trunk of an elephant is down, it indicates that one is docile as to will. When the trunk is up, this shows that one is victorious over the lesser will. If the elephant is in a state of attacking or charging him, this indicates that he is to be the victim of his own forceful will or to be exposed to the forceful will of another.

A certain man experienced an initiatory dream involving a snake. The snake appeared to be nonpoisonous. On drawing closer to examine the creature, the snake coiled and reared its head as if to strike. Following this the snake broke into chiding or teasing laughter. The interpretation of this dream relates to the snake as the symbol of kundalini or spiritual fire. The man, being formerly of a traditional religion and only being recently exposed to the inner sciences of the spirit, was being shown that the joke was on him; that his former traditional dogmatic defenses were to be transcended through the awakening of the kundalini fire, and thus inner spiritual knowing was to become his gift or prize.

INITIATION THROUGH PREHISTORIC ANIMAL SYMBOLS

Every two hundred and fifty thousand years the magnetic belt of the earth experiences a major slowing down. During one of these periods occurring over the hundreds and thousands of years consumed in such a gravity shifting, certain portions of the animal kingdom were sifted, weighed, withdrawn or obliterated. The mighty dinosaurs and other massive archaic creatures were all withdrawn into an etheric twilight state of life, ceasing to accompany the physical life of man. These archaic animals may be observed in dreams as floating etheric symbols forced up from the lower aspect of quelle or atavistic levels of the subconscious, and experienced as memory expanders during dreams.

During sleep in certain aspects of cosmic initiations, one is confronted with the atavistic life inhabiting the early phases of the earth's development, and thus coordinates with the meaning of life as it is presently experienced in consciousness on earth. In personalized instruction in dreams archaic animal symbols identify one's own degree of evolvement. Antiquated symbols in dreams on any level point to the need for one to move forward and to cease holding onto archaic decaying habits or ideas.

Dreams of animals usually relate a person to the lower subtle dream levels of grotesque, fantasy or wish. When one is preparing for higher degrees of initiation, he may research his past lives by observing in dreams the animals that lived in prehistoric times. He may also read the records of a past or prehistoric age through animal symbology. To do this he must rise above the grotesque, fantasy and wish levels in dreams.

One may learn of an important stage in his former embodiment through the symbols of the animals prominent in that particular age or time. Thus, if one dreams of the dinosaur or of the larger reptiles of ancient times, he is recapitulating his subconscious memory of these primitive days, and he is drawing upon a reservoir of association. Prehistoric animal symbols are used in dreams to open up the memory sheaths holding the clue to power in former atavistic lives.

The discarnate shells of all prehistoric animals now dwell as etheric shadowed forms in a twilight state in the ninth etheric layer within the physical earth. The Saturn Initiate, or the initiate being trained in cognizant night-flight, in night research travels to the etheric inner layers of the earth and there he beholds the animals who are now withdrawn and inanimate; however, when one looks upon them, they seem to be breathing, animate and living. From the autumnal equinox through January fourteenth one is more likely to have dreams of the prehistorical withdrawn animals.

SACRIFICIAL ANIMALS IN DREAMS

Inwardly man is aware of the Commandment, *"Thou shalt not kill."* This Commandment is ever close to the conscience and memory of all advanced souls. In dreams the initiate is reminded symbolically of the sacrificial nature of the animal offered up for him.

All animals are under the dominion of man. Throughout the ages man has used and misused the animal kingdom, that he may survive and rise. When God spoke to the Adam humanity, He gave no directives to man as to the eating of flesh meat. As men advanced through the varied phases of biological development, the necessity for survival, due to climatic and catastrophic disasters, compelled them to turn to the animal kingdom for food and sustenance.

DREAMS OF SACRIFICIAL ANIMALS

BOAR – A wild attribute of greed; the necessity to overcome one's greed.

BLACK BULL – A dream reminder of the necessity to cleanse the sexual nature through sacrifice and restraint.

WHITE BULL – Memory of Osiris in an Egyptian life.

DEER – Symbol of a sacrifice of a harmless creature, and of man's will to pursue and kill.

DONKEY – The symbol of a burden-bearer.

DOVE – Symbol of the sacrifice of the innocent.

HORSE – The sign of freeing and progression.

PIGEON – A sacrifice symbol of someone known to the dreamer who is dependent on man's charity.

ZODIACAL ANIMALS IN DREAMS

Animal symbols are portrayed also as they appear in the zodiacal significance of dream initiation.

The bull (Taurus) – initiation through earth matters, stewardship of earth objects; initiation as to coveting objects and possessions, also as to one's forceful sex nature. *High side* – to gain balance in earth attitudes; to learn generosity; to serve to carry the burdens of the weak. *The ox* – one of the aspects of the dream symbol of the bull – means to sacrifice and to grind and also to earn; *"The laborer is worthy of his hire;"* a burden-bearer person.

The lion (Leo) – to master the emotions; to be initiated to the higher will; to meet the teacher; initiation into conquest and restoration of the soul's record. To be hunted by a gold lion or white lion means that the teacher is seeking you. To hunt the lion means that one is seeking the teacher.

The ram (Aries) – to overcome assertiveness; to overcome the lesser will; to cleanse out acquisitiveness; to learn the consequence for direct action; to learn the first principles, and thus gain a first foothold in authority; reincarnation symbol of a former Israel life.

The centaur – half man, half horse (Sagittarius) – to overcome indecisiveness as to moral issues; to master the etheric elemental intrusions; to learn obedience in following true guidance; to mediate between animal and man; to see man as supreme only under God.

The goat (Capricorn) – initiations to overcome self-ambition; to evaluate pride; to bridle the desire to rule; to warm the cold, icy, undemonstrative temperament; to learn the difference between physical passion and spiritual love; to learn of the impersonal karmic law exacting penalties, thus to overcome the desire to take the law into one's hands and revenge.

DREAM AND MEDITATION SYMBOLS
AND THEIR CORRESPONDENCES
Animals – Birds – Fish – Insects – Reptiles

In dreams or meditation all four-footed animals represent the emotions, desires, feelings and senses. All two-legged flying creatures represent the mental: thought, thinking and telepathy. Fish represent etheric and astral action, also soul action. Insects represent bacterial action. Reptiles represent the sexual will's action and the kundalini's action.

ALBATROSS – Retribution. Symbol of a lesser-genesis dweller presenting the debt of scavenger thought traits from former lives; symbol of a dweller action and approaching death; an avenging person.

ALLIGATOR – Initiation to overcome lust; or may pertain to some person with lustful attitudes. Destructive, sentient, emotional will. Researching lust in one's own nature.

ANT OR ANTS – Initiatory health experience. Bacterial disarrangement in the physical body. Imbalance of health or high fever. Predictive of a sickness-to-be for self or some person or persons close by. Prediction of a mass epidemic. *Tiny ants* – a persistent fever. *Big ants* – malignancy gone wild.

ANTEATER – A personality who is a disturber and fear-bringer. One who is an agitator and disrupter of industry. Emotional body, sentient atom level. Overcurious person upsetting regulated routines.

APE – Malice. Unintelligible atavistic force. Sometimes seen before a tribal-genesis dweller experience or sentient emotional initiation. Brute force. Research into one's own aggressions and cruelty.

ARCTIC ANIMALS AND CREATURES – All animals and creatures living in frozen climes signify latent, dormant, or potential conditions, situations, or qualities yet to manifest. Exposure to unknown elements.

ARMADILLO – A shell creature denotes retreatist personality. Its habitat being southern indicates retreat into tribal-genesis inclinations and sentient emotional action.

ASP – Frustration of the emotional will due to a vicious person with a poisonous personality; symbol of self-destruction or suicide.

To see an asp through a *glass* means that one is being protected from his own thoughts of self-destruction. To see glass, as a glass wall in a dream, means that one is being insulated and protected.

ASS – A plodding personality of stubborn temperament; or stubborn, unyielding emotional force.

BAT – Negative, left-hand path telepathy from a person in the world with inverted, psychical powers or from a vampire force of the lesser astral regions. Such telepathy devitalizes or drains the feelings. Mental thought form. Symbol used by black magicians.

BEAR – Hibernation, emotional impenetrableness, and non-communication. Habitat northern indicates human-genesis level; *noncomplying*, hibernating men. An unclarified mystic and a retreatist.

BEAVER – Night service and unceasing industry in the higher astral planes with freedom in the use of the higher emotional body. A person of coordinated industry.

BEE – Spiritual telepathic industry; solar initiation; co-disciple. Freedom for action in the higher emotional body, etheric body and thought. *Beehive* – mediative Cosmos-Disciple action.

Bees in a dream are a soul-medallion symbol. The bees are under the command and direction of the great Solar Devas. The Solar Devas control the intricate mechanized functions of the bee. Honey, the product of the bee, is a unique food, especially healing and supporting the needs of the higher and lesser etheric bodies.

To see a bee or a hive of bees in a dream indicates that one is contacting the energy overflow or the honey wisdom of the medallions of the accumulative souls who are drawn together to produce the divine honey or wisdom essence of God.

Divine Mother especially works with Deva consciousness in certain solar initiatory powers.

The more highly evolved a person, the more he is capable of blending with souls of rare spiritual quality.

It may be seen that *lunar initiates* are unable to assimilate honey as a food. Being out of the range of the wavelengths of the Solar Devas, they must draw their intuitions and inspirations from the Flora Deva kingdom under the influence of the moon's night elixir rather than from the Sun or Solar Deva Angels.

All stinging insects are under the influence of the planet Mars. To see a stinging insect in a dream – with the exception of the bee, which is under the influence of the sun – indicates that one is to be wounded by a violent Mars attribute in his own nature or in someone close by.

BEETLE – Occultism; large beetles mean persons nourished in occultism; an occult power figure. Emotional telepathy. Initiatory powers from former lives in Egypt.

Black beetle – inverted powers.

Green beetle – healing of the astral.

Gold beetle – royal initiation or spiritual authority; relates to Egypt; work in Egypt of the past.

BIRDS – Flock of birds flying to the left means synchronization and mastering of negative-mind ominous forces. Flock of birds flying to the right means synchronization of spiritual forces coming to one's aid; also represents the reinforcement of the angels. Birds represent telepathy. *White birds* – spiritual telepathy. *Black and white bird* – the symbol of legal matters. Dream of *freeing a bird* – freeing the higher self; and telepathic powers. *Bird flying against a window glass* – a soul seeking to cross the barrier between life and death. *Bird being killed on hitting the glass* is a sign of an imminent death. *Bird overhead* – consciousness. *Bird dying* – sign that one is suffocating the life out of his higher self. *Bird in a cage* – higher self restrained.

BLACKBIRD – Negative telepathy or disturbing news of a subtle, mental variety. *Blackbird with golden message* – the test of money from devious persons.

BLACK WIDOW SPIDER – Woman of possessive, parasitical, malicious, or destructive nature with subtle, etheric, black magic knowledge and power. Destroying of one's own young. Destroyer of one's husband. Destroyer of home or family-atom. (see Spider)

BOA CONSTRICTOR – Parasitical, possessive, subtle danger from persons in the physical world or from entity powers of the astral world, paralyzing and frustrating the physical will. An evil discarnate entity, or one who cannot reincarnate, in possession of a person's physical will.

BOAR – A brutish, selfish, emotionally forceful person with an unreasoning and belligerent attitude. Abuse of the emotional will.

BUCK – A contesting, masculine, emotional force on the physical plane.

BUFFALO – Sentient emotional memories of decaying Atlantis. *Buffalo horns* – death of a strong person or tribal-like leader.

BUGS AND INSECTS CRAWLING OVER THE DREAMER – Warning about parasitical persons and the dangers of helping people before they are ready; also a warning that cell bacteria are out of control; danger of purification through fevers or infections.

BULL – Unresolved emotional sex force or over-dominating sexual power. Memory of Osiris Egypt.

BUTTERFLY – The symbol of the pituitary gland's higher telepathic power and also the symbol of the higher intuition. Symbol of reincarnation. A blessing as a disciple.

BUZZARD – A destroying, malignant entity related to the unresolved thoughts of the unrisen dead. A person who thinks of the death of others as a way to gain.

CAMEL – Nomad symbol. Desert habitat denotes tribal-genesis. Predictive symbol of change of place due to some sentient-atom relationship. If a camel is seen in light, it signifies a pure, selfless dedication of a polarity disciple, and is indicative of a spiritual sojourn or caravan to unknown places.

CANARY – Telepathy of a higher order. *Baby canary* – a young initiate.

CAT – Astral force; observing various degrees of energy; a psychic person who is draining off your vitality. Indicates one is subjected to the astral lower world through the region of the solar plexus, and also that the emotional magnetism and physical magnetism of the body are being depleted.
  White cat – astral religion.
  Black cats – women with malicious temperaments.
  One's own cat – a psychic protector of the home.

CATERPILLAR – The unformed and untrained will; a potential initiate.

CENTIPEDE – A disobedient escapist; an inverted emotional will; an abuse of hearing; a nuisance-minded intruder.

CHICKEN – Feathered creatures being the symbol of telepathy, a chicken is the symbol of domestic telepathy relating to home or family-atom.

CLAM – Non-cooperating person in the physical world. Materialistic, secretive and noncommittal attitude. A physical retreatist. *Large clam shell* – inner hearing; a blessing from Saint James.

COBRA – When attacking, is a symbol of a deranged psychical will. Dangerous psychical force or inverted use of the will. Danger from a hypnotic will. When the cobra is peaceful – kundalini power to be opened.

COW – Domestic situation; something to do with the family-atom.
  Sacred cow – symbol of Divine Mother's unending source of spiritual milk or food.

COYOTE – Stealthy and cowardly feeling action; a scavenger person and outcast.

CRAB – An escapist; an unreachable situation. A crab without a shell denotes a defenseless escapist; exposure to karma.

CRICKET – A small Guardian Angel of the family-atom. On the hearth, a protector for the mother of the home.

CROW – A trespasser and thoughtless intruder; a cunning mind; a destroyer of one's labors; a cynical materialistic bandit; a malicious gossip.

CUCKOO – A symbol of a silly, unrealistic person; also, the symbol of one of the polarities of the soul. The cuckoo in its highest aspect symbolizes the masculine principle seeking to blend with the feminine principle. The higher cuckoo symbol is sometimes called the nightingale of the soul. One can hear the warbling of this soul-symbolic bird in states of illumination. The soul may reproduce the sound of a bird through the audible current or cosmic sound.

DAUBER (Mud Wasp) – In its positive aspect, it means one is etherically exploring the minerals of the earth. In its negative aspect, it relates to an earth-sign person (Taurus, Virgo, Capricorn) with parasitical tendencies, building his life upon the life of another. The dream warning is that one will be stung if the parasitical person does not have his way.

DEER – A deer in a dream represents a defenseless person, or a victim of the cruelty of men; a peaceful and tender heart; harmlessness.

DESERT CREATURE – Indicates a retreatist person or a retreat situation; a symbol of self-research.

DINOSAUR – Indicates that one is undergoing a Saturn initiation, and is researching the withdrawn animal kingdom; also that one is using outmoded ideas in a modern situation.

DOE – Means a young, tender feminine disciple needing prayers and protective helps

DOG – A *white or light-colored dog* with kind and affectionate intent indicates unquestioned loyalty; faithfulness; a test of being faithful.

A *spotted dog* means a skeptical person, minus loyalty.
A *black dog* means a black or dark force; a threat from the powers of darkness; giving the truths to someone (who is not ready) who will ridicule you.
A *barking dog* indicates a warning of loss of physical possessions, honor or recognition.
A *mad dog* symbolizes an insane adversary.
A *vicious or snarling dog* means an atheist or an unbeliever; a contender; an ungrateful person.
A *pack of dogs* means vicious persecution.
A *strange dog with a rag or cloth face* means that the dreamer

is encountering an alien person showing a facade rather than his true nature.

To dream of *a faithful dog that is blind* denotes that the one dreaming has blind faith, or has a mystical nature.

A *woman carrying a little dog* indicates that the one dreaming subconsciously expects indulgence when he is faithful, or rewards for his favors.

When one dreams of *a dog he loved who no longer lives*, the dream indicates protection against alien telepathies and works. Such animals protect their former masters, in waking and in sleep, from subtle elemental attackers.

The breed of a dog and its significance in dream symbology:

An *Airedale* is the symbol of an inclusive person who feels that other persons are unnecessary to him; a regimented mind and attitude.

A *bird dog* – one having an extended sense of smell. A pointer indicates one who has discerning powers. A retriever indicates a return for good or bad.

A *bloodhound* is the symbol of a policeman; an angel of retribution; good to review the Ten Commandments.

A *bulldog* means stubborn loyalty; Guardian Angel; a jovial stubborn protector.

A *cocker spaniel* means domestic indulgence; a person with little imagination, expecting all of the comforts.

A *collie* means a shepherd, or a teacher.

A *dachshund* indicates a humorous situation with a happy conclusion; a person capable of crawling out of false accusations.

An *Eskimo dog* indicates one who has a controlled and rugged zeal; also an impersonal, unsentimental contact; a memory of ancient Arctic nights.

A *Great Dane* means an awkward and cumbersome condition; sometimes refers to a clumsy person.

A *hound* means the explorer, and the hunter side of one's nature; one who runs with a pack.

A *Mexican hairless* or *Chihuahua* indicates some embarrassing situation or connection with a Latin person.

A *husky* denotes a primitive memory of the glacial or ice age.

A *mongrel* means mixed loyalties; a person of mixed creeds.

A *Newfoundland dog* symbolizes a Good Brother; a loyal night server; the locale of a former life.

A *Pekingese* means a pampered situation and an unexpected contestant.

A *police dog* means the law; a Guardian Angel of the judgments and ethics.

A *poodle* means one is giving his time and his loyalty to vanity; an over-bred person with indulgent desires.

A *spitz dog* indicates a person who shows partiality and lack of hospitality; an unapproachable person.

A *Saint Bernard* means survival, and help from a large, lumbering, authoritative individual.

A *terrier* means inquisitiveness, tenacity.

A *white, young puppy* – a new loyalty.

A WARNING DREAM: I dreamed I was coming down a flight of stairs. At the bottom of the stairs was a glass door. I could see the face of a man glaring at me through the door. I became alert, for his look was unfriendly. Once outside, I hurried down the street and saw two policemen standing by the open door of a police station. I stood by the policemen, knowing I would be protected by them in case of trouble. Meanwhile, I observed that the man had several black dogs of different sizes. Some of the dogs were quite large. After I took my position of safety, I watched the dogs do to a person what they would have done to me; that is, the man had taught the dogs to surround a victim, rear up, and bark angrily in his face. The dogs were trained not to touch the victim; however, after being subjected to this weird attack, the victim would die of fear. After the man and his dogs left, there would be no outer sign to indicate the cause of death.

INTERPRETATION:

1. "Down a flight of stairs" indicates that the one dreaming is descending downward through the lower astral regions.
2. "Glass door" indicates insulation against astral negation.
3. "Unfriendly man" – astral underworld inhabitant.
4. "Two policemen" – two angels or two invisible helpers with spiritual insulation, power and authority.
5. "Black dogs" – elemental denizens of the dark; evil attackers.

6. The one dreaming is being shown the danger of astral powers of darkness who have power to kill without leaving a physical mark.

Note: When one speaks a mantram before sleep, he is protected from the night denizens of the dark, and prepared to overcome their challenges. In event of an astral attack during sleep, an initiate automatically speaks the mantram of insulation: "In the name of the Christ, I fear you not." Should one fail to use his mantramic speaking before sleep, he may fail to be insulated from the challengers of the dark.

DOMESTIC ANIMAL – Indicates some situation on family-genesis level. If the domestic animal shows violent tendencies, it is of dweller action. If the domestic animal shows friendliness, one can expect help from the Guardian Angel of the family.

DONKEY – Indicates some task is required of the dreamer in which he will carry a heavier load without complaint. In the negative, it indicates a stubborn and unyielding person or situation. (see Jenny Donkey)

DOVE – A spiritual co-disciple or a disciple; or a symbol of telepathy from another disciple; also the symbol of the power of the Holy Ghost.
Doves – fellow disciples.
White doves on the ground – earth plane disciple.
White doves flying around – means synchronization of a disciple nucleus.

DRAGON – Indicates that one is undergoing a moon's sphere initiation, and is researching the magnetic belt around the earth. The magnetic belt around the earth is the lower astral world which contains the negative emotional debris of mankind. This debris moves as a vast serpent, boiling, writhing and turning. After such a dream, the one dreaming should make a covenant to purify his emotions. Also represents lower astral region initiation.

DRAGONFLY – Indicates Saturn initiation as to the mineral resources of the earth, particularly the stone of amber and its healing properties; a study of exchange of magnetism, and the use of prana as a healing fire.

DUCK – A migrator; symbolic of one being trained to ride on the waves of the astral world; also indicates that one may migrate to a new place.

EAGLE – Means great initiative and daring, and a life that is not easy; a symbol of an initiate. An eagle also represents a loner-initiate.

A *brown eagle* means an initiation through earth matters or conditions.

A *blue eagle* indicates a mental initiation.

A *white or gold eagle* indicates a spiritual initiation.

To see *many eagles* indicates many fellow initiates.

To see a *young eagle* means a probationary initiate.

To see an *eagle flying* indicates the power to ascend above the astral world.

Large eagle – polarity-disciple and teacher.

EEL – Represents the atavistic or primitive fire in the spinal column; symbol of inverted electricity and malpractice through the sentient will. When one dreams of an eel, he is researching the primitive, prehistoric and atavistic memories connected with the sentient-atom action of mankind. Forceful use of kundalini fire.

EGG – Symbol of fertility. The greater cosmic egg relates to cosmos creation. An egg from a reptile is a warning and premonition of an imminent unwholesome and unhealthy astral effect upon human affairs. The egg from a chicken portrays ripe karma and a circumstance affecting domestic issues. An egg from a fish indicates pregnancy, or fear of pregnancy. Eating an egg in a dream means that one has absorbed universal life substance.

EGRET – Means one is abusing his emotions and mentality, or is endangering his spiritual life. An untrained attitude toward spiritual gifts. A symbol of false pride. A symbol of calloused destruction.

ELEPHANT – Means the will. *Trunk up* – means victory over physical conditions; the symbol of perseverance; strength, power, victory or success in learning a lesson. *Trunk down* – inverted, malicious, insensitive and unintelligent will; the use of force without compassion; defeat, or a lesson to learn from someone having a stronger will.

Elephant trumpeting or speaking – one will be called on to prove power; also kundalini rising in spine through median nerve.

Herd of elephants – making your own will to make the way.

ELK – Represents the fearless sentinel or protector; a dying event or end of a familiar phase.

EWE – A feminine follower or devotee of spiritual works. A woman called to do a special task.

EWE LAMB – Symbol of sacrifice and martyrdom by a pure, feminine person; an exceptional grace.

FALCON – Negative ambassador; one has given authority to the wrong person; a ruthless pursuer.

FIREFLY – Psychic flashes; a person who contains intermittent astral fire and intermittent mediumistic or psychical powers, rather than spiritual light. Such persons commune with the unrisen dead or with the elementals of the lesser astral regions.

FISH – *A fish swimming toward the right in pure water* – a convert of Christ. *Swimming toward the left* – an astral floater.

A *fish in muddy waters* indicates a confused situation caused by passive and deviating action.

To fish indicates a new disciple or initiate is soon to appear on the horizon.

To eat fish in a dream indicates that one is partaking of spiritual truths as given from the Christ. A certain sacrament action denoting union with the light.

Gills of a fish indicate one who lives in the obsolete past; research into the primitive memory; egotism in a person of unrealistic nature. *When moving* – denotes irritation from primitive sources.

Tropical fish denotes temporary plateau of evolvement.

Freshwater fish is an evangelistic convert.

Saltwater fish is one who will eventually work for the humanities.

Balloon fish – a boaster and braggart.

Catfish – an inhabitant of astral slime.

Dolphin – represents a neutral person; also a Cherubim Angel.

Goldfish – a hibernating personality in a secular religious body.

Marlin – a disciple with deep emotions and somber temperament, willing to accept discipline.

Note: A *deep-sea fish* indicates an initiate of deep emotions, with capacity to master astral conditions.

Minnow – the unevolved masses.

Porpoise – represents Cherubim Angels.

Shark – represents an astral, black magician; a discarnate entity.

Starfish – represents a karmic antagonist in a spiritual group. High side – represents a blessing and the opening of a spiritual portal.

Tarpon – a useless waste of time and abuse of Nature's forces.

Whale – represents the three lower planes of the astral world; a Jonah test of obedience.

FLAMINGO – A flighty, sensuous way of thinking or ideas to be withdrawn; obsolete situation.

FLEA – Signifies a parasitical, psychic irritating person who persists in agitating and disturbing the environment.

FLY – A parasitical, infectious communicant; a contagious carrier of unproven opinions; a spreader of malice; malicious thinking from someone; a contagious sickness; a carrier of psychic negation.

FOX – Cunning mind; a manipulator.

GANDER – A hypersensitive person with an inferiority complex; a sexual egotist.

GAZELLE – Indicative of harmlessness and gentleness. One dreaming of a gazelle is being told by his soul to be merciful.

GILA MONSTER – A confused, mystical retreatist with deadly, stinging, psychical powers.

GIRAFFE – Curiosity and harmless inquiry; an out-of-this-world idea; a suspicious vegetarian with a narrow outlook.

GNU – Research into tribal polarities and into the withdrawn animal kingdom.

GOAT – A stupid, stubborn and noncomplying person; one who uses force rather than the higher will.

A *baby white goat* – a young rigid mind needing a teacher or shepherd. (see Nanny Goat)

A *scapegoat* is one who falls unwittingly into a karmic trap, and thereby becomes a sacrificial agent or vicarious sufferer for sins of another.

GOOSE – Migration to another place; a change or migration caused by a compulsion stemming from the vibratory hum of the soul's medallion. In a dream, a person taking on the features of the goose means the person is under the domination of another. A silly idealist.

GOPHER – A vegetarian retreatist. A destroyer of good works.

GORILLA – A brutish, amoral person. When a gorilla is seen in a dream, this may mean impersonation, in that a discarnate entity can take the discarded shell of an ape or gorilla and appear in a threatening or frightening manner to the one dreaming.

GOSLING – A young, silly person; an immature, emotional person; an awkward male probationer.

GRASSHOPPER – Negative and acquisitive thoughts; an unsettled mind, unable to concentrate.

Many grasshoppers – a plague or curse destroying one's hopes and wishes.

GREYHOUND – A person with all muscle and low mentality; one who chases his quarry down without knowing why.

GRIFFIN – An elemental, protective guardian used by the Assyrians, Babylonians and Egyptians. When a griffin is seen in a dream, one is researching the records of past Babylonian, Assyrian and Egyptian times.

GUINEA PIG – Experimentation for the benefit of exploitation.

GULL – An astral scavenger or a discarnate entity living upon the vitality of a living person; a person living in the world with parasitical tendencies.

HART – Represents perfect balance and equanimity; one seeking to arise to God.

HAWK – A deliberate destroyer; one who searches for his prey with unremitting persistence; a clairvoyant using his powers without mercy.

HEDGEHOG – A symbol to prepare for a coming season and its initiation; a person who waits for fair weather to become a disciple.

HEN – Over-domestic woman; a gossip; a dowdy female.

HERON – A person half absorbed in the slimes of the astral world and the soil of error of the mental world.

HIPPOPOTAMUS – An easily aroused or quick tempered, armored, impenetrable, primitive, resisting person.

HOG – Selfishness, greediness, astral or psychical absorption; a thick-hided person who thinks only of himself.

> A *wild boar* – an uncontrolled astral force affecting a greedy person, causing destruction.
> *Pig* – a young untrained psychical, gluttonous, selfish, inconsiderate person; greed; sensuousness.
> *Sow* – a female, greedy, untidy person. A mother who thinks only of indulging her young.
> *Swine* – a person who is at home and happy within astral soil. Also a symbol of prodigal son who prefers the swine herd to his Father's house.

HORSE – Progress.

> *Brown* – material progress.
> *Black* – danger of death; or warning of death.
> *Black and white* – one is being warned that he is being indecisive and that his progress is being defeated by divided loyalty.
> *Gray* – retrogression; shady concepts.
> *Red* – a warning to prepare for coming aggressions; danger from a hostile and revengeful person with an afflicted Mars; also sign of war.
> *White* – spiritual progress and evolvement; an avatar and a teacher; usually seen at Easter.
> A *bay* – slow but safe conduct.
> *Mare* – a domestic burden-bearer; progress of a domestic nature; a woman fulfilling her duties to children and mate.
> *Palomino* – progress in emotions; symbol of new environments to come, containing beauty and harmony.
> *Pegasus* – (white horse with wings) means Mercury initia-

tion; symbol of Raphael initiation at Easter.

A *draft horse* or *Percheron* – means a steady uncomplaining helper; enslavement to conformity.

Pony – represents child's play; or self-delusion as to progress.

Roan – a symbol of one who is caught into traditional concepts interfering with spiritual progress; one who is self-satisfied with his progress; an overcomplacent person.

Stallion – a sexual challenge, and a warning to be more reverent in attitudes toward procreation.

Horseshoe pointing up – holy magnetism received from heaven; pointing down, magnetism from person on earth and from one's own emotions.

HORSEFLY – Cleaning out of the Augean stables; to bring the will back into purity.

HUMMINGBIRD – Sustained alignment with the higher etheric body; a levitation expert of the mind.

HYENA – A slinky, sly, amoral person or experience; a warning to be on guard against the cunning malice of some person nearby; a parasitical person; a person waiting for one to die.

IBEX – A primitive, self-willed intruder; also pertains to a forceful rise above the tides of common expectation; a social climber.

IBIS – An Atlantean and Egyptian memory; a research into the record of former lives in Egypt; a symbol of immortal life; a research into the medical therapies of Egypt; a protective symbol against sexual indecency.

IGUANA – One who gains by his cunning wits, one who lacks physical and emotional support or stamina.

INSECT – *Nuisance insect* – a warning that one has neglected reverence in his household or home; astral insulation has been removed.

Poisonous insect – a warning that one is devitalizing his energy level, and thus opening himself to malicious telepathy; to be alert to scathing or stinging personalities.

Quantity of insects – one has lowered his defenses against reproachful mass telepathies; bacterial world is being scrutinized before healing powers come.

JACKAL – One who lives upon the spoils of his fellow man.

JACKASS – A stolid, noncomplying, egotistical temperament.

JACKRABBIT – A harmless, hasty, seemingly timid person; a fast-thinking telepathic psychic.

JAGUAR – A ruthless, unethical force or person; an astral tyrant of the subtle underworld.

JENNY DONKEY – A patient, plodding woman; one who assumes the major burdens.

JENNY WREN – A domesticated mother with protective zeal.

JUNGLE ANIMALS – Atavistic and unpredictable impulses stemming from the lower emotions; challengers to the unwary.

KANGAROO – A defenseless, awkward, antiquated attitude. When seen in a dream, the person is holding onto sentimental attachments which will fail to fulfill his expectations.
> *Note:* The kangaroo is close to becoming extinct. Animals being withdrawn from the earth seen in dreams relate to unrealistic and passé conditions.

KATYDID – A ritualistic creeded person.

KITTEN – A minor, devitalizing, astral force; also means affections are being placed in a person emotionally immature.

KOALA – A useless indulgence in the home, consuming time, demanding care; a hunger and need to channel one's affection to a higher source.

LADYBUG – A domestic family-genesis symbol; a protector of the young.

LAMB – Lamb of God, or Jesus.
> A *white lamb* – a beloved disciple; a symbol of innocence and sacrifice; a symbol of an uncontroversial mind.
> A *black lamb* – a fallen disciple; one who has betrayed the Lord.
> A *lamb being led to the slaughter* – a symbol preparing one for a sacrificial role.
> A *lamb among many lambs* – a symbol of fellow disciples in the garment of the Good Shepherd or the Lord; a group of innocents or naive persons.
> A *lost lamb* – a disciple in danger of falling; one who should be prayed for.

A *lamb looking backward over shoulder* – a disciple reading his record of past lives.

LARK – The symbol of hope and of better things, and of an ascended consciousness.

LEMMING – A sign of famine in the land; a negative uncontrollable compulsion received from the destroying principle.

LEOPARD – A revengeful, discarnate entity; or a person ruthless in ambition.

LICE – An immoral and incestuous abnormality; a contamination from amorality.

LION – A male will-initiate.

A *black lion* – one who has yet to master his will. One who is using will to enforce the dark.

A *golden lion* – an initiate who has tapped his soul-grace; a Master.

A *white lion* – an adept; one who has command of his emotions and mastery of the astral regions and planes; also a Master.

A *brown lion* – one who is at home in the higher astral world; one who has physical plane manifestation powers.

Someone riding a lion – an initiate leading one over the astral world.

LIONESS – A woman will-initiate. (See reference to male lion for color interpretation.)

LIZARD – An ancestral sexual-compulsion; a lethargic person with a strong sex motivation.

LLAMA – The symbol of a dependable polarity-disciple; a memory of Eastern occult powers; a union with Tibet.

LOBSTER – A person who has armored himself against the light. If the lobster is alive, it is a symbol of being helped; if dead, an unpleasant experience astrally.

LOCUST – Danger of destruction through Community Dweller action.

LOON - An eccentric lunar mystic; a retreatist; an antiquated sage.

LOONEY BIRD – A negative moon initiation researching the emotions to overcome irreverence; silly telepathies.

LOVEBIRD (domestic) – Symbol that the Cherubim Angels are at work in the home.
A *dead lovebird* – one has slain the heart of the home.

LYNX – A sly, mysterious and self-contained person; an insincere person; a pretender.

MALLARD – A symbol of migration and change due to emotional impulse.

MANTIS – A destroying astral guru, bringing blight upon the life of a person. Danger of being led into left-hand path. An astral guru is one who has profaned initiation in a former life and thus is now of the dark.

MASTIFF – An over-display of loyalty; too much affection; an untidy or large person.

MEADOWLARK – A Cherubim reminder of the angels at work; a sunset hymn before a night's sleep.

MINK – Exploitation for an indulgent person; a false sense of the trait of pride at the cost of the innocent.

MOCKINGBIRD – A Cherubim Angel reminder. To penetrate man's unbelieving in the protection of universal love.

MONGOOSE – A fearless astral guardian who combats negative action; a guardian against the subtle dark.

MONKEY – Malice; gossip; overcurious or inquisitive person; a subtle, degenerate mental force.

MOOSE – Defender of the helpless; a person from the northern climes.

MOSQUITO – Astral, negative thoughts devitalizing the initiative. Many mosquitoes mean many enemies.

MOTH – A destructive and disintegrating astral visitant; one who is attracted to the light and fails.

MOUNTAIN GOAT – One who prefers an overlook. A stubborn-willed person with over-ambition.

MOURNING DOVE – A preparation to receive news of a death; one who grieves for souls sinning.

MOUSE – A sickness due to infection.
   Mice – symbol of poverty; fear of poverty.

MULE – A stubborn, neutral-field personality; slave labor; a barrier impossible to cross.

MUSKRAT – A hostile hermit.

NANNY GOAT – A woman confined to domestic labors.

NEWT – A frightening, harmless inhabitant of the lower astral regions, thriving within the murky depth of the astral world. A neutralizer of poisoned emotions.

NIGHTHAWK – An astral entity seeking a gullible prey.

NIGHTINGALE – A Guardian Angel of the night.

OCELOT – A ruthless, long-dead discarnate entity devoid of conscience.

OCTOPUS – A discarnate entity from the 8th sphere; a person having hypnotic power over the mind of another person; an entity attached to a medium using lower psychic powers.

OPOSSUM – A person without roots, and with transitory emotions; a parasitical, sardonic stoic; danger of being involved in an unproductive charity; sowing the seed in infertile ground; someone to avoid.

ORANGUTAN – An unintelligent mentality; a destroying, atavistic telepathic force; one who is alien to humanity; brute force minus conscience.

ORIOLE – A singer for the Cherubim Worlds; a messenger from the angels.

OSPREY – An atheistic mind which delights in goading a Christian; an examination into one's sensuality.

OSTRICH – An insensitive retreatist; a foolish, mystical left-handed attitude; one who expects others to do his work; refusal to face one's own weaknesses.

OTTER – A sensuous, graceful, pleasure-loving person; a former Sophist.

OWL – Wisdom; a symbol of the Number One Light Stream; also the symbol of a will-disciple; a symbol talisman of one of the great Masters.

OX – A victim of exploitation; a burden-bearer; a sacrifice imposed from without.

OYSTER – A time of trial and suffering to produce the pearl of the soul. An enforced retreat to learn a lesson. Initiation produced due to outer pressures.

PANDA – A useless person who believes himself to be an ornament to society.

PANTHER – An unrelenting, ruthless enemy of the night.

PARAKEET – A Cherubim help in the family-atom.

PARROT – A gossiper; talking out of turn or timing; one who talks to hear himself talk; one who is a repeater of loose words; one who has a negative Mercury.
　　Parrots – many gossiping; repetitive gossip passed on by many.

PEACOCK – Vanity; egotism; its higher aspect means the eyes of illumination through higher extrasensory perception.

PELICAN – The teacher; one who sacrifices his life for the young in understanding.

PENGUIN – A pompous, pious, harmless orthodox person.

PHOENIX BIRD – An adept with the power to rise in the higher worlds; one who is free of personal karma; one who has the grace to determine his embodiment cycles, or one who has the power to *"go in and out,"* the power to reimmortalize oneself, or the consciousness to remember past lives and to reembody at will.

PIG – (see Hog)

PIGEON – One of the multitude or the outer congregation; one who tries to besmirch or despoil a dove or pure disciple.
　　Rook – one who intrudes upon domestic faithfulness; a seducer; an ingrate.

PIGEON, HOMING – *Gray pigeons on ground* – physical-earth potential disciples not yet evolved.
　　Gray pigeons flying – transiting, potential polarity disciples.

PILOT FISH – A parasitical leaner or satellite person using the power and strength of a leader.

PORCUPINE – An aggressive, belligerent antagonist; one who is hypersensitive due to a guilty conscience.

PORPOISE – A Cherubim ambassador; a jolly angelic occurrence.

POSSUM – See Opossum.

PRAIRIE DOG – A clannish, retrogressed person; a retreatist.

PUMA – An astral antagonist.

PYTHON – Karmic, sexual insatiableness; a sex dweller.

QUAIL – A family-atom vulnerability; a composite of shrewdness and naivete; over-trusting.

RABBIT – Timidity; one in need of protection; a co-atom creature to the deer family; harmlessness.

RACCOON – A harmless sacrificial creature; signifies a person who sacrifices unknowingly; an industrious mischief-maker.

RAM – The symbol related to the time of Moses; also relates to the Ten Commandments; a sentinel of courage.

RAT – Poverty; a stubborn and unyielding poverty; a lesson to be learned through lack; a danger of becoming infected by poverty due to parasitical persons.

RATTLESNAKE – A warning from an enemy with a sportsmanlike gallantry; a person with venom.

REINDEER – A remembrance of Arctic polarity action; a warning to thaw out so as to progress.

RHINOCEROS – An impenetrable person; one who has an extended egotism; one who has a ferocious temperament; one having an armor against reasonableness.

ROACH – Astral soil and negation; lack of order in emotion and thoughts; a situation distasteful to good form.

ROOSTER – A symbol of denial of the Lord; betrayal; a sun clarion of new beginnings.

SABLE – A symbol of sacrifice; a needless sacrifice for a greedy person; being clothed in sable denotes one's etheric sheath of the night.

SALMON – A symbol of one who must go against the currents of life to accomplish his goal; one who dies that others might live.

SARDINE – A symbol of a congested domestic situation.

SCORPION – A symbol of an unexpected offense; the symbol of reproducing something which seems to have been destroyed; the symbol of an immortal rejuvenation.

SEA HORSE – A symbol of initiation into the astral deep.

SEAL – A harmless person who contributes to the world through sacrifice; symbol of an ending cycle.

SHARK – An astral, black magician; a subtle guru predator.

SHEEP – A follower of Jesus; also one of a flock of peaceful persons.

SHEEP DOG – A spiritual angelic presence protecting the flock of the Lord.

SHELL CREATURE – A symbol of insulation and protection due to hypersensitivity.

SHREW – A symbol of an officious, thoughtless, pressure-burdened woman.

SHRIMP – A symbol of a small, harmless, astral inhabitant; an insignificant person.

SKUNK – One who offends the ethic of charity; one who violates good taste. A person with a genius for doing the wrong thing in wrong timing.

SLOTH – A mystical, parasitical introvert subject to spurts of zeal; a warning from the soul to wake up and get busy.

SNAIL – A polarity disciple, or one who carries his house on his back; the power to observe the lesser etheric body and the physical body at work.

SNAKE – A serpent, when in a vertical position, or standing upright, represents spiritual wisdom, and denotes that the kundalini power is moving upward.

A *serpent in a horizontal position* represents an astral force; passive mysticism.

A *serpent coiled and ready to strike* indicates an enemy; also abuse of psychic force through one's own will.

Many snakes or *serpents intertwined and crawling* represent a hotbed of intrigue, confusion, deceit.

A *black snake* indicates some latent unresolved primitive sexual attitude; a subconscious fear of sex.

A *brown snake* is deception through sexual magnetic attraction; a prostitution of sexual powers.

A *gold snake* is the sign of a celibate initiate.

A *green snake* indicates one is depleting his life-forcevitality through wrong channeling and must be prepared for healing.

A *gray snake* represents a person who has devitalized his sexual power through abuse; an impotent person; also a shadow entity subverting one's will.

A *red snake* indicates over-aggressiveness in one's sexual competitiveness; lack of reverence in sexual expression; use of force through sex; abuse of sex; malpractice through use of sexual magnetism.

A *silver snake* indicates that one is being initiated through the lunar brain to purify his sexual attitudes; one is entering initiation of the lunar fire centered in the root of the tongue, the solar plexus, and in the spine.

A *white serpent raised* – generation power sublimated to spiritual powers; use of the white kundalini light.

A *red* or *greenish-brown serpent, coiled* – temptation in sex; a challenge to divert the spiritual life.

Venom of a snake – death thrust from an enemy.

SPARROW – Symbol of mercy for the masses.

SPIDER

A *small spider* – telepathic manipulation received from a psychic person.

A *large spider* – symbol of material increase in supply; prosperity; a widening of the orbit of action; a warning to observe one's ethic as to prosperity.

A *black widow spider* – means a coercive female person who delights in devouring the will of a male.

A *blue spider* – spiritual prosperity with financial help; a mental creator inspired continually.

A *brown spider* – a loss of possessions.

A *gold spider* – a disciple weaving his life out of his own grace resources.

A *white spider* – spiritual progression and prosperity.

A *nest of spiders* – danger of a psychical pitfall.

To dream of a *spider in the bed* – to covet with lust; adultery.

A *spider on the wall* – the symbol to watch stewardship in the home.

A *spider in a web* – the symbol of a danger of being over-gullible.

A *spider web* – a symbol of the medallion of one's soul spun out of one's own soul-light; in its negative aspect means the spinning of negative, restless thoughts.

Monkey caught in spider's web – indicates one is dissipating his thought energy.

Venom of a spider – a poisonous person contaminating purity.

Tarantula (see Tarantula)

SQUIRREL – One who hoards. One who is provident toward the future.

STALLION – A warning of a primitive and violent sexual trial.

STARFISH – A Christian, stigmata initiate; symbol of planets and their night helps. (see Fish)

STINGRAY – An astral entity with power to physically harm; or a person who is sadistically inclined.

STORK – An angelic protector; a home increase.

SWALLOW – The symbol of a timid, inoffensive, meek disciple with the power of rhythm.

SWAN – Mastery over the astral world.

A *white swan* represents the levels of the saints.

A *brown swan* represents a person who has the power to receive certain practical helps from the Hall of Learning.

A *black swan* – a black occultist or magician posing as a peace-giver.

TADPOLE – A cosmic symbol of dormant, germinal life; atavistic memory.

TAPIR – A tribal-genesis greedy person.

TARANTULA – A malicious and deliberate side-stepper who places the burden upon others; a malicious and poisonous slanderer who spreads the poisoned word without thought of its result and consequence.

TARPON – A harmless astral inhabitant dependent upon astral association rather than upon man.

TERMITES – A mental erosion caused by continued negativity and irresponsibility; an undermining situation or person.

THRUSH – A symbol of faith in God.

TIGER – A ruthless person destroying and devouring for the sake of lust; unleashed senses.

TOAD – Black magic; black magician; black arts of alchemy.

TOMCAT – A sensuous, amoral male.

TORTOISE – A plodding disciple; one who measures or gauges his senses by the act of withdrawal.

TSETSE FLY – A symbol of threat from tribal-genesis revenge; an alert to be careful in strange territories.

TUNA – An anointed sacrificial disciple.

TURKEY – A symbol of a sacrifice offered up in thanks for having survived; also a symbol denoting an important event in the autumn, corresponding to the time of Thanksgiving; scavenger person.
   Many turkeys – race situation.

TURTLE – A methodical disciple; guidance to go slow. *A turtle with head withdrawn* – a retreatist disciple.

UNICORN – A Cosmos Disciple with the power of manifestation.

VERMIN – A soiled intrusion disturbing peace and sanctity.

VICUNA – A sacrifice. One's etheric sheath; if healthy, this is reassurance of one's care of inner bodies.

VIPER – A friend turned enemy.

VULTURE – An astral vampire feeding upon negativity and depression. The vulture relates to an antichrist force, preying upon the decaying sins of men, their indifference and their inertias.

WALRUS – A slow-thinking, pompous, social-minded person.

WASP – A jealous, vindictive, revengeful, antisocial, hostile and possessive retreatist person.

WATER BUFFALO – A sensuous, slow-moving, drudge-like person.

WEASEL – A harmless miser; a Uriah Heep type of person.

WHALE – A symbol of maneuverability in the astral world; a Jonah initiation.

WHIPPOORWILL – A sorrowing introspection and irreparable nostalgia for events of the past. To dream of a whippoorwill is to be shown that things of the past are out of one's control.

WILDCAT – A retrogressed, crosswalk, primitive person with destroying, ruthless tendencies.

WOLF – A relentless, revengeful person who manipulates the wills of his cohorts to inflict revenge; a stalker; hunts only in a pack; an untamed friend or undeveloped communication.

WOLVERINE – A person with a dual temperament, close to schizophrenia; without moral concepts; dangerous to society.

WOODCHUCK – An affectionate hoarder.

WOODPECKER – An introvert disguising himself as an extrovert; making a lot of noise to cover up one's insecurity; an exasperated feeling that one is pushed into an undesirable situation.

WORM – A warning of a repelling astral experience; guidance to set one's house in order; a spineless or weak-willed person.

YAK – Symbol for Tibetan research; memory of Tantric practices.

YELLOWJACKET – A symbol of one who is continually on the offensive, who contributes little to industry, and thinks only of himself.

ZEBRA – One who has become a hybrid in the races, part dark and part light; one who is pulled in dual race-currents; a dualistic person.

ZOO – To dream of a zoo where animals are confined – a symbol of one's animal nature being restrained; to be made an object of curiosity or come under the thoughtless scrutiny of the masses.

Chapter 8

TREE SYMBOLS

*I turn to sleep with trust, and give thanks for the many
mediative joys, the happiness of knowing and recognizing the
sacred intent ruling my world.*

THE TREES OF HEAVEN AND THE TREES OF EARTH

Trees are healers, comforters and friends. Trees have been with
man since the beginning of his memory in the earth. Trees are
valiant sentinels speaking of God's immortal way.

The symbol of a tree is used frequently in dreams because the
tree, while often taken for granted, is still deeply rooted in man's
memories of progression and evolvement in this earth and in his
memories of heaven.

The tree of life, so often portrayed symbolically, dwells in the
higher reaches of heaven. The tree of life is the archetypal tree of
generations, and is called in the higher worlds *the genesis tree.*

The tree of the Ancient of Days is the tree of the archetypal
scrolls. Through the archetypal scrolls one is initiated into the seven
branches of archetypal life memory of the earth.

The tree of life and the tree of the Ancient of Days are etheric
trees, and are active only in heaven. All trees in the physical earth
are united with the heavenly archetypal trees. Thus, the trees in
the physical world are not only talismans of everlasting, germinal
life, but they are also the uniting link between man's intuitive
memory and the symbologies within the archetypal trees in heaven.

In the pre-Lemurian times, the fruit-bearing trees and the nut-
bearing trees appeared in the earth. When one sees such a tree in a
dream or in meditation, he is opening the portals of his memory to
man's earliest dietary habits; and he also learns of the Agrarian
Angels who directed and led men into fertile places where nour-

ishment could be found. In these dreams one is being reminded of the true nourishment ordained by the Father.

All trees with short tap roots are pre-Noah trees; their atoms were quickened in the earth in the latter Lemurian times. From these trees the great forests came, and man moved out of his cave habitation and found shelter in wooded places. Some of the ancient Lemurian trees will be withdrawn with the slowing down of the magnetic belt around the earth. This will occur within the next 500 years. When a tree with a short tap root is seen in a dream or in meditation, it signifies that one is making alignment with an archetypal memory.

After Noah, in the beginning of the Aryan Age, the Flora Angels quickened the archetypal atoms for the long-root trees, such as the willow, the bamboo and the banyan. These trees will flourish in the earth, and will eventually attain a short tap root. They will accompany man's future evolvement. Should one dream of a tree having exceptionally long roots, this indicates that he is touching the world-soul record of man in the earth.

Trees having semi-tap roots, growing their roots in all directions, are transit trees; they become extinct at the end of a 10,000 year cycle, called a *moving archetype*. Any tree set in surface soil with widely scattered roots, when seen in a dream or as a meditation symbol, relates to the lack of stamina in man's emotions. Such trees with scattered roots absorb some of the emotional passion of men.

When man transplants a tree in receptive and loving soil, the angel of the tree will protect it in its new environment.

THE THREE FIRES IN A TREE

To use the wood of a tree as firewood is healing; the fragrance opens the buds of the pineal gland. Philosophical and spiritual illumination may come when one is sitting before a fire of burning wood.

Each tree has a distinctive healing aroma penetrating the breath, the lungs and the blood.

When a forest is fired by lightning, this is a cleansing from the Balancing Angels. When a forest is set afire by man through accident or caprice, this is a cleansing for astral sordidness. Men's negations collect in the astral electricity, causing astral humidity. Each year certain communities in large cities suffer the ravages of fire, due to the need for cleansing away of astral humidity. Thus a cleansing comes to a community, to a people, to a family and a new beginning is made possible.

All trees contain three fires. The first fire in a tree is mineral-fire. This is particularly healthful for the breath of man. The second fire is the life-fire connected with the sacred atom centered in the root of the tree. This life-fire works with the ages, thus enabling the tree to live beyond the years of man. The third degree of fire is the light-fire. This is the fire which enables the tree to be an antenna of telepathy for man.

While dreaming, one may behold the different degrees of fire in a tree. Should he see the mineral-fire, this indicates his need to unite himself with Nature and her healing resources. Should he see the life-fire within the tree, he would have access to the reading of the akasic records of the tree and of the ages past, in which the tree had its first beginnings. Should he see the light-fire of the tree, he would be uniting his dream telepathy with Nature's telepathy; and he would be receiving instruction as to the transposing of thoughts.

TREES AS DREAM AND MEDITATION SYMBOLS

When the symbology of a tree appears in a dream, the first symbolic level of the tree is archetypal; such a dream means that one either has been given instruction about the greater archetypes or he has observed the working of the archetypes. When one sees the *top of the tree*, he is observing man's mentality. When he sees *the limbs of the tree and their branches*, he is relating himself to a family-atom. When he sees *the root of the tree*, he is researching the memory of the ages.

When *snow is upon a tree*, this indicates that one is in a static state; he is being warned by his Guardian Angel that he must yield more to circumstances around him, and to give more fervently of his love.

When *a tree is bare of leaves*, one is being alerted that he is out of timing or out of season. A dead tree indicates that a situation has ended.

When one sees *birds in a tree*, it is indicative that his thoughts are ready to enter into a state of telepathy.

If one sees *a leafy tree being cut down*, it is the symbol of a divorce, or the end of a marriage. If one sees *a dead tree being cut down*, this is the symbol of the end of life.

If one sees *a tree with ripened fruits*, this is the symbol of spiritual gifts. If one sees *a nut tree*, this is the symbol that he has certain mental images waiting to be opened. The symbol of *a ripe berry tree* indicates that one should accelerate his hospitality action.

If one sees *a tree laden with flowers*, this is the symbol that he is to receive spiritual gifts from a former life.

To dream of *sitting in the higher limbs of a tree* indicates an observing and overlook as to the evolvement of communities. It also shows that one is preparing to gain a wider perspective. To dream one is *sitting upon a lower limb of a tree* indicates that he is communing with the family-dweller action and learning its true cause.

To dream of *dried twigs* indicates that one has finished a situation and is ready to burn away the hampering memories of the past.

To dream of *bushes in swampy places* indicates that one has certain astral frustrations and deceptions that he must seek to overcome.

When one dreams of *sour fruit on a tree*, the soul is preparing him to receive a well-earned bitter lesson.

To dream of *unripened fruit* indicates that one must be patient and await the timing of fulfillment.

To dream of *tall trees in blackened water* is to recall early Lemurian times; also indicates a guilt-laden mind.

To dream of trees denoting a season of the year means:

1. *Spring* – a virginal beginning.

2. *Summer* – (a) a harvest time and its rewards; (b) a dramatic and fortunate ending of a situation.

3. *Autumn* – a necessity to re-evaluate one's attitudes and thoughts.

4. *Winter* – When one dreams of bare trees and snow on the ground, this indicates a climax or end of long-standing associations; the finality of a hopeless, nonresponsive and static situation.

To dream of *a fig tree with dead leaves* denotes that one has researched the power of cursing and dweller action in the family-atom.

To see *a tree with icicles* indicates that one has become frigid in his attitudes toward life.

To see *a tumbleweed blowing in the wind* indicates that one is rootless, homeless.

To see *the leaf of a tree* means to hear sounds that are not heard with the outer ear.

To dream of *a tree pruned back* indicates that one is in need of elimination in association and thoughts; he should be prepared for discipline.

To see *a tree with sucker branches* indicates that one has become subjected to parasitical persons who negate his vital energies and thoughts. One is being shown that he has a blind side of penetrableness.

To see *an insect-laden tree* indicates that one has hidden infections devitalizing his life-force.

To see *an orderly forest* reminds one that he is ready for a retreat, or a time of spiritual surrender and privacy.

To see *a thicket of trees* reminds one that he has need of clearing out his thoughts, so as to provide him with a pathway to greater thoughts of light.

To see *an elephant clearing a path in a forest* indicates that one is to have massive helps from strong persons and presences.

To see *wood ready for the fire on the hearth* indicates that one is to enter into a protective and happy domestic situation.

The shape of trees in a dream is important. A rounded willow tree indicates a feminine tree. Trees having more angular vertical lines in a dream represent the masculine side of symbology. Short trees indicate stunted life; tall trees, longevity.

Trees having dead limbs indicate neglect, death vibrations, termination. *Trees in a container or box* indicate human interference with natural law. *Trees covered with ice or snow* indicate non-communication and death.

In the higher astral planes trees may be seen sometimes in an upside-down chimera; that is, the roots appearing at the top and the foliage at the bottom. This indicates that one is viewing an earth archetypal-tree relationship, that is, the earth is receiving power from an archetype.

TREES

ACACIA – An Egyptian memory of ritualistic power.

ALDER – A hidden strength protecting one from the astral world.

APPLE TREE – Represents the law of gravity; through a collective, myth, allegorical memory, the one dreaming of the apple tree is being warned of a temptation to come; his soul is reminding him that he lives in a gravity world, where his spiritual freedom is hampered by sensuousness.

ASH – A temporary pause on the higher regions of the astral planes, enabling one to have introspection in the night's sleep; a symbol of domestic harmony.

ASPEN – The symbol of Judas and his death; the symbol of betrayal by a Judas person; the symbol of a Judas-like person being contrite.

AVOCADO TREE – The healer with anointing grace.

BALSAM – A symbol of release from guilt, and the overcoming of prejudice; an anointing of mercy.

BAMBOO – A symbol of a former Chinese life; family-genesis entanglements.

BANANA TREE – A symbol of providence and nourishment for the physical body.

BANYAN – A symbol of inseparableness; a symbol of a teacher's protecting love.

BIRCH – A symbol of discipline rendered by some austere person or circumstance.

BO TREE – A symbol of illumination, and communion with the higher worlds; a symbol of spiritual initiation, and of relinquishing the world.

BREADFRUIT – A symbol of a tribal-genesis memory; reverence for the feminine principle.

CARNIVOROUS TREE – A symbol of a parasitical person nearby depleting the magnetism within the lesser etheric body.

CEDAR – A symbol of peace, grace-timing, anointing, and perfect faith; preservation.

CHERRY – A symbol of childhood memories, and the need to return to simplicity in actions; love; emotions; chastity.

CHRISTMAS TREE (Decorated) – Heart disciple; initiation during the Christmas season (from the period of December 14th through January 8th); overcoming the Herod materiality.
Christmas tree ornaments – symbols of festival grace.

COCONUT – Lemurian memories; instinctual unappeased hungers.

COTTONWOOD – The symbol of astral nothingness, or dead-end actions.

CYPRESS – The symbol that one should enter into a state of fasting, restraint and surrender.

DATE – A symbol of Arabic memories, and of Islam revelation.

DOGWOOD – A symbol of the Lord's resurrection and of the resurrection power of healing to be given to the one dreaming.

EBONY – An African memory; also, a symbol of opaque impenetrableness.

ELDERBERRY – A symbol of healing etheric toxicity.

ELM – A symbol of domesticity, tact.

EUCALYPTUS – A symbol of racial and national impartiality; an indication that a cleansing initiation is before one as to race and nation; migration.

EVERGREEN – A reminder of everlasting life.

FIG TREE – A symbol of the racial seed or germ.

FIR – Symbol of nobility; inheritance through tradition.

FRUIT TREE – A symbol of spiritual gifts.

GUM – Symbol of the adhering principle.

HEMLOCK – Symbol of self-destruction or enforced suicide.

HICKORY – The symbol of rugged family-genesis.

HOLLY – Symbol of the crown of thorns awaiting the brow of the Saviour.

JOSHUA TREE – Symbol of Lemurian tendencies expressed through the family-atom; an etheric-psychic quality and temperament.

JUNIPER – A reminder that one should discipline or purify his will.

LEMON – Symbol that one is to undergo restraining in speech; an astringent or caustic occurrence; sour; sour facts.

LIME – A symbol of purification of the blood; a reminder to look to the nourishment of the cells in the physical body.

LINDEN – Symbol of joy and domestic peace; healing by the angels of the family-atom.

LOCUST – Symbol of manna or food on the desert.

MAGNOLIA – Symbol of purity, chastity; a regal reminder that certain things of the Spirit are untouchable by profane men. Feminine flower and tree.

MAHOGANY – A symbol of strength, durability and survival; a Lemurian tree.

MANGO – A symbol that one is researching Lemurian times.

MANZANITA – A Lemurian tree indicating Lemurian memories received psychically through the nervous system.

MAPLE – A symbol of early American memory; also a symbol of the blood stream and its contents.

MIMOSA – A symbol of impulsive emotionalism; feminine flower; mystic sexual seduction.

MISTLETOE – A symbol of Elysian-mystery initiation memory.

MONKEY TREE – A symbol of tribal telepathy; gossip; malice; mischief; one's unbridled thoughts.

MULBERRY – Symbol of a Chinese memory in ancient Cathay.

MUSTARD – A symbol of Jupiter expansion and manifestation prosperity.

MYRTLE – Symbol of traditional reticence; domestic self-assurance.

OAK – The symbol of honor, integrity.
The acorn – the symbol of the fruits of honor.

OLIVE – A symbol of the Lord's Passion at Gethsemane.

ORANGE – The symbol of Mediterranean memories.

PALM – To see a short palm tree in a dream indicates that one is being helped by surrounding persons and circumstances to bear his burdens.
Palm leaf – the symbol of praise and praise-giving.

PALMETTO – The symbol of an opportunity needing cultivation.

PEACH TREE – A bittersweet experience, in which one realizes his wrongdoing, but also knows the wisdom of correction.

PEAR TREE – A symbol of dependability; also indicates the time of autumn as holding significance for the one dreaming.

PECAN TREE – One is learning of the oily residue in Nature, and of its potential fire and helps for cells of the physical body.

PEPPER – A symbol of the Lemurian ages; the research into the heavy minerals and ores of Lemurian times; a symbol of helps from an ancient, reverent person.

PERSIMMON TREE – To dream of the persimmon tree is to be reminded that there is an astringent or cleansing help from Nature, as well as a nourishing help to be found in foods. One is being reminded that he should cleanse his physical body, and thereby receive the rewards of his self-discipline.

PINE – A symbol of Atlantean times; also of the need to research the combined humanities and their meaning. A symbol of the Mars initiate.

PLUM – A symbol of ruggedness, dependableness.

POMEGRANATE – Symbol of the Lord's bitter trial; also a reminder to the one dreaming that he will be asked to drink a bitter cup.

POPLAR – A symbol of exclusiveness or of lack of communication and articulateness; also a symbol of haughtiness.

PUSSY WILLOW – A symbol of Cherubim tenderness and affection.

REDWOOD – A symbol stirring the grace-memories of Atlantean and Lemurian times.

ROYAL PALM – A symbol of an initiate who has the gift of healing the astral poisons of a city.

RUBBER TREE – To dream of a rubber tree indicates that one is researching the inertia in racial encasement.

SASSAFRAS – A symbol of blood purification, and cleansing in the lesser etheric body.

SPRUCE – A nudge from the Guardian Angel that the one dreaming should become more tolerant, more charitable.

SUMAC – Poison-sumac – a memory stemming from Druid initiatory ritual.

SWEETGUM – To dream of a sweetgum tree is to receive a special benediction from a special angel.

SYCAMORE – The symbol of memories of Cathay; the symbol of extending one's intuitive powers of mediation.

TEAK – A symbol of old Cathay; an indication that one is preparing to receive a resurgence of oriental memories, which will be experienced outwardly as an interest in the oriental cultures and arts.

TUPELO – A symbol of a healing therapy to the lesser etheric body, and of receiving a third vitality from the invisible elixirs of the spirit.

WALNUT – A symbol of sturdiness; of a masculine nature; helps from a paternal person.

WEEPING WILLOW – The symbol of healing in the night for those who have taken their lives, and also to help those who would take their lives. When a great depression is felt on seeing this tree, it is the symbol that someone very dear to the one dreaming has taken his own life, or that the dreamer has taken his own life in some former time.

YUCCA – A symbol of Lemurian memory; an indication that one is researching the transition of certain plants into trees; also a symbol that one is preparing for desert initiation.

Chapter 9

FLOWER SYMBOLS

*The ministering angels shall say, "Come" – and the sick
shall translate their fevers into joyful fervors for God.*

FLOWERS AS SYMBOLS OF GRACE

There is a kinship between all living things. God uses the greater archetypal fiats or archetone tone-commands or His Word-vibration to send forth in varying degrees of tone the species blueprints for flowers and plants. One may observe with awe and veneration the Law of God manifested in the kingdom of plants; for in plants and flowers individuality reigns, even as in the life of man.

Each flower has its particular species insignia or definition. Each flower has been differentiated and individualized by the varying vibrational tones sent forth from the floral archetypes. Thus, the rose is unique unto itself, in that heaven has determined it to be a rose.

No matter how much man may tamper with the plant world (its leaf, its bud and its flower) – and no matter how he would pollute the plant kingdom – the archetypal worlds have the last word in determining the differentiation in the plant, in the leaf, in the bud, in the flower.

At the root of each plant or flower is a life-atom which correlates to the floral archetypes residing in heaven. This life-atom is a sustaining atom. Regardless of how men abuse the soil or neglect their stewardship of the plant world, the seed holding the sustaining or life-atom will ultimately find its way into fertile or willing soil. Here it will flourish, awaiting a reverent hand and a beauty-seeking eye.

The flower is a vessel of grace given to man that he might receive in his most depressed hours a confirmation of God, His beauty and His glory everywhere.

When one sees flowers in dreams, he has partaken of a special
token of grace. The saints and the angels, using flowers as telepathic symbols, often lead those who travel in the night to expan-
sive fields of flowers; and one may awaken refreshed and renewed
by the virginal life of these heavenly gardens.

All tender things correlate to the level of the saints. Children,
flowers, butterflies, the tender bird on the wing – all of these are
out-picturings of the Kingdom of Heaven, reminding men that the
world is neither barren nor desolate, and that man, if he will, can
make it holy, beautiful.

Flowers are a feminine aspect of Nature. All Flora Angels work
with the feminine side of their androgynous powers. Thus, flowers are a tender testimony reflecting the beauty as given of God.
When one is stirred by the beauty within a flower, something of
compassion, of tenderness, and of reverence enters into his being.
Therefore, he comes closer to the angels when he is surrounded
by flowers. His soul-capacity is enlarged and his mind ennobled
when he contemplates the origin and intent of flowers and their
service to man.

In each flower there is a tone correlating to the life-tone of the
atom whence the flower stems. Despite the ravages of the ages
and man's destruction, flowers continue to bloom in the world.

When one enters into floral symbology in the dream world, he is
nigh to the verbal logos of his soul. All flowers seen in a dream are
part of the emotional body's expansion during sleep. Flowers seen
in higher dream state are always a token of grace or a blessing
from the heaven worlds.

The saints use the fragrances of certain flowers in their saintly
helps. Thus, when one enters into the floral kingdom in heaven,
he is near the saints.

When flowers are seen in meditation, one has entered into a degree of evolvement wherein he stands upon the threshold of greater
love-expression.

In each flower there is an inner flame. When one attains the
inner sight, he may research this flame and determine the *Light
Stream* or planetary action that affects the particular flower. There
are varied Venus-violet shades in the flame of the red rose. There
is the Neptunian pale green flame in the white rose. And the aquamarine flame in the violet correlates to Uranus. The flame in each

flower correlates to a Flora Angel, the Guardian Angel protecting the flower, and to the Light Stream of the planet influencing the life-duration of the flower.

Flowers correlate to the healing musics of heaven; and they also correlate to the Cherubim Angels, because flowers are ambassadors of healing and of joy.

SPIRITUAL MEANING IN FLOWERS

Every person has a physical flower correlating to his natal sign, and he has a spiritual flower correlating to his Light Stream and to his sacred name. Through continued meditation and alignment with his higher self, his spiritual flower will be revealed to him. When a person desires to plant or to grow a certain flower in his yard or in his garden, the flower is in some manner associated with his emotional evolvement.

When one is repelled by flowers with heavy odors, such as jasmine or tuberose, he is fearful of the world of the dead. When one is irritated by pollen from certain flowers, he has something unresolved in racial understanding.

When one feels attracted to flowers yielding a velvet moisture in their petals, he has a grace aspect from the lunar or moon cycles. He is ardent, tender, and inclined toward a pure mystical reverence. Some of these flowers are the arbutus, the violet, the dogwood, the sweet shrub.

The rose is the purest flower in the floral kingdom. It is a protective flower creating an atmosphere of purity. It also sanctifies the environment, as the powers of dark cannot come nigh to a pure rose.

Cut flowers which have been kept overlong by florists are detached from their angelic communication. Such flowers in a room are harmful rather than helpful.

When men create artificial flowers out of fabrics or synthetic materials, these become, in time, an irritant to the senses and an offense to the pure ether in the eye.

Flowers with thorns are symbolic of man's stigmata gained through initiation.

The color of a flower is very significant. To mutate or to use dyes on flowers offends the sustaining atom within the plant producing the flower.

Wild flowers are purifiers. He who seeks the wild flowers in their seasons is being directed by the angels, that he might be anointed in a seasonal time. Wherever there are wild flowers untouched by man, this is a spiritual polarity overflowing with anointing grace.

Where there are moist fern beds, the small elfin beings and the miniature Flora Angels work to bring harmony and serenity to the world.

When trees bearing fruits produce their blossoms, the geometries between the purity and precision of the snowflake and the budded fruit blossom become as one. In the mood of spring, men behold the wonder and the promise of creative life.

A flower seen in dreams or meditation is not only a symbol, but one has an experience with the flower itself. To see a flower in dream or meditation does something for one – either to give an anointing or to give a stirring. On seeing a flower something is built within; something is created in one's emotions. Flowers are not mental; they are emotional and always relate to emotional symbols.

THE PALETTE OF COLOR IN THE FLORAL KINGDOM

All life sustaining atoms in the flower kingdom correlate to the fourth Light Stream. However, the color of the flower correlates to a separate value of the fourth Light Stream. For example, white flowers correlate to the first value of the fourth Light Stream; pink and red flowers, to the second value; orange flowers, to the third value; blue flowers, to the fourth value; flowers with tints of green, to the fifth value; violet flowers, to the sixth value; and yellow or gold flowers, to the seventh value of the fourth Light Stream. When a white flower has a tinge of green, it would correlate to the first and the fifth values of the fourth Light Stream.

All seeds, bulbs and roots correlate to the fourth Light Stream, which is under the direction of the Father principle. If the seed contains a living atom, the seed will propagate, and produce its floral progeny.

The fourth Light Stream is the forming and shaping Light Stream. The Father principle uses the floral archetypes to manifest the flowering plant. One who has a true alignment with the fourth Light Stream, or who is working with a fourth value in any of the Light Streams, has what is known as a "green thumb." He is a sacred steward of plant life and plant form. Plants respond to him with a living awareness. Plants, particularly flowering plants, will not respond to those who have harsh wills and caustic temperaments.

When one gives flowers to another person, he should seek to intuit the flower bearing the healing fragrance for the person. Flowers to the sick may be healing ambassadors. When the sick have absorbed the complete healing fragrance of the flowers, the Flora Angel accompanying the flowers withdraws his presence. Such flowers should be discarded upon their first wilting.

In plucking or cutting flowers, one should always be aware that he is the recipient of a healing talisman overshadowed by an angel. He should try to avoid bruising or bending the stem upon which the flower blossoms. He should seek to minister to the plant bearing the flower – and joyfully receive the fragrance, the form, the beauty and the message within the upturned face of the flower.

NUANCES IN THE FLORAL KINGDOM

When flowers begin their season of dying, the living ether surrounding the sustaining atom at the root of the plant is used by the Angelic Kingdom to produce introspective moods in man.

When flowers are budding, preparing to fulfill themselves in their beauty and their fragrance, this inspires men to be poetically creative. Men make contact with the Cherubim Angels, and the masterbuilding potential in man is stimulated and stirred.

When the stamen within the plant prepares the seed of the plant, there is a healing balm in the atmosphere, giving off a pungent fragrance into the lungs of man. When the last portion of pollen has been extracted by the bee and the bird, the seed in the flower becomes mineralized; the fire within the life of the seed is shut away from man's absorption.

The weed, the antagonist of the domestic flowering plant, works with the destroying principle to combat and stimulate the chemical vitality of the plant. Flowers do not respond to man's cultivation where there is antagonistic weed life; however, there is a healthy competition between weeds and wild flowers or plants, sustaining the mineral fire within the seed. Thus, wild flowers reproduce themselves each season, and need not the hand of man for their planting.

Flowers having velvet-like petals are especially identified with man's emotional evolvement. Men choose velvety-petaled flowers for weddings and special occasions because such flowers are influenced by the Venus planetary Light Stream action, and thus are conductors of emotion and love.

Plants producing flowers that have milky or white substance in their stems are astral plants, and soak up or absorb the astral poisons in the community or environment. Among these is the poinsettia, which in the season of Christmas acts as a shock absorber for negation challenging the Nativity drama in the world.

Certain poisonous flowers are astral plants, healing diseases of the mind and emotions. These poisonous flowers are mediators for man's unknowing. In time, the science of chemistry will learn how to distill these poisons to cure diseases of the soul, mind and body. Man often looks upon these flowers, and knows them not to be poisonous: the sweet pea, lantana, hyacinth, morning glory, lily of the valley, iris, foxglove, wisteria, mountain laurel, castor bean, yew and rhododendron.

SPIRITUAL EQUILIBRIUM WITHIN THE FLORAL KINGDOM

When cataclysms come to the earth, plants grafted by man fail to survive. Only the original flora atoms survive. Thus, with each cataclysm cleansing, plants start anew in Nature's world – regardless of how men shape, cut, graft or plant.

The seasons of autumn, winter, spring and summer are used in the plant kingdom to prevent Nature from possessing the earth. When *cosmos-genesis* has been achieved, and men have built their emotional bodies – and they are filled with the living spirit rather than with the bruising curse – Nature and flowers will move out of seasonal growth. When the planets, the moon and the sun have changed their orbits of influence upon the earth, there will be perpetual growth and flowering of plants. However, the earth will not be overrun by growth, as the plant world will be controlled by inner spiritual restraints.

Chapter 22, verse 5, in the Book of Revelation states: *"And there shall be no night there..."* While in the present time this relates to the heaven worlds, there will be a time in the far distant future when men will live in a daylight state, having moved beyond the duality alternates of the seasons and cycles in time.

Flowers are the bridal garment of Nature. Whenever flowers are in season, there is a wedding between the soul of man and the angels.

FLOWERS AND RITUAL

When men use flowers in their worship, the Cherubim Angels and the Angels of the Presence sustain the love, the hope and the prayers of the congregation. And if the minister be sincerely dedicated, his logos becomes inspired by the Holy Ghost.

Flowers used in the death ritual enable the Luminosity Angel of the one who has died and the Resurrection Angels to work with those who grieve for the dying. To omit flowers for the dead produces an austere and sterile ritual.

During the ritual for the dead, the fragrance and the life emanation from flowers enable the angels working with the dead to shower a blessing of faith, and also enable the angels of the dead to come closer to those grieving – thereby comforting them.

Men who ignore the floral kingdom – in life or death – fail to unite themselves with the harmony and the blessings given of God.

Flowers have been used by the knowing since time immemorial, because they have intuited that flowers are close to the soul within the life of all living things.

To place flowers upon the grave of a person does not earth-bind the one dead. Such tokens of love are received in heaven as a communication, and as a confirmation of the belief in a spiritual life after death.

FLOWERS AND THEIR GRACE

There are twelve layers of ether around the eternal sustaining atom in each seed. These layers of ether are as follows: the innermost point of ether, or the cosmos ether, retained from the former eternity system from which the atom in the seed came; the second layer of ether retained from the sun; the earth layer of ether; the moon layer of ether; the Saturn layer of ether; the Jupiter layer of ether; the Venus layer of ether; the Mercury layer of ether; the Mars layer of ether; the Uranus layer of ether; the Neptune layer of ether; the Pluto layer of ether.

When the earth was separated from the sun, all seed life remained in the fiery gelatin-like substance of the earth-to-be. When the earth became solid and moisture began to penetrate the earth, the flowers came forth to make a carpet of beauty for man to see, and to remind him of his eternal self. The trees came forth with their flowers and their fruits awaiting man's own solidifying into matter.

God has so prepared it that animals and plants go before man to serve him and to sacrifice their lives for him. When men come to look upon the animal kingdom and the plant kingdom as a mark of grace from God, they will enter into grace, and their souls will receive the fulfillment of the bountifulness seen at every hand through flowers and plants.

FLOWERS

ACACIA – A Neptunian flower reminding one of the immortal genius in man. Seen in a vision, it is the symbol of hope, resurrected thought, and an inspired mind. If blossoms of the acacia are placed in the hands of the disciple during sleep, it is a token from heaven that one is entering into immortal ways of action.

ALYSSUM – Understanding of spiritual blending in Nature; part of the healing of the saints and of working with the saints.

ANEMONE – A symbol of timidity, sensitivity; a precaution against abusing the sensitivity of others; of cherishing the tender times.

APPLE BLOSSOM – The promise of spiritual fruits to come; a talisman of encouragement for the effort one has expended; also a reminder that there are spiritual seasons as well as physical seasons.

ARBUTUS – The symbol of new beginnings and of virginal promise, and of healing to be gained from the absorption of Nature. It is also the symbol of purification, virginity.

ASTER – The reminder of man's communication with the starry cosmos; also a symbol of personal inoffensiveness; grace from community; outgoing temperament. *Unopened aster* – grace for coming autumn.

AZALEA – A symbol that one needs a special environment in which to develop or to evolve, even though the environment seems alien to others; homesickness.

BACHELOR'S BUTTON – The symbol of isolation, nonconformity and frigidity; retreatist.

BEGONIA – The symbol that one is dependent upon external circumstances or outside helps for his personal prosperity and expression; an unyielding extrovert person.

BIRD OF PARADISE – When seen in a dream, it is the symbol that one has united within himself the correspondences between the bird life and the flower kingdom, and thereafter he sees all living things as unified expressions of God.

BLEEDING HEART – The symbol of the suffering of our Saviour; and a symbol that one is approaching a plateau of sacrifice. One of Mary's grace flowers.

BLUEBELL – A symbol of elfin creatures for a childlike heart; a joy derived from belief in invisible, pure helps; a promise of extended, inner hearing; a summons from elfin-like creatures to learn more of their kingdom.

BUTTERCUP – A symbol of childlike naivete, malleableness.

CACTUS FLOWERS – A symbol of healing through repentance; of dedicated retreat to absolve the prominent errors made apparent through initiation; a healing purity gained through right perspective; sturdy awareness.

CAMELLIA – A confirmation of evolvement above the pituitary or psychic level; a symbol of healing of the astral emotional tumults; a pungency of peace.

CARNATION – A domestic flower signifying the protection of the Divine Mother and the Guardian Angel of the family.

CHRYSANTHEMUM – A symbol of conventional or man-made courtesies, lightening the competitive challenges in the world; autumn initiation.
Bronze – symbol of autumn felicity.
White – symbol of aristocracy, and of right deportment.
Yellow – symbol of the physical sun; of pungent healing to the lesser etheric body to be gained from the rays of the sun.

CLOVER – A symbol of peace and refreshing grace; symbol of giving and of having; healing of the impossibles.

CREPE MYRTLE – A symbol of tradition, of home life, of homesteading, of family-genesis.

DAFFODIL – A symbol correlating to the Angels of Mercury; a symbol of joy and adoration.

DAHLIA – A symbol of spiritual enlightenment in higher or mountainous environments.

DAISY – A symbol of humanity thoughts accepted as commonplace, yet significant as a goodwill message between men; also a symbol of hope and honor; of humanity; of human-genesis; grace from family.

DANDELION – A symbol of unseen grace; also, of healing through Nature; correlates to the planet Mars and to the physical sun.

DELPHINIUM – A symbol of a joyous and sturdy friend; a reminder that one should observe friendship without possessiveness or claim.

DOGWOOD – A symbol of the Lord's crucifixion, and the reminder for one to *"deny himself, and take up his cross, and follow me."* A pathos symbol of inner grief, and dying to one's selfish will.

FERN – Symbol of protection; also indicates future comfort and comfort logos; the symbol of the psychic power to be raised to the spiritual.
   Frond or bud of fern – this symbol indicates the power to comfort others; the Comforter Logos (St. John 14:16).

FLEUR-DE-LIS – The symbol of Mary, the mother of Jesus; symbol of telepathy from a Cosmos Disciple; symbol of immortality, spiritual purity; symbol of eternity and eternal initiation.

FLOWER – Blossom of the soul; some memory.
   Flower bud – undeveloped soul powers.

FORGET-ME-NOT – A telepathic symbol or reminder of one who no longer lives or of someone forgotten or neglected; a reminder to be grateful for past friends who have proven helpful.

FOXGLOVE – Symbol of undercover activities; the herb flower correlating to the heart atom and to the health of the heart.

FRANGIPANI – A symbol of astral initiation; of emotional lessons accepted by the ego; of marriage or betrothal disciplines to follow. Worn on the left ear, the sign of useless sacrifice. Worn on the right ear, the sign of acceptance and willing sacrifice.

FUCHSIA – Close alignment with the Nature Spirits; devotion to the pure.

GARDENIA – A symbol of short-lived popularity; also a symbol of a brief period of grace.

GERANIUM – A symbol of a self-sufficient person, or the need to be self-sufficient.

GLADIOLA – A symbol of royalty, of nobility, of dignity, and of authority earned through the use of ethic.

GOLDENROD – A symbol of harvest, of knowledge of the races; a symbol of herbal research within the inner planes.

HEARTSEASE – Healing from a saint; conscience rectified; a comfort talisman from a fellow disciple; and a symbol of healing close by.

HEATHER – A symbol of healing gathered from courage grace in other lives; a symbol that one will be valiant in time of coming trials; symbol of chaste exclusiveness, or being singled out to fulfill a pure work.

HELIOTROPE – A symbol of an unseen tempter; also of an earthbound entity. To see a heliotrope in a dream indicates that one has been researching the world of the dead. To see it or experience it in meditation, one should be on guard as to the origin of his thought process.

HEMLOCK – A symbol of danger from the wills of brutal and ignorant men; a symbol to prepare one to suffer at the hands of the ignorant.

HIBISCUS – A symbol of naive tribal-genesis; a symbol of intuition gathered from pure tribal-genesis origins; a symbol of the pure instinctual memory which protects one from the four vices of lower genesis: malice, avarice, lust and greed.

HOLLYHOCK – A symbol of rise and ascent with ethic, portraying Jacob's ladder. All tall plants represent individualized and non-mingling persons.

HONEYSUCKLE – A symbol of telepathic antennas attracting fellow disciples. The fragrance from a honeysuckle in a dream symbolizes that one has the grace of sacred intimacy or atom alignment with a fellow disciple.

HYACINTH – A water hyacinth – a parasitical or astral condition suffocating the life stream. The hyacinth plant symbol relates to a temporary situation requiring care and diligence. The fragrance from a potted hyacinth is influenced by the planet Neptune, and produces healing for the spinal nerves.

IRIS – The spiritual symbol for the royal fleur-de-lis, relating to healing, purity, immortality; the feminine principle.

JASMINE – To dream of the vine or night-blooming jasmine indicates that one has touched the purgatorial regions of the astral world. The flowering, larger jasmine is a token of spiritual purity; in dream or meditation, it is a symbol of having overcome the purgatorial regions of the astral world.

JONQUIL – A Cherubim flower; being of the bulb family, in the dream world it is a symbol of immortality and resurrection, of hope and betterment.

LADY-SLIPPER – A symbol of communion with elfin-like creatures.

LARKSPUR – A symbol of mental chastity, of thoughts free from lust.

LILAC – A symbol of remembrance; a symbol that memory is to be healed.

LILY –

Calla lily – a symbol of moon initiation affecting the ear or hearing; a symbol of inner hearing received as a grace token from former lives.

Easter lily – a symbol of resurrection, of purity, and of Mary the Virgin.

Lily of the Valley – a symbol of marriage; of pure initiation to gain spiritual powers.

Tiger lily – a symbol of primitive memories inherited through ancestry.

Water lily – a symbol of the First Heaven or the realm of the saints.

Lily and bud – a soul gift from Mary and another gift (bud) coming forth.

LOTUS – A symbol of Eastern or yoga initiation; also a symbol of Buddhistic or Brahmin memories. If the lotus is pure white, it is a symbol that one has contacted or made alignment with the Bodhisattva plane or First Heaven.

LUPINE – A symbol of family-genesis memory of Anglo-Saxon origin.

MAGNOLIA – An Atlantean lily. The higher-world record shows that the lotus and the magnolia have the same archetypal root-atom. In the East, the lotus remained under the influence of astral light, and became a product of water and mud. In the Atlantean time, the magnolia moved above the astral light, and became a tree in the Western world. When one sees a magnolia in a vision or a dream, it is symbolic of initiation into Atlantean memories. When one sees a lotus in a dream, it is a symbol of Lemurian memories, also some contact of Buddhistic nature.

MARIGOLD – A symbol of pure, homely familiarities; a symbol of the child Mary before she became Mary, the mother of Jesus; a blessing from the feminine principle for all small or young girls.

MILKY-STEMMED PLANTS – Astral absorbers; warning of a person fat with astral magnetism. In the dream, the person is usually one who is devitalizing the magnetic fluids of the lesser etheric body – and thus sustaining his own magnetic vitality; a warning against an astral, parasitical person with whom one is associated.

MIMOSA – Flirtatious; exotic; tribal marriage union; overwhelming sweetness; saturation.

MISTLETOE – A symbol of initiation into the darker Celtic rites. One who dreams of mistletoe is being warned against pagan orgies and their dangers.

MORNING-GLORY – Uniting with the elf kingdom on early morning arising.

MUSTARD – Symbol of bountifulness, and of healing for the chemistry of the body; a reminder to attain a selfless austerity while sitting in the medallion of bountifulness.

NARCISSUS – Self-love; self-conceit; self-engrossment. Narcissus is the symbol of one who thinks that he is the most beautiful one in the world; that he is more intelligent than anyone.

NASTURTIUM – A symbol of healing for the vitamin C content of the body; a purification of the pituitary gland through invisible helps of the night; a reminder that one is being oppressed by someone close by with too strong a will.

ORANGE BLOSSOMS – A wedding; an initiation into enlargement of one's self through yokefellowship with another.

ORCHID – A parasitical plant, indicating in dream or meditation that one has contacted a level of the astral world where certain entities, denizens and elementals look to man for their sustenance. It also can mean that one has an idea which has neither soil nor roots – that is, of short duration. The orchid is a glamour, astral plant, living upon the noxious gases exuding between the astral world and the earth's atmosphere. The beauty of the orchid is deceptive, and is symbolic of many things in the astral world which appear to contain beauty, but have not enduring life.

PANSY – To see a pansy in a dream indicates that one has contact with Cherubim; a symbol of geometrical or symbolic and parabolic thinking.

PEACH BLOSSOM – When seen in *meditation* or dream, it indicates that one has touched the propagation powers of the Flora Angels. Also, a symbol of a promise of new and pure events.

PEONY – A symbol of a small child, and naivete.

PERIWINKLE – A symbol of music and the Cherubim worlds, and of the fairy kingdom; a myth-key to the unseen worlds.

PETUNIA – A symbol of healing for the lesser etheric body through the prismatic rays of the sun and soothing rays of the moon.

POINSETTIA – A symbol of the victory of the Spirit's fire over the astral abyss.

POISON IVY – Thoughts creating allergies of the body and mind.

POPPY – Symbol of the negative imagination; the influence of subtle habits from previous lives. When seen in a dream or in meditation a warning of an insidious or habit-forming influence demoting the will.

POTTED FLOWERING PLANT – A symbol of one's confinement and over-domesticity. A feeling of one's soul imprisonment.

PRIMROSE – Symbol of timidity, of delicacy. In a vision or a dream, when the primrose is seen with slimy *mud* or decaying matter, it symbolizes a fall into a life of vice through procrastination.

QUEEN ANNE'S LACE – A symbol of mental perspective, and poetic inspiration; a symbol of freedom to think without restriction; a blessing from Saint Anne.

RHODODENDRON – The symbol of family-genesis in primitive places; a cyclic reminder of family progress.

ROSE –

> *Pink* – the symbol of devotion; of help from the saints; of reverence.
>
> *Blue* – grace from the soul.
>
> *Red* – the symbol of the bloodstream; of humanity; of the human spirit. One is presently under the saints and learning of heavenly food for the humanities.
>
> *Black* – black-magic powers. When surrounded with gold means black powers are overcome or under control.
>
> *White* – the symbol of purity; of peace; of ethical ritual. Expression of the ego in pure spirit fire.
>
> *Yellow* – the symbol of intimate friendship; of a covenant and agreement between disciples.
>
> *Rose thorn* – symbol that one is to undergo some form of suffering that he may ascend into spiritual alignment.
>
> *Wild rose* – to dream of a wild rose or to see one in meditation is to open the memories of man's freedom in Nature; also to remind the one dreaming that he should return to virginal wellsprings of Nature.

SNAPDRAGON – The symbol of impulsiveness; preparing one for the unexpected.

SUNFLOWER – The symbol of a sun initiate; of courage; obedience.

SWEET PEA – Symbol of the saints and their helps.
White sweet pea means grace; to be inoffensive to others.

THISTLE – A symbol of a rough issue facing one, and a reminder to be firm.

TUBEROSE – A symbol of death; also indicates that one is researching the world of the dead.

TULIP – A telepathy from the Cosmos Disciple called the Hollander; a symbol of religious mediation; pure religious worship devoid of ecclesiastical prejudice.

VIOLET – Symbol of the 7th Light Stream; of a spiritual healing being consummated through one of the seven sources of healing mediation.

VIOLET, AFRICAN – A symbol of the Master R; a healing for bigotry and prejudice.

WILD FLOWERS – Symbol of aeonic memories, and a reassurance of protection through Nature's providence.

WISTERIA – The symbol of Oriental former-life memories; the symbol of tender moods from poetic memories in past lives.

YUCCA – A Lemurian memory.

ZINNIA – Symbol of a spinster or unmarried woman noted for good works and virtue.

Chapter 10

INTERCESSORY SYMBOLS

> *There are few mighty mortal men. God gives authority*
> *to those who love, and who know the true authority to be the*
> *Law of God and the Will of God. He who names himself as*
> *an authority walks toward brambles and pitfalls, for he has*
> *a mind filled with fantasies and a will centered in self-*
> *delights. Earn thine authority by first cleansing away the*
> *small petty things, as thou wouldst sweep away irritating*
> *fragments which make unsightly thy house. Believe on the*
> *greatness of thy soul, so that thou might unite thyself with the*
> *greatness in the souls of immortal men.*

Through depth initiation in dreams and meditation, one touches the symbolic storehouse of heaven. In time, he will become familiar with certain *intercessory symbols*. Such symbols identify one's degree of evolvement, and inform him of the source of his intercessory helps.

Intercessory symbols may be received during dreams or daytime contemplation and meditation. One should familiarize himself with the intercessory symbols so that he may know the source and level of his spiritual training and instruction.

INTERCESSORY BEINGS AND THEIR IDENTIFYING SYMBOLS

ARCHANGEL RAPHAEL – A white horse; a white rose; the rising sun; a sapphire.

ARCHANGEL URIEL – The aurora borealis; an emerald; a tree upside down (archetype of humanity generation).

ARCHANGEL MICHAEL – A golden flaming sword; armor and breastplate; scales; a diamond.

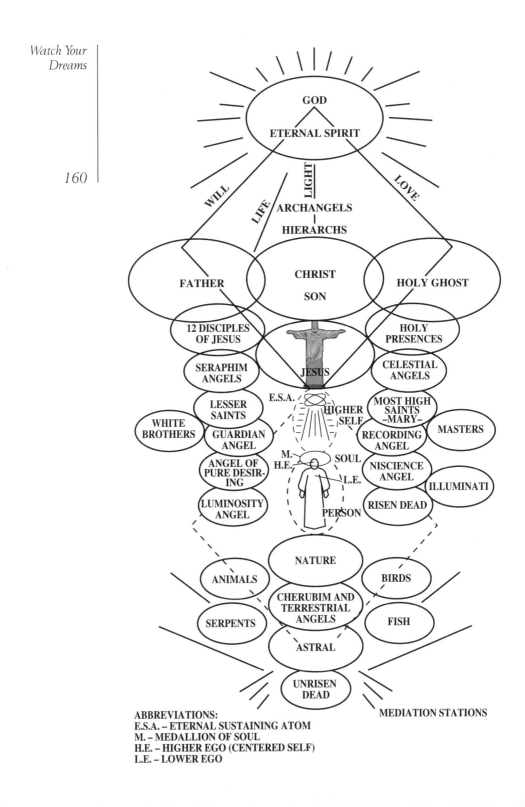

ABBREVIATIONS:
E.S.A. – ETERNAL SUSTAINING ATOM
M. – MEDALLION OF SOUL
H.E. – HIGHER EGO (CENTERED SELF)
L.E. – LOWER EGO

MEDIATION STATIONS

ARCHANGEL GABRIEL – A horn; a golden horn; a red rose; a ruby; an infant child holding the hand of a man; the Madonna.

BODHISATTVA – A lotus; a cave; a diamond rod; a white serpent; a bamboo cane.

CELESTIAL ANGELS – A golden harp; a diamond.

SERAPHIM ANGELS – Six wings on the angel; many eyes making up a medallion; a golden peacock's feather; crystal. Six-winged Seraphim symbologies have to do with ideas; the Lords of Mind or archetypal ideas research; an adept's vision.

CHERUBIM ANGELS – A cube; a bar of music; a musical sound heard in the inner ear; a freshet poem; all great composers receive their musics through the help of the Cherubim Angels. All great cathedrals are built through the help of the Cherubim Angels. The Cherubim Angels are the masterbuilders of heaven; protection; manifestors for building the unmanifested; sounders of the soundless into musics; they open the wisdoms in the use of akasia.

RECORDING ANGELS – A book; a scroll; a golden chain; scales; a lesson in timing.

GUARDIAN ANGELS – A perpetual flame; a hearth; a pure white hand; a lesson in the mystery of space.

TERRESTRIAL ANGELS – A vision of the sphere of the earth; an upright tree; a human heart; a knowledge of gravity; a bird.

JESUS – A shepherd's staff; a seamless garment; a fish; a loaf of bread; a table with white cloth; a white dove; a dove in violet light; a cross; a crown of thorns; a small boat with white sails; an open tomb; a white pearl; a door; a white seamless robe; a healing hand; a sandal; a Christ child; a ring of gold.

MARY – A white lily; a mother and child; a donkey with mother and child; three women and a cross; an intercessor for a miracle.

SANAT KUMARA OR ANCIENT OF DAYS – The all-seeing eye; a golden chair; a diamond staff; a rainbow; a throne.

MAHA CHOHAN – A domed room with tiers; a screen; a red-carpeted central stairway; a tube ascending upward.

RISEN DEAD – A feeling of pure love and a remembered scene or face; a vision to warn, to protect.

THE SAINTS – A rainbow; seven golden chalices filled with anointing oil; seven golden steps; a golden slipper, blue shoe or sandal.

ILLUMINATI – A golden quill pen; a library of books; a scroll; a physician's vial; an artist's paintbrush; a compass.

THE GREAT IMMORTALS OR INWARD MASTERS

Master M – Light Stream #1. A book; a transparent crystal-like staff; a golden wedding ring; an hourglass; an archetypal tree; a diamond; a unicorn; a grain of rice; a golden bowknot, if one has earned protective telepathy; a silver bowknot, if one is under discipline; an owl. If the owl is looking east, the disciple is remembering Eastern lives. If the owl is looking west, the disciple has opened the Christ Light within his mind. If the owl is looking south, the disciple is yet bound by ancestry. If the owl is looking north, the disciple is to be sent to a new polarity, requiring him to pioneer in a new spiritual theme.
The Venerable One – Light Stream #2. A white staff; a pink rose; a white dove flying in rosy light; a ruby; an acorn; a grain of corn.
Master Serapis – Light Stream #3. Solomon's Seal; three interlinked loops; an amber stone; an amber staff; a dove flying in orange or amber light; the Star of David; a stalk of millet grain.
Master K.H. – Light Stream #4. A jeweled throne-chair; Hippocrates' symbol or a serpent on a cross; a red rose; a surgeon's bowl and white towel; an emerald; a dove flying in etheric, Neptunian green light; a grain of rye; indigo blue light.
Master Hilarion – Light Stream #5. A white butterfly; symbol of Uranus; sapphire; a dove flying in sapphire blue light; a grain of oats.
Light Stream #6 (see reference to Jesus)
Master R – Light Stream #7. A white rose; an African violet; scales; pyramid; obelisk; an eagle; phoenix bird; an amethyst stone; a dove flying in amethyst light; a key; a grain of wheat; a bunch of grapes.

A TEACHER OR SACRED GURU – A pelican; a snow-top mountain; a string of pearls or jewels. A teacher clothed in white garment surrounded by diamond-like light is an etheric guru of the highest order. A teacher with the lower part of his garment colored from the rosy earth ether, the upper part of the garment diamond-like, is a teacher still living within the reach of gravity, as in the First Heaven and Second Heaven; such teachers come only to advanced initiates.

ADDITIONAL INTERCESSORY SYMBOLS

To shake the Master's hand in a dream is to be accepted as a probationer; to make a covenant to accept one's karmic cleansing and thereby render a service to aid in the soul liberation of others.

When the Master kisses one on the cheek, the one being kissed has become an accepted disciple or initiate. The initiate should be prepared thereafter to render the kiss of communication and salvation to all others.

Vision of Great Being at top of staircase – Master K.H. leads one up to healing work; to be trained in night healing; to blend with Hippocrates' ethic in healing; to learn etheric healing techniques. A surgeon's bowl and towel; a red ruby; a red rose; a surgeon's scalpel; geometrical designs; the initiate is being trained in the techniques of etheric anatomy and solar light healing.

To turn right and to walk up a spiral stairway means that one is preparing to meet Master K.H. and to be instructed into the 4th Light Stream of healing the impossible; also is preparing to move into higher planes for self-research and akasic soul-record research.

Walking downstairs – a memory of returning to the body after sleep.

To see a blue light while meditating means one has made contact with one of his angels close by. He also has seen a portion of his spiritual atom portal open in the throat or between the brows. This may mean that one is making a contact with a pure presence of the light, such as an angel, an invisible helper, a higher guru, one of the Masters, or a beloved risen dead. One should always give thanks for this vision so as to extend the time of the blessing from the presence.

Rainbow – Cherubim; a saint's protection; also Ancient of Days; the power to rise to the First Heaven and receive help from the saints.

Teacher or a Being with feet on floor – means the one seen is living in the earth. If his feet are above floor, he is in the etheric or omniscient state. If he is seated in a yoga posture, this is the sign of Master-omnipresent powers or being permanently conjoined with his protégé apprentice in the earth.

Feet on earth – earth worker and earth teacher; also invisible helper and night server with visitation powers.

Feet above ground – teacher with ascension powers in the spiritual worlds. Such teachers give to the earth initiate levitational powers, that he may rise into greater ranges of light, and lift those in the world from their sicknesses, griefs, sorrows and awkward ways.

Breath in a vision or dream – the Holy Ghost; uniting with prana or cosmic life force; the need to unite with the pulsation point of the soul's medallion so as to be at one with the vibrationless power of God.

Jesus seen in a vision giving off a beautiful indigo blue on inner rim of His head nimbus means one has made contact with Christ consciousness.

The Eternal Spirit fire or mind's light of Jesus is always seen in a cerulean blue light of cool, peace-giving, celestial fire.

SPIRITUAL TELEPATHY

Spiritual telepathy is the art of communication and communion between physical and spiritual minds on similar light-waves of life. In spiritual communion through telepathy, there can be no communication unless the communing minds have similar or equal degrees of light. One is totally sealed away from spiritual telepathy if he short-circuits his degree of light through doubt of God as the uniting One in Will, Life, Light and Love.

In spiritual telepathy, the scale of thought velocities between souls may vary, but the degree of light must be the same. A Greater Being has the power to slow down the velocity and intensity of his light. Thus, a Greater Being may communicate with one having a lesser degree of illumination.

A person raises his degree of light by having an unwavering faith in God. In this manner, he can receive telepathic thoughts of light from Beings having greater degrees of light than he. However, when one has skepticism, doubt, hate, anger, fear, hostility or arrogance, he opens his mind in dreams and waking to a horde of negative telepathic depleting, demoting and inverted ideas.

In telepathic communion through faith in God, one receives un-interrupted inspiration and guidance. In seeking to receive psychical communication telepathies by placing one's faith in mechanical objects, such as Ouija boards, crystal balls, Tarot cards, or halluci-natory drugs, one opens himself to darkness, mental derangement, psychic abnormalities.

The Life-of-God telepathies are transposed through life-restoring, life-sustaining, life-providing and life-knowing.

The Light-of-God telepathies are transposed through the Christ Mind into omniscient minds and into the higher mind and soul-light of the ego. Through the Light-of-God telepathies one receives transcendental powers.

The Love-of-God telepathies are transposed through the Lord Jesus and the Holy Ghost–reassuring, comforting, forgiving, heat-ing; these are experienced by man through faith in God. Through the Love-of-God telepathies one is transformed.

SPIRITUAL LEVELS OF TELEPATHY

GOD – Eternal Spirit; the Will-of-God telepathies are transposed through Heavenly Beings as vibrationless powers and still-ness, bringing peace and making it possible to *know* God.

CHRIST SPIRIT – Works with the archetypal and greater ideas telepathies; vibrational revelation.

FATHER – Works with the imaging, making and creation telepathy.

HIERARCHS – Work with the temperament and prototypal will-ing-forming telepathy, using the planetary, cosmic, zodiacal constellation energies accompanying our earth system.

JESUS – Works with Saviour, love, healing, forgiving, manifes-tation and ethic telepathies; commanding eternal cosmos forces, cosmic energies, astral currents through His etheric body as an instrument of mediation.

DISCIPLES OF JESUS – Work with the prototypal-ethic telepathies; apostle gifts, powers, prototypal ethics and soul-record grace.

THE FOUR ARCHANGELS (Raphael, Gabriel, Michael, Uriel) Telepathically release the archetypal ideas during the four sea-sons; move men out of karmic fixations. The three remaining

Archangels – Raguel, Zerachiel, Jeremiel – release telepathies to increase the spiritual power of the Holy Ghost into the souls of men so that men may forget not their God.

CELESTIAL ANGELS – Work through initiates and adepts to reveal the inner wisdom-truths of God.

HOLY GHOST (Command of the Archetones) – Works with the archetone or the sound stream, audible sound or vibration, the WORD; works with charismatic telepathies and power, signs and spiritual wonders. The Holy Ghost may be heard in dreams and meditation in supra-dimensional echoes as the voice of God.

SERAPHIM ANGELS (6-winged) – Protectors of the great archetypal ideas; in dreams and meditation one encounters the Seraphim Angels so that he may receive initiation into the higher mind. The Seraphim Angels work with the six soul-portals of the mind, opening the higher rational spirit in thinking.

PLANETARY LOGOS ANGELS – Work with higher planetary telepathic tones and Spheres-of-Light telepathies. In dreams one is initiated into the reflected planetary Spheres of Light, uniting with universal and cosmic creation. Each planet contains a variation of tones that an initiate must master. From life to life the initiate incorporates the tones of the planets through the help of the Planetary Logos Angels. The mastery of the tones of the planets gives the power of synchronization.

SUN ARCHANGELS – Work with Mary; the adept's protectors; work in the night and during meditation and in the night during dreams to free the solar fire in the right hemisphere of the brain. The chief solar angel is called Metatron.

MARY – Miracle telepathy; levitation powers; transmutation powers; visitation power through command of the four-body eternal atoms; the power to appear in crisis to petitioners or supplicants; to see Mary is to touch the Second Heaven and to commune with the Most High Saints who are under her charge and the charge of her Son. Her symbol and her signs are more often contacted at high noon each day. To dream of Mary is to be cleansed, purified of hostilities. To see her in a vision is to be blessed with very special sanctification powers.

24 ELDERS – Patriarch telepathy; authority for the worthy; the dual Hierarchs or Elohim working with the chromosomes of man.

ANCIENT OF DAYS – Timing telepathy; advanced initiatory trials and happenings; the benign Father principle expressed by an omniscient progenitor of the heavenly Father. He is seen in dreams when one is to learn something of timing and its command, and thus to become timeless.

JEHOVAH – Tribal and racial telepathies in dreams and waking; family-atom cleansings. In meditation Jehovah, working over the lower aspect of the divine thalamus, sends the guilt pictures of the world onto the mind's screen of the initiate, that the initiate may covenant to give soul liberation to mankind.

LUNAR ANGELS – Propagation telepathies; recalling of lesser-etheric-body forces. In dreams and meditation, a lunar psychic using the lower psychic forces receives fearful apprehension, visions and predictions from the Sharp Angels. The higher lunar psychic receives from the Lunar Angels foretelling of true things, realistically oriented to man's vital need and comfort.

MOST HIGH SAINTS – Miraculous telepathy and works; in meditation assures the initiate of comfort, peace and protection. In dreams the Most High Saints or Bodhisattvas *take* the initiate to scenes of the record of martyrdom; most specifically the martyrdom of Jesus is revealed by the Most High Saints.

CHERUBIM ANGELS – Building and creativity telepathy; telepathic stimulation of humor; telepathy through music; healing the depressed. To be aware of the Cherubim Angels in meditation and dreams is to know that one will have supernatural helps in his development on the physical, mental and spiritual planes. The Cherubim support all servers for God by sustaining them with flawless skills.

LESSER SAINTS – Healing telepathies; healing the persecuted; may be seen in meditation as invisible gift-bringing friends from the invisible planes. Their mercy helps in dreams give assurance that one is blessed, led and comforted. Every person has a saint who works with him in certain times of meditation and dreams. The saint wears a duplicate face to his own, but is not himself. In time one learns by divine intuition what his saint is saying to him.

DIVINE MOTHER – Telepathies are received as guidance to love more, to be giving, tender, to enlarge the love principle through the feminine principle. Her symbols seen telepathically are the white lotus, the white rose. Through telepathy she cautions a male initiate to be more tender, forgiving, loving, merciful. To a woman initiate she gives telepathic guidance to be more charitable, forgiving, giving. Through telepathy she guides a woman initiate to use sacredly the feminine functions of her body, such as motherhood, giving birth, the sexual act, household tasks, the handling of food, the training of children.

MELCHISEDEC – Manifestation and de-manifestation telepathies. He initiates through fire.

MAHA CHOHAN – Heavenly-governings telepathy. He initiates through organizing the law principle.

JUDGMENT ANGELS – Guilt and conscience telepathy. These initiate through the conscience.

LITURGICAL ANGELS – Activate worship telepathies. They work with Holy Ghost vibrations.

LITANY ANGELS – Ritual telepathies. They work with rhythm.

WHITE BROTHERS (Men in White Apparel) – Protectors of the Risen-Dead telepathies. They work with higher emotional body.

RISEN DEAD – Protective telepathies. Exorcisms. (Note: In spiritual experience it is necessary to understand and interpret the telepathies from the *unrisen dead* in order to gain exorcism powers. Unrisen-dead telepathies relate to misdirected obstructions, karmic telepathies and dark-magic telepathies.)

TERRESTRIAL ANGELS – Wisdom telepathies regarding grains, plants and all reproducing things in man's and the animals' domain.

ILLUMINATI OR HIGHER ADEPTS – Creative telepathies. They are mentor telepathic directors over all artists.

GREAT IMMORTALS OR THE MASTERS – Instruction telepathies. They work to keep the disciple on the Path; to bring unmanifested ideas.

MAN'S PERSONAL ANGELS – Man's companions since the beginning of this eternity system.

> *Luminosity Angel* – care of body and time-of-death telepathy.
> *Angel of Pure Desiring* – emotional response telepathy.
> *Niscience Angel* – pure thought and ethic of thought telepathy.
> *Recording Angel* – akasic-record telepathy.
> *Guardian Angel* – apprehension and protection telepathies.

HIGHER SELF – The eternal reality telepathies.

SOUL – Akasic grace-record telepathy and vibratory-hum telepathy.

HIGHER EGO (Centered Self) – Past-life accomplishment telepathies.

INVISIBLE HELPERS – Healing, ethic, reassuring and prompting telepathies in sleeping or waking.

THE HOLY GHOST INTERCESSION AND THE SEVEN GUIDANCE BRAINS

The Holy Ghost power enters through the arches of the feet, moving upward through the biomagnetic brains or two sacral plexus centers at the base of the spine. The Holy Ghost utilizes the third guidance brain, using the navel plexus and the solar plexus to unite man with solar Hierarchy power. Holy Ghost next enters the fourth guidance brain, the heart, to unite man with the kinetic and electromagnetic energy, freeing man to receive the supernatural helps of the angels. The heart, the high guidance commander over the solar plexus guidance brain, uses the cosmic energy of this eternity system. The heart is seated in an exalted love position above the liver, pancreas and spleen – uniting one with the cosmic love of the Father.

Each guidance brain has its own memory and techniques for revealing things to come. The seven memories overdirecting man's physical and spiritual compulsions are as follows:

(1) The serpentine guidance brain or interior earth brain, located under the arches of the feet – the memory of man's Edenic consciousness. Note: Walking on earth, soil, grass opens this.

(2) The two sacral plexus or biomagnetic brains – the memory of glandular impulses, instinctual kinetic powers inherited from ancestors. The two lowest or biomagnetic brains, uniting with

the glandular memory of one's ancestry, produce offspring with the help of the Procreation Angels releasing pranic healing and lunar fire.

(3) The navel plexus or solar plexus is the center for the Hierarchy guidance brain. It contains the memory of Hierarchy forming and shaping of the physical body.

(4) The heart guidance brain working through the liver, the spleen and the pancreas. The heart contains the memory of man's physical-body atom experiences and of his prototypal impulses in former lives and in this life.

(5) The quelle psychic guidance brain at the base of the skull correlating to the throat contains the memory of the higher reflexes of the lesser etheric body and the instinctual memory gained from many lives. The psychic or quelle guidance brain also contains the memory of hostile and alien actions and thoughts.

(6) The pituitary guidance brain between the brows contains the memory of imaginative works in former lives and in this life. It also contains the memory of manifestation akasic power working through the feminine or Divine Mother principle.

(7) The pineal guidance brain or gleaming brain centered in the crown of the head contains the memory impulses of creative and inspirational works in this life and other lives. It also works with the memory of manifestation powers through the masculine or Father principle.

Holy Ghost power moves upward through the soles of the feet, stimulating the wealth of memory contained within the seven guidance brains. To be ignited by the Holy Ghost or to open the tone of the Holy Ghost in any particular guidance brain is to undergo a creative experience directed by the Holy Ghost. The Holy Ghost works with tone and power. The Holy Ghost manifested His powers before Jesus. Through tone, the Holy Ghost stirs man, cleansing the passageways of man's forming and shaping, that man may become a vessel for God and a mind through Christ.

Since the coming of Jesus, the Holy Ghost has increased the sounding of His tone on the solar plexus guidance brain, using the heart and lungs of man, that man might breathe in the power of the Holy Ghost, and eventually give the breath of life to all things shaped and formed through creative love. Since the coming of the Christ Spirit, the Holy Ghost powers have expanded the memory impulses of man's heart, that man may open his mental higher-mind atoms to a foreseeing of mighty things to come through Christ. When this occurs, the physical brain will become a perfect instrument for the higher mind of man. All phases of higher intuition are activated by the Holy Ghost, that man may become a perfect seer for God.

HOLY GHOST AND THE ACCEPTABLE TIME

Through the feet man is a magnetic willing instrument. In nomadic or tribal-genesis, Holy Ghost guidance-brain impulses thrust upward the subtle, serpentine, kundalini astral fire through the feet into the nervous and muscular systems of tribal man. The sacral biological impulses compel men to propagate and to beget tribal offspring expressing *sentient thinking. Tribal-genesis thinking seeks to protect the tribe rather than the individual person.*

In human-genesis or family-genesis, Holy Ghost, working with Elohim Hierarchy, centers His power upon the navel-plexus guidance brain of family-genesis men, causing them to become specific zodiacal thinking prototypes, such as Aries, Taurus, Gemini, Cancer, etc. *The thinking of the family-genesis man is directed to society, community, family property, and prestige of family.*

In lesser self-genesis, Holy Ghost plays His tones of power upon the solar-plexus guidance brain of man, where may be found the individualistic atom. *Lesser self-genesis thinking pertains to thinking one's self to be all-important, thinking of one's own interests before the interests of other men. The lesser self-genesis person is acquisitive and self-centered, producing selfish works. Hardened hearts produce unteachable minds.*

In the higher self-genesis person, Holy Ghost centers His work upon the sacred atom of the heart. The love emotions of the heart are then channeled into all of the feelings, thoughts and organic centers of man. Holy Ghost works that the heart of man may produce the twelve apostolic forms of love, and thereby enable man to attain higher self-genesis thinking. *Such persons will have access – in essence only – to the guidance-brain preservative and protective instinctual-thinking telepathies and instinctual tribal memories, and thus be free from the hostile quelle impulses of the past.*

In higher self-genesis, the love body is united with the higher mind. The thinking of evolved men moves through the pure, etheric, cosmic mind matrix of souls, where separations of minds are impossible – blending all minds in the flowing Christ-vortices of the Spirit. *Higher self-genesis thoughts see all men or souls united under God – akin as sons of God.*

Note: The seven guidance brains beginning at the feet of man are not the same as the kundalini portals of the spine.

Chapter 11

ETHERIC-ANATOMY SYMBOLS
Part I

*May the lame find their walk joyous in the hours of sleep.
May the halt be accelerated into joy. May the sick rise above
their fevered thoughts and receive the balm of healing bliss.*

HALL OF LEARNING

In initiatory dreams all initiates must research the physical body, the etheric bodies, the astral and emotional body, and the mental body. The great Overlords of instruction meet their protégés in the Hall of Learning or the Universities of the night. Here, in laboratories of superconscious planes, their protégés are taught as to the functions of all bodies. All initiates having such night instruction become more aware of their need to learn of the processes of all bodies so that they may render a service on all planes.

In the First Heaven, where the Hall of Learning is centered, initiates attend night classes during dreams and sleep. These classes are overdirected by the Masters, the Illuminati, the Master Saints or Bodhisattvas, and also by some who while living in the earth are invisible helpers or instructors of the night.

In the Hall of Learning may be found everything that man must know and experience in the earth concerning his body and the use of his body. In the Hall of Learning in the present time a greater activity is occurring. This pertains to science and man as he will be in the earth in the next 3,000 years. Everything that man is to manifest in the physical world is first worked upon and blueprinted in the Hall of Learning before it is utilized by the ingenuity of responsive, competent minds in the earth.

Many initiates on recalling their dreams put into action their diagrams and blueprints received while being instructed in the laboratories of the Hall of Learning.

All ideas of the night initiation eventually drift downward into the receptive, higher intelligible minds and souls in the earth. To have cognizance of such dreams and night instructions is a confirmation that one is indeed fulfilling his true task in the physical world.

In dreams and meditation, each part of the body has an interrelated symbology which correlates to the emotions, thoughts and actions – past, present or future.

When one dreams of etheric-anatomy symbols, or of certain areas of his body, he should ask himself, "From what level am I receiving this instruction, and why am I receiving this instruction?" If one conscientiously responds to the instruction he receives in dreams, in time his dream cognition will unite with his night initiation and instruction. He will come to define whether his etheric symbol in dream stems from his conscience, his Guardian Angel, his own initiation, or the invisible healers of the night.

The psychosomatic field of medicine is now beginning to probe the subconscious portals connected with and functioning through the etheric side of anatomy. Psychiatry is testing and exploring the psychic terrain of the subconscious. Their findings will eventually lead them to depend upon the basic master archetypal symbols supporting all symbols. All symbols are written into the etheric or inner part of man. As the Rosetta stone opened the reincarnation memory portals of Egypt, so will the knowledge of man's unseen and inward citadels come to light. In one's etheric body and consciousness a universe lies concealed.

Initiatory revelation concerning the physical and etheric anatomy is experienced during dreams and meditation. Acquiring mastery of dreams and of meditation symbols opens the door to prescient wisdom concerning the evolvement of man on levels of the soul, mind, emotions and the body.

The most primitive of men, as well as advanced men, have throughout the ages relied upon symbolic reminders as a means of correction and guidance. As men give more thought to the interrelationships between the soul and the body, they will recover the ancient symbolic knowledge in the name of science. All initiates versed in the science of the soul are adepts in dream and meditation symbols.

In dreams each portion and function of the physical anatomy

has a correlating significant symbolic meaning. These symbols tell the dreamer that each organ and each action of the body are directly influenced by a positive psychical and negative psychical energy. They also reveal that each physical organ, appendage or portion of the body has a supporting etheric counterpart, and that the planetary energies influence and subtly affect the etheric counterpart of each limb, organ and cell of the physical body.

The initiate of the inner life, in time, will come to discern the karmic and etheric causes and also the initiatory processes as related to sicknesses, maladies, ailments or accidents. He will observe that man in the world is subjected to constant and varied stages of contesting from visible and invisible sources; and through these conflicts – exterior, interior and anterior – he is developing a perfect body and an individualized consciousness so that he may manifest and create within the earth, thus fulfilling the design and Will of God.

ANKLES

There are three etheric axis poles in the body: (1) the ankles, (2) the area from the knees to the hip bones, (3) the area from the heart to the crown of the head. These three etheric axis poles are the penetrable initiatory points of the body. The first, or the area of the ankles, correlates to the Hierarchy or zodiacal energy axis poles within the earth. All polarity Satanic Dwellers, which are the combined evils of men formed into an evil intelligence, direct their telepathies through the first axis located at the area of the ankles. The negative satanic power seeks to overthrow the disciple and the spiritual power he represents. The second axis, or the area from the knees to the hip bones, correlates to the Father axis pole in the core of the earth. Should the disciple be irreverent or critical toward the worship of others, he is the recipient, through the knees, of telepathies from the shadowed body or Dweller of Religions. If the disciple has retained one particle of irreverence toward sex, he will become the recipient, through the thighs, of telepathies from the Generation Dwellers. The third axis, the area from the heart to the crown of the head, correlates to the Christ axis pole in the core of the earth. When one is out of alignment with his heart, soul-grace and mental triad atoms, and has one fragment of doubt in his consciousness as to the Christ, during certain initiatory trials he will be the recipient of materialistic and satanic telepathies contesting his spiritual beliefs and actions.

The ankles are immersed in a horizontal energy zone of force consisting of the cross-currents between astral magnetism and earth gravity. As long as man inhabits a physical body, his ankles will be subjected to this horizontal energy zone of duality action between earth gravity and astral magnetism. The command of these duality cross-currents through the ankles or the first etheric axis pole, which correlates to the Hierarchy axis pole within the earth, will enable him to eventually gain polarity powers as related to the polarities of the earth and to ultimately direct the Hierarchy dual powers into perfected androgynous powers. When a man has at last mastered the duality currents, he will be in alignment with the Jesus One, and Satan shall be bruised under his feet. (Romans 16:20)

If a person suffers an injury to his ankle or ankles, this is an indication of imbalance between the lesser etheric body and the emotional will, and also an imbalance between the emotional body and the thought. For instance, a prejudiced mind, a faultfinding mind, or lack of understanding as to justice in the world will cause a person to be subjectively prone to accidents to the ankles.

It is commonly thought that a spiritual life is a protected one. How may one account for accidents to his body, such as an injured or broken ankle?

In daytime action when one suffers an accident to the ankle, he has opened himself to resisting the forces of gravity. He is contending with these forces so that he may attain a greater etheric range of flexibility and a broader etheric range of polarity action for the future.

THE ANKLES AND THE POLARITY DWELLERS

The ankles are the receivers and distributors of all polarity and duality forces, energies and powers. There are five types of Polarity Dwellers that can penetrate the etheric ankle axis: (1) Continent Polarity Dwellers, (2) Nation Polarity Dwellers, (3) City Polarity Dwellers, (4) Community Polarity Dwellers, (5) Environment Polarity Dwellers. The Nation, City, Community and Environment Polarity Dwellers can penetrate the etheric ankle axis of any person or disciple who has a specific spiritual work to do for the world. Such an attack occurs in rare instances of ripe timing and is part of the disciple's initiation previous to his dedication for a greater work directed toward a larger sphere of accomplishment.

Continent Polarity Dweller. Spiritual powers are gained step by step. All highly evolved or spiritual persons must contend with little-known forces of the invisible worlds. Just as there are gains and losses in great battles or wars in the physical world, so must the dedicated disciple contend with the contesting forces of darkness; and, step by step, he must earn, fortify and strengthen what he is and what he stands for in the world. When one shows his readiness and ripeness to assume greater responsibilities, the atheistic, malicious actions and materialistic concepts of man move against him in the form of a Continent Polarity Dweller – an apparition built out of aeons and ages. Each time one contends with and overcomes an intensified Dweller's action, he has made a greater sustaining in Light, not just for himself, but for the world.

There is a Continent Polarity Dweller for each continent of the earth. Continent Polarity Dwellers work in or with polarity orbits correlated to the subtle and satanic forces in the anterior layers of the earth. Being fed by an artery of negation, the Continent Polarity Dwellers are the closest dwellers to Satan himself. When a disciple has reached a certain phase of evolvement, and is ready to acquire greater disciple powers, he is contested by a Continent Polarity Dweller. This initiation for the disciple has no minor aspects; it has to do with a major action. The Continent Polarity Dweller works to obliterate the light of an initiate, and therefore may endanger the life of the initiate. When this initiation occurs in wooded, mountainous or virginal places, the Continent Polarity Dweller is assisted by certain subtle Panlike forces attacking the vulnerable point of balance, the disciple's ankles, literally seeking to throw him from the Path. In some instances, the initiate may become the victim of an accident to his ankle or ankles. An initiate suffering such an injury to an ankle escapes very lightly, as compared with some who suffer death in such initiations. One who loses his life may be said to suffer a martyred death, and in some coming life will gain grace to sustain works of spiritual power.

An attack from a Continent Polarity Dweller may occur more than once in an advanced initiate's life, but such attacks only occur just previous to a greater serving, in which the initiate will touch vast numbers of people rather than a minority. The advanced and dedicated person, who has successfully experienced his initiatory trials with the Continent Polarity Dweller, will produce a more positive and sustained etheric alignment, and incorporate a broader etheric range, thereby becoming more qualified to work visibly and invisibly in all portions of the earth. Such an initiate may remain in one place and still be communicable through telepathy to any continent in the earth.

Community Polarity Dweller. The combined evils and negative mass thought, and the powers and principalities of darkness working through them, telepathically affect the uncertain and vacillating minds of persons, causing masses of persons to waver and doubt as to their beliefs and faiths. These insidious telepathies penetrate people through the area of the ankles. A Community Polarity Dweller is made up of the combined evils and also the atheistic and materialistic beliefs of a community. The Community Polarity Dweller telepathically challenges the spiritual belief and faith of a student or would-be initiate. When the would-be initiate finds that he is too often comparing his spiritual beliefs with materialistic and atheistic viewpoints, it is because he is the recipient of waves of doubt sent telepathically by the Community Dweller. The expression, "To take a stand," is derived from the knowledge of this telepathic action directed against the etheric axis or penetrable area of the ankles.

There are many times in which a Community Polarity Dweller may seek to challenge an initiate and deplete and devitalize him with negative telepathies, especially when the disciple's faith has yet to become a fully working and manifested part of his expression. These negative telepathies may cause the initiate to feel alone and unsupported as to his spiritual life. When such a telepathic challenge occurs, the disciple should reaffirm his beliefs, reestablish his faith, and rededicate himself to the Light; and he should seek the help of the Guardian Angels of the community, as these angels represent the grace and good of the community.

An initiate learns, after his first period of grace has been fulfilled, that dedication alone is not enough, for he must continually take his stand and constantly reaffirm his faith so that he may bring into the world vital and living works of Light. If the disciple will sustain himself in the Christ Light, and make his stand for the Light and the Christ, he shall still the Community Dweller telepathies. Each time the faith is reaffirmed and the belief clarified, an initiate grows stronger as to his faith or beliefs. It is especially important that one comes to know that these Dweller telepathies come not from himself but are from a combined action of countless unbeliefs and nonbelievings in the community. Jesus was unable to produce His miraculous works in His own community of Nazareth because of the unbeliefs of His community. So also should the disciple be alerted, that he may sustain at all times that which he is and that which he knows and that which he can be in the Will of God.

An initiate may be spiritually sent to a new community to begin a new phase of spiritual work. All of the mass malice from atheistic and materialistic thoughts will move in against that which he represents in the Light. He thus is subjected to a Dweller challenge through the axis of the ankles. While this may not result in an accident, it will affect the initiate in a form of self-doubt as to his worthiness, his ministry and its purpose. Such an initiate must contend with this Dweller or combined community antichrist by sustaining and maintaining with renewed vigor and strength what he is. Often the initiate will feel that he is fighting a blind and senseless force; but if he is aware of it as a tangible intelligence directed toward thwarting his works of Light and ministering helps, he will protect himself from this malignant intelligence which would seek to devitalize the essential ether sustaining his thought. Each time the initiate receives such a challenge he will make a new alignment to substantiate and reaffirm what he believes in and what he has to give to the world – and he will become stronger in that which he is and knows. In his sustaining of the Light, he will render a service to the community, in that one part of his work is to stir and to change the community's crystallized patterns of thought and action. And, from this, the community will receive, over a period of time, benefit and healing grace.

Suggested mantram to overcome Community Polarity Dweller telepathy:

> I reaffirm my belief
> and take my stand
> in the Light of the Christ.
> I am supported and sustained
> in the mighty Will of God.

In seeking the help of the Guardian Angels of the community, one may say:

> If it is the Will of the Father,
> may the Guardian Angels of this community
> still this nefarious work of the dark.
> And may I stand in the Light of the Christ.

In the event of any telepathic negation affecting the polarity ankle axis, the Luminosity Angel may also be called upon as well as the Guardian Angels of the community. For example:

> If it is the Will of the Father,
> may my Luminosity Angel come unto me
> so as to protect me
> and shield me from harm
> in this Dweller experience.

Small accidents to the ankles are sometimes reminders that one is out of alignment with his spiritual balance; and he should seek to search his thoughts and the motives in his actions.

To dream that one is receiving *a blow to the ankles* reveals that some subverted force is seeking to trip him so that he will lose his spiritual poise.

To dream that one's *ankles are fettered* indicates that he is imprisoned, limited and restrained.

To see the symbol of *the wings of Mercury* on the level of the ankle assures the dreamer of freedom in night-flight.

If one is *wearing shoes with tops* reaching to the level of his ankles, this indicates that he is being demagnetized through negative currents affecting the atoms of his feet, and that he is being prevented from receiving the benefit of healing currents moving upward through his feet; also that he is thinking antiquated thoughts pertaining to progress.

To stand in water up to the ankles means that one has need of more courage, that he might move more deeply into the purifying waters, and thus experience the healing and cleansing of the pure rivers of life; indicates procrastination and timidity.

To see one with *broken ankles* infers a martyrdom with persecution.

If *the ankles appear strong,* balanced and upright in a dream, this is saying that one has attained the true spiritual poise, has taken a stand, and will not be moved.

To *break one's ankles* in a dream indicates that he has been challenged by a subtle dweller seeking to overthrow his upright spiritual position. The spiritual aftereffects of such an initiation are equanimity, poise, self-assurance, confidence.

In a certain meditation posture, *crossed ankles* form a mudra or a sealing in of prana so as to charge the various chakras or soul-portals with higher frequencies of energy. Crossed ankles also protect a person from overly psychically-charged astral currents from another person. One should place the right ankle over the left ankle to sustain a positive point of insulation.

APPENDIX

The appendix is an astral organ collecting the astral seepage or overflow from one's psychic unruly emotions. It is a primal organ working with the lower quelle aspect of the subconscious.

To feel *pain in the appendix* in a dream or to see the organ of the appendix in a dream is symbolic of astral infiltration into the emotions. To see the area of *the appendix in the light* during a dream or in meditation symbolizes that one has earned the right to insulate himself from darkened astral forces.

ARMS

The *arms lifted as in supplication* in a dream indicate that one has surrendered his will to God, and henceforth will be initiated into laws of obedience.

When *arms are outstretched horizontally* in a dream, it is a symbol that one is to offer himself up as a supreme sacrifice, and will thereafter take upon himself the griefs and wounds of others.

When one feels that he is *holding someone in the shelter of his arm,* he has received tenderness grace, and henceforth becomes a shelter for those who are weary or burdened.

Should one *hold a creature,* an animal, tenderly in his arms, he is emulating the Lord Jesus.

To dream of *meeting an adversary who wounds or bruises the arms* indicates that one is to meet an adversary seeking to take away from him his initiative.

To *embrace someone with passionate love* in a dream shows that one is experiencing an evaluation of his sexual desires and love intent.

Should one *embrace a person tenderly in his arms* while dreaming, this reveals to the dreamer he has attained the reverent side of love.

If one sees *the armless statue of Venus de Milo* in a dream, this indicates that he has abused love on a sexual level in former lives, and therefore is incapable of retaining a faithful mate or a rewarding personal love. He is being told that his love will be thwarted.

If one is *swimming vigorously* with a rhythmic stroke, this reveals that he has mastered the astral currents and is a true swimmer in the spiritual sea of life.

Any *athletic activity with the use of the arms* emphasized in a dream indicates that one is preparing himself for crises or perils ahead. The *elbow* indicates self-defense.

Should one dream that he is *being branded, tattooed, or vaccinated* on one of his arms, or *if a snake should bite him on one of his arms,* it indicates that he has exposed himself to malicious undercurrents of the psychic underworld.

Should one dream that he is having a *vein opened* and sees a flow of blood, this indicates the loss of a blood relative.

BLOOD

Blood is a combination of ether, prana, akasia and energy. Blood is a fluidic ego vessel, enabling the ego to remain fluidic and flexible within a body of flesh in the gravity world. The etheric energy in the lesser etheric body, the heartbeat, the pulse points of the body, the cells, the veins, the nerves, the arteries, the muscles, the glands and the organs of the body are utilized according to the mental and will intensity of the ego. The blood as a fluidic agent is a photographic field registering man's impressionable emotions and thoughts.

The condition of the blood in a state of health is under direction of an ego will. In case of an ego being apathetic or indifferent to the life currents and life force supporting the blood, one becomes anemic and listless. In the case of the ego living too much ahead of time, high blood pressure is experienced. In case of one resisting life, living too much in the past, refusing to give full play to life's current through the blood, the result is low blood pressure, tension, stress, emotional and mental.

The cosmic plasma or pranic ether supporting the bloodstream of man seeks to convert the energy processes of cell life and functional life in the blood into pranic intelligence, and thus use the more vital processes in the blood for the higher mind's action.

Cosmic plasma in the blood supporting the ego processes of the blood is a coagulating spiritual substance. The influence of the physical expression of the ego and the karma of the ego cannot utilize fully the cosmic plasma substance in the blood. Transfusions of physical blood plasma do not intrude upon the higher ego. Ordinary blood transfusions contain the prototypal pictures or karmic imprints of the one giving blood in transfusion. When one receives a blood transfusion, he incorporates temporarily the identity photographs of the person who gives the blood. Very often, even though the type of blood may be correct, if the pictures in the blood representing the one who donates the blood are filled with dissonance or inharmonious colorings disagreeable to the one receiving the blood, the result is that the patient may be thrown into a violent fever due to failure to assimilate the ego transmission in the blood. Forty-eight hours are required to master any dissonant effect received from a blood transfusion.

In dreams one may feel that he is *receiving a transfusion of blood.* This does not mean a foreseeing or prophecy of an actual blood transfusion; in its positive sense it signifies that one is being reinforced with a higher rejuvenation of the cosmic life force.

One's own identification with the karmic levels of humanity can be found in his blood type. The type of blood one has determines the type of humanity karma he is seeking to master.

In a dream when *blood flows from a wound,* this indicates that one is being cleansed of impure prototypal pictures registered in the blood. A prototypal picture contains a picture of the former life or personality, also the record of the ancestral line.

To receive *a blood transfusion* in a dream indicates that one has devitalized the vitality of his lesser etheric body supporting the prototypal and ancestral record, and is receiving resuscitating and healing ministering helps from heaven.

When a woman dreams of *menstruating or hemorrhaging,* this indicates that she is seeking purification and is turning her faith to the Lord Jesus that He may heal her of any feeling of guilt through procreation or sex, even as He healed the flow of blood (St. Matthew 9:20). So do all women heart-disciples in the beginning of their initiations turn to the Lord Jesus for absolution and chastity strengths.

To see *bloodstained garments* or blood upon the garment of any-

one else in a dream indicates that one is in danger of being involved in some unpleasant condition related to amoral acts.

BRAIN

When the brain is seen in a dream, one is researching the brain
zones. He is being taught that the brain contains a honeycomb of
energized zones or stations for the mentality rather than the organ
of mentality. During etheric-anatomy initiations in the night he
sees *the mental or mind atoms* supporting the brain zones at work.
He also learns of the power of imaging (frontal lobe), the power of
the will (the crown of the head), and the power of memory (base
of the skull). Should he see *the brain saturated with light* in a
dream, this indicates that he is spiritually active, communing with
the illuminative side of his soul.

To dream of seeing *the back of a person's head* or the back of
several heads means the end of one's association with them, or of
a refusal of the one seen to acknowledge him as an ego or person.
When only the back of the head of a Master is seen, one is being
rejected by the Master.

To dream of *an operation for a tumor of the brain* signifies the
removal of thoughts of guilt.

A cerebral hemorrhage in a dream is a warning that one has an
overburdened conscience, and thus has uncontrolled life impulses.
The ego desires to relinquish responsibility as a thinking person.

In dreams *a white skull* means initiation or death to the worldly
or materialistic nature; *a brown skull* is a warning of physical body
death; *a black skull* is a warning of an obsessing dark force.

The physical brain is a honeycomb mesh of cells, tissues, arteries, nerves. In the spiritual life the brain is the focal point for a
mightier function: the three mental triad atoms are seated in proximity to the brain; and the soul's medallion also overdwells the
brain.

To *research the brain* in a dream or in meditation, or to dream of
being engrossed with any particular portion of the brain, indicates
that one is being instructed as to certain initiations whereby he
may gain additional knowledge of his interior nature supporting
his soul and his mental consciousness.

There are five initiatory portals of the will. The first portal is
seated at the base of the spine. The second is the occipital portal of
the brain supporting the base of the skull. The third is the medulla-

oblongata portal, called the mouth of God, containing the ego breath, initiating one into the primitive or primordial will and the cosmic will. The fourth initiatory portal of the will is the cerebellum portal supporting the quelle subconscious life where one is initiated into the emotional impulses of love or hate, likes or dislikes. Through this initiation one learns to overcome hostility and to master the negative side of his emotional will. He also takes unto himself certain degrees of courage and fearlessness. The fifth or cerebrum portal initiates one into the highest degree of thought action, and unites one's thoughts with the Will of God. Through this portal initiation he becomes a conscious identity, spiritually willing his life, his emotions, his thoughts; he becomes a poised and perceptive instrument for God; he becomes a creator rather than a creature.

To dream of one's brain or to see the brain in a vision indicates that one is being instructed in the higher worlds as to the purpose of the brain, that he may gauge its capacity and influence on the soul, the mind, the emotions and the body.

When *the brain appears magnified or enlarged* in a dream, one is beginning to be initiated into the occipital portal of the brain. This portal is the second door to the will, and holds the key to the memory of the origin of life. Through the occipital portal the river of life moves. The source of occipital initiatory impulses begins at the root of the spine. These impulses move upward through five major chakras into the occipital initiatory door and stimulate the will to live, to survive. When one begins to observe these conjoining currents at the base of the skull, he is evaluating his origin; he also is increasing his will to live; his survival powers are increased; he has access to longevity grace; and his will to live is united with the cosmic restoring and revitalizing life.

The root of the spine, correlating to the occipital door, receives its most powerful influences and compulsions from the generation archetypes. These archetypes or blueprints press upon the base of the spine, stimulating one sexually to beget and to procreate.

The occipital portal supports the skull. This portal is the door into the medulla-oblongata initiations, where one is initiated into an understanding of the vital nerve centers controlling his breath and also linking him with the incoming and outgoing pranic life tides of his soul. In the occipital and medulla-oblongata initiations one unites with humanity's etheric origins; he has access to the memory of the primordial beginnings of humanity.

When the portal at the root of the spine, the occipital portal and the medulla-oblongata portal are externally penetrated out of timing, the result is derangement of the mentality. When one uses incorrect meditation practices or willingly exposes himself to irresponsible hypnosis, these portals of the will are injured and some form of irrationality will result. If a person offends these laws, he will fall into subversive and dangerous mental pitfalls. If he has the grace of protection, he will receive prevention-grace dreams, and he will observe where the weakness lies in the use of his will.

When one experiences the will initiations through the etheric brain receptivity, he observes man as a being free to will; he learns that will is the highest attribute given to man from God. He also observes that there are penalties exacted when one abuses the will.

Concentration, contemplation, pure meditation, the speaking of mantrams and prayers in right timing, enable one to free the life force conduits or chakras within the etheric processes of the spine, keeping open the door of the will so that one may become a will-initiate for God.

Dream symbols are the vocabulary of the soul. When one has the initiation of the will through etheric magnification of the brain, he should be alerted to outer circumstances which would challenge him as to his will impulses. He should pray that he may be chaste in his sexual attitudes and actions; that he may be charitable and loving toward his fellow men; that he be responsible for his own acts; and that he use his will as an instrument for God.

THE GLEAMING BRAIN

Night-flight and dream experience with cognition are established when one has reached a degree of spiritual evolvement whereby his emotions are pure, his mentality wholly dedicated, and his works are devoted to good. If one has immature emotions or traces of egotism, dream experience is distorted and discolored through psychical function stemming from the phallic symbols of the lower astral world.

In night-flight the silver cord is relaxed and slackened in its anchorage over the spleen, the liver, the heart, the throat and the crown of the head. In uninterrupted night-flight the initiate freely releases himself from his body through the loosening of the silver cord.

With night-flight coordination, one leaves the physical body and lesser etheric body resting upon the bed. His higher etheric body processes take command of his emotional body and mental body. Out of the physical body, he is able to observe, to study, and to serve in the higher wavelengths of the inward life.

In the study of etheric anatomy, at night one learns of the gleaming brain situated directly beneath the crown of the skull. The gleaming brain is the product of the pineal gland. In night-flight, one observes the function of the higher brain and sees its functions to be similar to an eternity system – the pineal gland being the sun, and the twelve spherical projections of light orbiting around the pineal gland are as the planets. When one is in deep meditation, and has made alignment with the pulsation point of his soul's medallion seated at the crown of his head, the gleaming brain is activated – and the total brain is flooded with illuminative light. The process of imaging is magnified, and the will of the initiate and the Will of God become as one. Memory then begins to function in a state of timelessness wherein the initiate may behold eternal things and eternity conditions and see things as yet unmanifested – and thus know them to be a part of the Eternal Plan and Will of God.

There are times during the first stages of meditation when one experiences a spiral-like circular or rotational movement within the crown of the head. This is the beginning of the activity of the gleaming brain. Sometimes, when one has attained this state of meditation, he feels a flow of warmth in the crown of the head. This occurs because he has succeeded in uniting the soul's pulsation with the gleaming brain.

When the gleaming brain is thus activated, the gravity-laden senses are drained off, becoming semi-dormant; and the soul-faculties or higher sensory perception take possession of one's thoughts. One should be alerted to this experience in meditation so that he may remain receptive during this period and retain the consciousness of his meditative experiences. Should he permit himself to give way to the rotational movement of the gleaming brain, he will find himself out of the body. In etheric-anatomy brain initiation, one must remember that it is necessary at all times to retain consciousness as to what he is doing, seeing, hearing and speaking.

When one is overtense in meditation, through the intensity of the will he may project himself from his physical and lesser etheric body out of timing. He should at this time protect himself by speaking a mantram so as to keep his bodies stabilized, and thus avoid a psychic shock or disturbance.

The gleaming brain when free in action enables one, in time, to harmlessly release himself from his bodies while awake. It also enables him to experience daytime etheric visitations called astral projection, and record what he sees and hears while in command of his consciousness. Adepts are capable of releasing themselves from their bodies and of traveling etherically to great distances, giving help to those who have need in time of crisis, or accomplishing a particular thing for a fellow disciple. They use their gleaming brain without interruption, being in constant alignment with the higher wavelengths of the inner world, remaining consciously aware of their proximity to the unseen forces. Such adepts are free to do unusual things in the world while yet accomplishing the things of Spirit.

THREE GREAT INITIATIONS

Until all men function through their heart atoms equally with their spiritual will and mind, they will continue to undergo three outstanding phases in initiation: *primal brain initiation* through lower quelle or Center Q situated at the base of the brain; *lunar-brain initiation* through the solar plexus; the divine sun or *gleaming-brain initiation* working through the crown of the head.

Primal-brain initiation, when first experienced by the spiritual initiate, is a clarifying and terrifying experience. In primal-brain initiation one must undergo a recapitulation of the genetic impulses, the procreation impulses and the individual sexual impulses of man. Through the primal-brain initiation one unites with the moral issues of his time. His own moral values are weighed. His past-life sexual motives and moral instincts are retrospected. On the physical planes he is presented with many issues pertaining to sexual desire, sexual attitudes and sexual reciprocity. In certain levels of initiation in the inner planes, the male initiate meets the temptress; or if female, the initiate encounters the tempter. To dream of a temptress or a tempter, or to take part in a sexual act during sleep is to evaluate one's own sexual chastity.

The initiate learns through spiritual instruction in the inner planes that sex is given to man in the physical world as an act of love. He masters the primal-brain initiation when he accepts the laws governing love in the sexual life. If his sexual acts of the past have moved reverently with the rising side of evolvement, that is, becoming more intuitively selective with each life's action, his propagation grace will protect him during the primal-brain initiation. He will gather the essence of chastity into his sexual relationships, thereby contributing to the world purity.

Beginning students of the inner science of the soul are compelled in dreams to research their sexual compulsions, to weigh their sexual motives. For assurance they should look to the Jesus ethic concerning sex; from this they may accept what their Recording Angel tells them in the night's action during sleep.

Solar-plexus or lunar-brain initiation magnifies one's response to the lunar rays acting upon the lesser etheric body. The lunar-brain initiate must undergo many trials of sensitivity that he may understand the cycles of his periodicity responses. He also must understand the functional tone-rate of the physical body, how it is made and how it functions in waking and in sleeping. The initiation through the lunar brain controlling the etheric processes of the physical body introduces one to the energies of the different planes of life: mineral, plant, animal and man. All crude or raw cosmic energies are mastered to some degree through lunar-brain experience centered in the solar plexus.

When emphasis is upon lunar-brain experience, one becomes clairsentient to all life; he increases the magnetic field of the emotions or astral body. It is necessary that one's magnetism be increased and ego-controlled so that he may function in a wider sphere of awareness as to his own emotions and feelings and as to the emotions and feelings of others. Until one has mastered certain initiatory powers through the lunar-brain initiation, he is incapable of knowing an empathy for others in the world, thereby making it impossible for him to heal or contribute with lasting consequence to the happiness and harmony of others. The time must come in the life of all initiates when the Master comes forth to ask, "What have you done for others in the world?" Only then will the third phase of initiation begin to open to the initiate.

The gleaming brain remains behind the cloud of unknowing until one has offered up his devotion, love, sympathy and selfless desires to the intent of God. Then and only then will the cloud obscuring the brightest light of his own spirit, fashioned after the eternal Spirit of God, come forth.

Gleaming-brain initiation is the highest initiation given to man in this cosmic eternity system. Gleaming-brain initiation takes place after long fastings of the spirit, hungers for the spirit, and famished longings for the spirit and spirit only. When one's body, emotions and mind are readied, spirit becomes the total possessor of the soul housed in the body, emotions and mind.

Prayer, devotion, purification, self-discipline – all self-imposed and accepted – are the steps to free the gleaming brain. All initiation begins by one step. No physical process of earth can initiate into the gleaming brain initiations – only direct contact with Eternal Spirit is the Initiator. On the rise upward, illumination draws one into greater and greater expansions of insight, revelation and knowing. To be initiated into the gleaming brain, one masters the mental and soul telepathic nuances of all souls of the world, of souls yet unborn, of souls in heaven. The initiate must take command and master the duality powers in thought, that he may use with full awareness the third or spiritual capacity of his mental atoms, emotional atoms and physical atoms.

In the era approaching men, the Aquarian or highly evolved initiate will be initiated simultaneously with all three processes of initiation: primal brain, lunar brain and gleaming brain. The divine Son, or the Christ Light, will speak into the initiate's mind and instruct him. All initiates and students of the spiritual and soul sciences should strive to balance their lives, that they may come under the converging stream of initiatory receptivity as given by the Light of the Christ.

The initiatory foresteps to receiving the gleaming-brain initiation incorporate the first two major initiations: primal brain and lunar brain. Woe unto him who seeks the gleaming-brain initiation without preparation, without honesty, without pure desire. To such will come the fall – and only God knoweth the time of his redemption.

BREAST

In dreams *the symbol of the breast* when seen with detachment relates to the nourishing feminine principle giving sustenance or milk of spiritual truths. To see in a dream *a woman absent of breasts* is to be reminded that the feminine principle is being denied or the channel of life nourishment is being thwarted. To see *the Amazon symbol of a warrior woman with one breast* is to recognize through dream code that a female person is using more of the masculine principle than the feminine. The breast, seen as a symbol in chimera-like dreams, sometimes is experienced through sexual sensation. In such dreams, one is researching his sexual nature as to lust.

The *temptress symbol* seen in the dreams of the night by the male initiate very often reveals a seductive portion of the torso of the female body. A male initiate exposed to the temptress in dreams is being warned that he must be alerted to the outer physical experience testing his attitude toward sex and his self-control and reverence toward sex.

To dream that *one is an infant once again at the breast* of his mother is a sign of emotional immaturity and a warning that he is refusing to meet the mature demands of life.

When a woman dreams that she is *nursing a babe,* this is a symbol that she is uniting with the Divine-Mother principle.

One of the most prevalent etheric-code symbol dreams in the life of an initiate is *the symbol of a baby.* To be in the process of having a baby, holding a baby, seeing a new baby, or cuddling a baby, is the symbol that one has been born to the higher self. In the dream he is being told by his angels and the monitor of his higher unconscious that he has given birth to a new self and in the future will put into practice the pure first stages of the spiritual life, or that he is being born anew. All such dreamers should be alert to the outer manifestation of the new self in their lives.

To refuse to take the babe in a dream means that one is turning away from the responsibilities demanded of him in initiation to the higher self.

BREATHING

Ancient astrologers, understanding the expanding powers of the soul, stated that the first breath at birth recorded one's solar identity. It was said by these great seers that the ego-initiative began with the first breath.

Through Hall-of-Learning dream research, one learns that breathing during the day is stimulated by the solar energies; breathing after dusk or sundown, by the lunar energies.

Daytime thoughts stimulated by the solar energies are thoughts of survival, perception, discernment. Thoughts stimulated by lunar energies are reflective, detached and pertain more to moods rather than to active thinking.

Some persons having lowered etheric vitality in the lesser etheric body are more subjected to lunar energies during the waking or daytime hours. These persons breathe with the upper portion of their lungs, rather than with the full capacity of their lungs; they are more responsive to lunar breathing – and therefore are more introspective and inclined to moods. Persons using their full breath capacity, having a high vitality in their lesser etheric body, are more realistic in their thinking.

If there have been strong racial prejudices or rigid racial patterns in thinking in previous lives or in the present life, one is more likely to breathe through the lunar vitalities, and thus suffer through respiratory ailments or forms of congestion in the lungs.

The use of the lungs for breathing correlates to the soul's effulgent, emanating power. When one has balanced the soul rhythms, the mental rhythms and the emotional rhythms, he has command of solar and lunar breathing. His breathing is united with the medulla-oblongata ebb and flow of the soul's pulsation. His lesser etheric body and higher etheric body, having attained equilibrium, give him freedom to draw into his thoughts cosmic creative ideas saturated with pure pranic vitality.

Untrained and precocious breathing techniques for the Western disciple, when absent from a teacher or a guru, overexpand the imaging faculty between the soul and the mental antenna atoms. When a Western disciple uses Eastern advanced methods of breathing or pranayama without an instructor, he accelerates the vibratory hum of the soul's medallion, and opens atavistic, psychical powers – endangering his physical health and also his psychical health influencing his moral attitudes. One should never use the advanced techniques of breathing unless he has the supervision and direction of a true teacher.

The Western disciple can best balance the solar and lunar breath action through the less advanced yoga or cosmic exercises – walking, speaking of mantrams; through prayerful containment, meditation and quiet.

CALVES

The calves of the legs reflect the zeal and the momentum of the body. *A weakened calf* indicates a fear of defeat. A muscular *cramp in the calf* denotes a recoil from participation or doing one's share in the world. During the daytime hours, *spasmodic cramps in the calves* are caused by a depletion of ether; a disconnection from the psychic flow affects the calcium in the body and produces the need for calcium. If the zeal or "go" impulse has been thwarted, there is a lack of etheric alignment between the muscles and the bones of the legs. To awaken in the night with a spasmodic cramp in the calf of the leg is an indication that the higher etheric body has failed to release itself perfectly to the night work and that there is some hidden psychic block caused by noncomplying action as related to physical duties or responsibilities.

If one will speak a mantram and thus align himself with his Guardian Angel before sleep, he will begin to order his life as to timing; he will overcome haste and impulsive decisions; and he will overcome his hidden timidities pertaining to insurmountable obstacles. Therefore, he will relax muscular tensions and free his higher will into all movements of his limbs, producing poise, coordination and grace.

CELLS

In dream or night initiatory instruction, the initiate is taught to observe, scrutinize and study the cell life in the bloodstream. He is shown that each cell contains three points of life working in a pyramidal or triad action. He studies the cellular balance between the three points of life within the cell. He watches the movement of the cell in the blood; and he is shown through initiation how the cell maintains its exchange points of balance, and how the cell in each organ has a higher or spiritual function, an ego or individualistic function and an ancestral instinctive function. He notes how the cells of the liver, the heart, the spleen, the brain and all other organs respond to a tone suitable to each organ. He sees how the sacred atom in the heart maintains the tone within each cell. He also sees how the master atom in the heart over all cells, when out of focus or deranged, imbalances the physical body. Degeneration in the cells is multiplied; ether supporting life in the organ collapses, the cells becoming sluggish, weak, and sometimes malignant.

The organs of the body are so constituted that each organ works in a positive or negative polarity to another organ. For example, the spleen and liver are antagonists to one another; the pancreas, to the adrenal glands. When the various antagonistic functions are balanced in their polarity function, there is health in the organs and in the body. The cells also work in positive and negative functions in their triad points of life.

The sacred-atom tone within the heart commands the negative and positive actions of the organs and of the cells. The sacred-atom heart tone also commands the rejecting rhythm of the cells, that the old cell may die and a new cell take its place.

If the prototypal image supporting the ego in the sacred atom of the heart moves out of accord with the rhythm of the sacred-atom tone, the triad cellular function becomes a purging fire. Inharmony between the prototypal image and the sacred-atom tone of the heart is caused by a continuing desire to escape from life, or a continued wish to die. Through initiation the disciple learns that persons having such suicidal wishes lose touch with the coordinated rhythm between the cell, the organ and the prototypal function of the ego.

Vital cells sustaining the norm of health in the body work with the blood in a continual flowing state of movement. Cells moving with the bloodstream are weighed and assessed infinitesimally by the sacred atom in the heart where the ego prototypal pictures gathered from the three points of life in the cell are recorded on the prototypal image in the heart. Should the mirrored picture of the cell reflect the ancestral cell as being predominant, the sacred atom records this emphasis onto the prototypal image. Here it is registered that it may be retained. Should the cell mirror the picture of over-accentuated activity in the individualistic point of life in the cell, the result is recorded upon the etheric, cloudy substance of the egotistical shell. (The portion of the egotistical shell surrounding the etheric encasement of the heart contains all of the self-willed actions in this life and in former lives.)

When the lowest or ancestral point of life in the cell is predominant, the health of the physical body is subjected to inherited ancestral sicknesses. When the emphasis is upon the individualistic point of life within the cell, the physical body may undergo many undefined or undiagnosed states of sickness. If the picture of the spiritual point of life in the cell is inactive, the picture fails to mirror itself upon the sacred atom of the heart; this is due to one's having depended solely upon the instinctual will rather than upon the spiritual will. One is thus shut away from the spiritual flow of the soul.

In the study of the cell through initiation, the disciple will in time perceive the answer to the riddle of all cellular structure.

In the *latter part of the self-genesis age,* a fourth point of life, as yet latent in all cellular life, will become active in the blood, tissue and organs of highly evolved men. This fourth point of life in the cell will correlate to an omniscient cell in the brain. The functioning of this *omniscient cell* will produce the spiritual man.

In the Hall of Learning, men study minute subjects, such as the cells, during the time when the constellation rays focus their velocity upon the planet Mercury. This in turn is stepped down into physical laboratories of the world, that all of the minute or microscopic forms of life may be researched.

Initiates having Mercury elevated in their charts may be found at night in their dreams working under the direction of the greater cosmic presences. From such instruction and apprenticeship come men who have talent for the intricate and infinite, or patience with a side of life ordinarily unobserved by other men.

In one portion of the Hall of Learning there is a mighty, transparent domelike roof or covering. The material forming this transparent ceiling is supercharged with pulsating energy that acts as a vibrational receptor and distributor of the great planetary and constellation rays of Hierarchy beamed from the outer constellations in space. These Hierarchy rays beam into the vibrancy mental coils of researchers of the night, giving an informing action. These great energy rays determine what men are to learn in particular times in the cosmic laboratories in the Hall of Learning.

Chapter 12

ETHERIC-ANATOMY SYMBOLS
Part II

When sleep falls unto me, the claims of the day will cease to bind me, for in the night I am free to immerse my heart in the renewing pool of God's perfect peace.

COLON

When one is spiritually receptive, he may be warned in dreams of impending ill health, for all illnesses are first registered on the etheric counterpart of an organ. In dreams the etheric replica of the physical body is magnified to a dream initiate. When this occurs, if there be grace, during a dream the negative tone rate of energy in the organ may be transposed; rectification of the etheric organ may also be made possible through prayer and intercession, and thus the physical organ is restored.

One's Guardian Angel and Luminosity Angel will sometimes yield the divination of etheric imbalance; and if there be grace, one receives the way of relief or remedy through whatever agency may hold the key to healing helps. On applying this guidance, health is restored.

To dream of *the intestinal corridor* is to be initiated into the ingestion laws on the physical level. Dreams revealing *physical disturbances of the colon* signify an unyielding lack of cooperation or resistance to releasing. Dreams portraying *emotional-level disturbance of the colon* signify false concepts of chastity and failure to accept the functional processes of life. Dream research into the etheric disturbance of the colon, pertaining to infants or young children, discloses that the etheric weakness is the product of past-life resistance to the rules of life.

The etheric duplicate of the colon works with the gravity function of the constellation of Virgo, the planet Mercury and the planet Mars. Inner research confirms that all elimination processes in the body are also influenced by the magnetic ebb-and-flow tide actions of the moon.

To constantly dream of one's *elimination process* in any part of the body means that one is being purified, cleansed. To dream of *bowel or kidney elimination*, and to feel embarrassed in the dream, means that one is to be cleansed, but will also be chastened publicly in some manner. As all ingestion begins in the mouth, elimination dreams sometimes mean that one must be cleansed of needless conversation.

Spiritual health is holy; perfect bodily health is a reflection of well-earned holy actions, emotions, thoughts. Dreams will speak the corrective healing word when one rests his dreams with the angels.

DIAPHRAGM (see Larynx)

EARS

The uniting sound current sustaining all life is experienced in dreams as well as in daytime action. The audible sound or the Word is first experienced in the right ear in energy ecstasies in the body. During meditation one unites through the portal between the eyebrows with the Nadam or great vibration, his body becoming a vibrational hum of divine joy. The starry portal or the command center between the eyebrows is opened when the great Nadam or Word is contacted.

To be united with the sound current is to be at one with the Holy Ghost and to be alive within the divine-life current. This current opens for the initiate the inner eye wherein one sees dimensions unknown to physical man, and also whereby one hears the great Nadam or name or Word. Sometimes he hears the mighty logos of the Christ. More often he hears a Nadam conversation with his Master. Sometimes he hears the angels. If he has opened the full Nadam vibration of the Holy Ghost, he has the power to spiritually see, hear and speak – and in speaking, to change the karmic currents in the lives of those to whom he speaks.

To experience the great Nadam in sleep is to be instructed, cleansed, revitalized. In dreams one can open himself to Nadam if he has understanding of the master sound currents.

The sense of hearing in the physical plane in dreams is magnified. If one has undeveloped extrasensory perception, he is more likely to hear in dreams through *the portal of his left ear*. Thus, the voices he hears in the night will be subtle, insinuative voices. To be leaning in the direction of the true sound currents and to come under the tutelage of one's Master is to use the sound current, and to hear the cosmic music of the eternals, the angelic voices and music, the Seraphim archetypal ideas. Words heard in the night-Nadam or sound current are meaningful, penetrating, lasting. One should be aware, and determine to remember the tone of the voices he hears in the night – whether they fall upon his fears or upon his enlightenment and encouragement.

In dream symbols the ears denote receptivity, communication, pleasant or unpleasant. Should a voice speak into *the orifice of the left ear* during a dream, this is the symbol that one has opened himself to the subtle undercurrents of the unseen worlds. In a dream, should one feel that he is being touched on *the lobe of the left ear,* it indicates that he is being misled. Should he feel a touch upon *the upper portion of the left ear,* it indicates that he has moved too deeply into nefarious levels of the dark.

If one sees *the lobe of his right ear* in a dream, it is a symbol that he has approval from the angelic worlds as to his daytime material actions. When one feels that someone is speaking into *the orifice of his right ear* while dreaming, this indicates that he is being called to do a specific work. To feel that *the upper portion of the right ear* is being touched while dreaming means one is being assured that the spiritual worlds are blessing him and fortifying him in his spiritual works in the world.

When one dreams of a person with *fawn-shaped or pointed ears,* he is being told that the person is an instrument for the lower astral or dark. He is also being shown that the person is a psychic agent for the Pan creatures or elementals.

THE EARS AS ANTENNAS OF SENSITIVITY POINTS IN THE LESSER ETHERIC BODY

There are seventy-two thousand nadis constellation or zodiacal sensitivity points in the lesser etheric body. If one has earned *constellation grace* from a past life, the telepathies of the angels are communicable to the constellation antenna or nadis points in the lesser etheric body. Constellation grace has been earned in former lives through obedience to spiritual guidance. The ears are highly

sensitive constellation antennas for the lesser etheric body. The
Guardian Angel sometimes uses the antenna sensitivities of the
ear to guide and direct a person who has constellation grace. This
token of grace from the angels is a sacred grace; therefore, one
should be careful to be attentive to the *silent logos* pertaining to
this particular form of guidance and help from the angels. Silent
logos is freed by the act of contemplative listening.

If one has prayed for wisdom and guidance, and if he has perfect
alignment with his Guardian Angel, he will be fortified by angelic
directives. Sometimes he will be aware of *a warmth or a tingling
sensation in certain areas of the ears*. This is caused by the angel
sending his light to that particular portion of the body.

The constellation or nadis sensitivities of the ears are used by
the angels either to warn or to encourage and bless. If the tingling
or warmth occurs in *the lobe of the right ear,* the angel is saying
that one is fulfilling a certain positive action in the physical world.
This means that one has turned in the right direction and that what
he is doing is approved by the angelic worlds; it also may mean
good news or positive telepathies from physical persons. Should
he receive the tingle in *the orifice of the right ear,* his Guardian
Angel is telling him that he is to have an audible confirmation of
acceptable good, and that some form of praise in the physical world
will help him to spread his work. Should the tingle occur in *the
upper part of the right ear,* one is being shown that his prayers
have been answered, and that he is reinforced by heaven; that he is
on the threshold of doing something which will open grace for
him and his works; he is being given good news or positive
telepathies from the higher worlds.

When one feels a tingling sensation or warmth within *the center
of the right ear*, this is an approving signification that the angels
watching over his spiritual progress are working to screen out the
negative. This powerful asset of constellation nadis power is protective and is a form of timesaving grace. If one is aware and alert
he will come under this screening process of the angels. One should
be alert to these nadis stimulated velocities of approval on his *right
ear* or on *the right side of his body.*

If the harmony or guiding circumstance affirms the green light
for a place or location where one is to be, or to have a physical
thing one desires, this is experienced as a feeling of warmth in *the
lower tip of the lobe of the right ear.* If it pertains to a place or a

work of grace one is to receive, the vibration is felt in *the inner
opening of the ear*. If *the higher most exalted portion of the ear*
becomes intensely warm or electrified, one should know that he
has extreme approval for an act or for a condition. This invariably
denotes a spiritual blessing.

If the tingling or warmth occurs in *the lobe of the left ear,* this
indicates that one is turning in the wrong direction or is out of
timing to something material or physical; it also is a warning of
physical danger. When one feels a tingle or warmth in *the orifice
of the left ear,* he is being evilly spoken of by negative persons or
tongues, or he is on the verge of receiving unpleasant news or
communication from a negative source. If *the upper portion of the
left ear* insistently itches or tingles, this is the symbol that one
should pray to be protected from subtle, unseen forces; hc should
search himself to see if there is any cupidity or acquisitiveness in
his mind; it also is a warning of negation telepathies. The Guardian Angel is alerting the person that he is under a negative barrage
from the subtle worlds, and thus could have an accident or experience some unpleasant occurrence. The accent upon vibration in
the left ear is also to keep one from doing something wrong, or
beginning something that will be an unnecessary waste of time or
energy, or alerting one to negative or selfish persons whom one
will meet for the first time.

If the warning tingle comes in *the upper portion of his left ear*
while he is traveling in a vehicle, he is being warned that he is in
danger of an accident due to the carelessness of an approaching
driver, or some other form of accident caused by a person who,
expressing as a neutral field, could be used by the forces of the
dark to commit violence on one's physical person.

ELIMINATION SYMBOLS IN DREAMS

If one dreams that he is *clearing his nose or sneezing*, it indicates that he has stepped into inverted currents of the astral world,
and thus has opened himself to dangers of attack from the dark.

If one *clears his throat* in a dream, it is a symbol that he is undergoing a pressure initiation upon the logos atom of the throat.
He should be cautious in the days following the dream that he
speak only with the love logos, and with the silent logos wait to
speak in timing.

Coughing up phlegm in the throat in a dream means that one is overcoming the lesser levels of genesis; genesis elimination; emotional restriction placed by family or friends.

If one dreams that he is *weeping,* or there are tears upon his face, this indicates that he should be prepared for an approaching grief or loss of someone who has the power to wound or to grieve him.

If one is *nauseated or vomiting* in a dream, it indicates that he has reached an impasse in which he must eliminate the resentment and bitterness which have been stimulated by the bile of his hates and hostility.

To dream of *bowel elimination* indicates that one is overcoming and eliminating the poisonous memories and conditions of the past.

Toilets, so often seen in lower dream-level dreams, always mean eliminating the outgrown. A *toilet bowl* indicates that one is preparing to eliminate one's acts of the past.

To dream that one is *undergoing a bowel cleansing* while standing up to the waist in water is a symbol that he has had a Hindu life in which this practice is considered a sacred ritual. This symbology may also refer to the present life and tells the one dreaming that he is presently engaged in cleansing the soiled matter in emotions and thoughts.

To dream of *kidney elimination is* indicative that one has failed to use self-control and has need of discipline as to his lesser will.

When the male initiate experiences a *nocturnal emission* in a dream, this indicates that the Race Angels working with Jehovah are seeking to relieve and to purify the propagation compulsions working through him. When such dreams are accompanied by sensual pictures, it is a symbol that there are some degrees of lust yet to be mastered and overcome in the sexual nature of the initiate.

When there are *skin eruptions* on the face or any portion of the body in a dream, this is a symbol that one has injured his self countenance or image picture in the lesser etheric body, and that his ego is being penetrated by the fiery telepathic astral bacteria of the subtle worlds. Such persons will find that the Guardian Angel is telling them that they are subjected to some person or condition in the waking world depleting their self-confidence and vitality. One should remember that he should resist any person who would demagnetize his etheric vitality, for such demagnetization causes open wounds or penetrable places within his lesser etheric body. *Pimples* seen in a dream denote scars on the etheric body from repression and difficulty.

If one should be *born with a birthmark* on any portion of his body, he sometimes looks for and receives the meaning in his dreams. One may be shown in a dream that *a birthmark on the hand* may be a stigmatization of a former life action of grasping or taking. *A birthmark on the face* indicates that one in some manner has stigmatized his countenance through vanity or over-narcissistic love of the personal self.

All birthmarks are recorded originally upon the etheric body of the embryo. They come as a mark upon the physical body as a reminder of error or omission causing suffering to others in former lives.

To undergo *surgical operations* upon any organ of the body in a dream is a symbol that one is being freed from some mental fault or emotional obstacle standing in the way of spiritual progress.

If one is being *operated on for goiter,* he is having greed and envy amputated from his nature.

If one is having *a liver or gall duct operation* in a dream, he is being shown that hates or bitterness flooding his emotional will are being brought into control so that he may activate the higher will in his emotions.

If one is receiving *spleen surgery* in a dream, this indicates that he is preparing to be initiated into certain levels of ancestral memory and actions. He should also prepare for a new relationship to the demands of individuality.

If one dreams of having *surgery upon a sexual organ,* the ovaries, the womb, or the testes, this is a symbol that he should be prepared for certain external restraints upon his sexual expression, that he may become more conservative and reverent in the sexual act; such dreams can also signify self-mutilation in a former life.

If one is receiving *surgery upon the pancreas,* this is a symbol that he has entered into a corrective phase in his evolvement pertaining to his understanding of other persons and their motives, and also to overcome his failure to incorporate other persons into his own emotions.

EYEBROWS

When seen in a dream, *heavy eyebrows* growing close together toward the nose are a symbol of the Mars initiate who seeks to pursue his course regardless of obstacles.

Widely spaced eyebrows seen in a dream denote a benign person, more of an observer than an actor.

Bushy eyebrows overshadowing the eyelids are a symbol of reticent wisdom. When seen in a dream they indicate that one has come close to a person who has counseled many.

Arched eyebrows indicate incredulity and sophistication.

One eyebrow raised higher than the other symbolizes a person who is intellectually biased, or who is unevenly balanced in his emotions and mind; also indicates snobbery.

Thin or sparse eyebrows indicate over-frugality in giving or sharing of the self.

To see *the portal point, or centered star between the eyebrows* means one is opening the command center in preparation to hear the "audible sound."

EYELASHES

When one sees in a dream the eyelashes of a person as being *long, thick, luxuriant,* it is indicative of over-idealism.

When one sees *spearlike projectiles of darkened light* surrounding the eyes, he is beholding a sub-elemental, non-incarnate creature or an entity having contact with such entities.

FEET

To see *the feet in a dream or a vision* symbolizes progress, advancement, support, understanding. If *the feet are still,* they represent support or understanding; if they are walking, they represent progress.

When *the feet are walking on uneven stones*, this indicates that a difficult portion of the path now faces one. If the stones are smooth, this indicates that one will experience a recurrence of something of a familiar nature he has experienced in other lives. If the stones are sharp, this denotes a painful new and unfamiliar experience requiring sacrifice and self-restraint.

If *the feet are climbing rocks,* this indicates that one is beginning a new trial whereby he will master the art of vertical thinking.

When *the feet are supine or in a lying position,* this denotes a dying state or a state of inertia.

If *the feet are running with joy,* this indicates that one is close to his goal. If he is *running a race* with someone else, this indicates that the dreamer is to be challenged by a competitive person or situation. If one is *running from some shadowy pursuer* in a dream, this indicates that the dreamer has a feeling of having wronged another person and therefore must rectify his actions – for his pursuer is his own sin or guilt.

When one is *dancing* in a dream he is being taught the law of rhythm in the inner planes. Dancing in a dream also shows that one should learn how to relate himself rhythmically with close persons or fellow initiates. If the dancing is tribal, this indicates that one has yet something of the sensual tribal-genesis moods to overcome.

If one is *tiptoeing* in a dream, he should proceed in his affairs with tact and diplomacy.

If one is *jumping rope,* he is learning to use the lesser rules in life.

If one is *pole-vaulting,* he is being taught the power of levitation, that he may ascend over the tumultuous regions of the astral world.

If *one stubs his big toe* in a dream, it is the symbol that he is in danger of committing a social faux pas.

If one sees *a foot in a kicking position,* this indicates that the lower will is being asserted; if *kicking an object,* it is the symbol that he is refusing to face his own weaknesses and shortcomings, and is therefore emotionally immature. If *kicking a person with the right foot,* it indicates that he should search his heart as to revengeful tendencies. If *one is being kicked by a person,* this is telling him that he has misplaced his love or admiration.

If one is *tripping a person,* he is being shown that he is using the cunning side of his will.

If *one's foot is stepped on by a person,* it indicates that he has intruded upon the will of another. *If an animal steps on one's foot* in a dream, this indicates that he has overstepped the boundaries between animal and man, and has interfered with the Animal-Species Angels' work.

If *one steps into mud* in a dream, this is a sign that he is to be involved in a slander.

If one sees *the heel of the foot in a dream*, this indicates that he has made himself vulnerable, or has exposed himself in some manner to danger or condemnation. He is also being warned that he has a weakened place in his ego which makes him vulnerable to flattery. If one sees *the right heel beneath the foot,* it is a symbol that he will overcome his weakness and crush it. To see *winged heels* is the symbol of night-flight.

If one sees *the arch of his foot,* he is being shown that he is ready to overcome a situation.

If one's *feet are bare,* and there is a feeling of freedom and joy, it is the symbol that he has attained spiritual humility. If the feet are bare, and there is a feeling of embarrassment, it is the symbol that he is to be ridiculed or exposed.

If one's *feet or ankles are tied in a dream,* he is being shown that he is a prisoner of a situation, and unfree to act.

If there is *an open, bleeding wound on either foot,* it indicates that one has attained stigmata, and is now a true disciple of the Lord Jesus.

The right foot in a dream or vision is the progressive foot. If it is clad in a *golden sandal,* it is the symbol of spiritual progress; a *white sandal,* a symbol that progress is being made in spiritual purity; a *blue sandal,* a teacher to be met; a *pink sandal,* a devotional attitude will be observed.

The left foot in a dream or vision means one is lagging, even though he has spiritual potential.

The following symbols pertain to shoes on both feet:

> *Black shoes* – the one dreaming is being led into the dark path.
> *Green shoes* – one is making progress in health.
> *Dark blue shoes* – one is being led into the path of discipline.
> *Sapphire blue shoes* – one is being led into the path of mental illumination.
> *Brown shoes* – one is being led into the path of materiality.
> *Vermilion red shoes* – one is being exposed to psychical excitation.
> *Orange shoes* – one is being asked to fulfill an ancestral obligation.
> *Ruby red shoes* – one is preparing to walk in the path of integrity and honor.
> *Pink shoes* – one is being prepared to walk the path of devotion.
> *Boots* – one is protected from astral slime or soil.

To touch the feet of the Master in a dream indicates that one is saluting his own Master and surrendering his own will to God through the Master's will. As Mary of Bethany washed the feet of Jesus, her Master, so do all disciples recognize the feet of their Master to be sacred under God.

FINGERS (see Hands)

FOREHEAD

To dream of a *rounded forehead* indicates joyousness, joviality, generosity.

To dream *of a domelike forehead* beneath an enlarged skull indicates that one is expressing bigotry, egotism, fanaticism.

To dream of *a forehead shaped on square proportions* indicates that the person is a slow learner, but well organized.

To dream of *a narrow forehead* sunken at the temples indicates an ascetic nature.

To dream of *one having hair too low on the forehead* indicates that one is to receive a mental shock or some restraint upon his imaginative faculties; also indicates tribal-genesis tendencies.

To dream of *a band or ribbon on the forehead* is a symbol of restraint due to authority.

To dream of *being kissed on the forehead* is the symbol of an anointing blessing giving peace.

GALLBLADDER

The physical and etheric gallbladder bears the emotional brunt of disappointment and bitterness. In dreams it is the symbol of bitterness, or resistance, of failing to respond to love, of being frustrated in emotions, of damming up the inner flow between love and being loved.

If one dreams of the gallbladder, he is being shown the need to research his inclination to bitterness, to subtle resistance within his emotional nature. He should prepare for the humility initiations, and thereby gain humility. A dream of this nature is sometimes experienced as a parable or allegory. The one dreaming may walk in mud, in muddy water; he may see colors of soiled green or astral slime. In such dreams he is being warned by his soul that he must learn to forgive *"seventy times seven."* He is also being shown that he is placing a stumbling block or stone against his own progress.

All healing of the night to be manifested in the day begins in the etheric counterpart of the physical body. Dream symbologies are used by the soul to remind one to rectify his acts, emotions and thoughts. When one responds to symbolic guidance, healing begins in the etheric counter part of the physical body. Physical doors also open, and he will receive healing helps in the physical as well as in the spiritual worlds.

THE GIRDLE OF LIFE

The girdle of life consists of the liver, the pancreas and the spleen. The girdle of life is sometimes pictured to one dreaming as representing the unseen positive forces influencing life. To dream of the three as one indicates that the one dreaming is researching his courage as to will, life and light.

The liver in dreams is a symbol of emotional courage and emotional will. *The pancreas* in dreams is a symbol of life forces; for example, the form of man, or the blueprint design for man. *The spleen* is shown to one dreaming as a vitality source-maker or restorer of light and vital currents in the body.

He who offends or abuses the girdle of life in daytime neglects of the body will be reminded in dream symbols that something is awry in the triad balance of these three organs.

To use force on the physical planes as a means of expressing one's emotional will produces a weakening and a degeneration of the liver.

To refuse to participate in firsthand experience and association with other persons in the world results in a discordant function of the pancreas.

To be indifferent to the laws of Nature, to refuse to adapt and to use Nature's laws, to seek to detach one's self from Nature's vital restoring gifts, will set up armies of alien bacteria in the ether supporting the cellular system of the body. The result will be devitalization of the blood system controlling the cells of the body.

Dreams come to warn when one has offended the moral and ethical laws. To observe dreams on the soul, the religious and the spiritual levels is to enter into a foresight whereby one may accelerate his consciousness, and thus work constructively with his soul in the night's reflections and the daytime contemplations.

The Guardian Angel of sleep directs the dreamer to look into his weaknesses and his strengths. Though response is often delayed one will inevitably respond to what the Guardian Angel says in the night. For the Lord has said to each one: "All things begotten in the day and all things remembered in the night are my voice; and when obedience comes, healing comes as a winged peace, prompted by the Angels of Love."

GONADS

To dream of *the gonads* symbolizes that one is researching his sexual impulses and evaluating the necessity for chastity, purity.

HAIR

When one observes in a dream *the hair texture, thickness, color,* he is seeing a person who lives in the earth. He may determine what sort of person he is seeing by the vitality within the hair. Should he perceive *a woman with flowing blonde hair or with titian red hair,* he is beholding the temptress, and should prepare for a sexual trial.

When one beholds *the locks of the Cherubim Angels,* he is aware of nimbus-burnished golden light on the ringlet head of the Cherubim. He will have received nimbus Cherubim grace, and may look forward joyfully to a lifted sense of joy in coming days. His own nimbus grace will be seen by those around him with the inner sight.

When one sees *the balding head of the aged,* he is being shown that he is preparing to come under the tutelage of longevity wisdom, and should thereby develop prudence, character, faithfulness, veracity.

When one sees *black, wiry, bristling hair* in a dream, he is receiving tribal-genesis knowledge. He will thereafter better understand the origin of tribal-genesis. Extreme primal-fired psychic energy is used by such persons.

When one touches *a vibrant lock or head of hair* in a dream, he receives a transfusion of etheric fire into his own lesser etheric body.

Washing the hair in a dream reveals that one is cleansing the lesser etheric body, thus relaxing and neutralizing etheric energy static. Primitive atavistic dreams often occur to one who has yet to balance his moral nature. In these dreams one may see an ape or baboon, or persons whose bodies are *Esau-like, hairy.* Such dreams come to remind one that he should make more pure his ethic as to sex, and should search his motives as to lust.

To see *a thick head of hair* upon a person in a dream indicates that the one seen has a healthy lesser etheric body, or one who is immune to certain physical weaknesses and depletions.

When one sees *brown hair with tints of golden light,* this is the symbol of a highly evolved humanitarian.

When one sees *dry, unhealthy, listless hair,* this is the symbol that the lesser etheric body is demagnetized and cannot regenerate itself during sleep.

When one sees *glistening locks of black hair* with tones of blue, this is the symbol of a person who has a piquant sense of humor, plus a traditional exactness.

When one sees *hair dyed a fiery red with orange tones,* it is a symbol that the person is under the tutelage of astral subverted powers.

When one sees *healthy blonde hair,* it indicates fearlessness, warlike traits; also a supersensitivity as to pride.

If *hair is arranged artificially* in dreams, it symbolizes vanity and self-love.

If *oily hair* is seen in a dream, this is a symbol of the cunning mind; one is seeing a person with a large body who desires to force himself through small openings.

If one sees *a person tearing his hair,* it is a symbol of madness, derangement.

If *a person is seen combing or brushing his hair,* this symbolizes introspection and cleansing.

If *vermin are seen in hair,* this indicates fevers of an infectious or contagious nature. It is also the symbol of procrastination, licentiousness, amorality.

If *the hair is being shaved or cut,* this is a symbol of sacrifice, renunciation.

If one is seen to be *wearing a wig* in a dream, this is a symbol that he has two personalities; one he knows himself to be, and the other is a deliberate affectation or the desire to conceal something of himself.

If one sees his own *hair graying,* or the hair of another person graying, it is the symbol that time is running out, and that one must hasten to keep pace with the soul's demands.

HANDS

To *shake hands* with someone in a dream or a vision means that one is making a covenant. If *the hands are in a shadow* while they are being shaken, it means one is making a covenant with the dark. If *the clasped hands are in the light,* one is making a covenant and has agreed to accept the discipline accompanying greater illumination.

To see *a clenched left fist* in a dream or a vision indicates a threat; *a clenched right fist* indicates a need for firmness and a promise of protection.

To see *the outstretched palms of both hands* in a dream or vision indicates one's surrender, and his recognition of his own helplessness. To see *the outstretched palm of the left hand* indicates that one is in danger of being deceived. *The outstretched palm of the right hand* indicates that one is being asked to receive and to give more than he is presently giving.

Praying hands are the symbol of intercession from the higher worlds. When *healing hands* are placed upon an ailing organ or a weakened part of the body, this is the symbol that one is receiving heavenly, invisible healing helps.

FINGERS

The thumb is the authority finger. When *the left thumb* is seen in a dream or vision, it indicates force, aggression, dominance, tyranny. When *the right thumb* is seen in a dream or vision, it indicates that one is being initiated into the higher will, and therefore will receive certain lessons relating to the modification in the use of the will; and in time will attain spiritual authority.

The forefinger is the influence finger. When *the left forefinger of another person* is seen in a dream or vision, this indicates the danger of submission to hypnotic influence from the astral guru level or from some psychical person using hypnotic powers. If it is *the left forefinger of one's own hand*, he is being shown that he is using the hypnotic will to nullify the will of another person. When *the right forefinger* is seen, one is being given the assurance that he is under guidance, and that he is preparing to learn true discrimination.

The middle finger is the mentality finger. When *the left middle finger* is seen in a dream or vision, it indicates that one is using the negative side of his intellect. If *the left middle finger* is of another person, this denotes that one is exposed to the untrained thoughts of the person, or that he is receiving negative telepathies from an inverted source. *The right middle finger* indicates that one is using his mental faculties on a higher level, or that his thoughts are approved by the heavenly Presences.

The left-hand marriage finger relates to physical partnership lessons. To dream of a ring upon *the left-hand marriage finger* means that one has made an agreement to walk the left-hand path. *The right-hand marriage finger* relates to spiritual initiation, or spiritual marriage between the soul and the spirit; seeing a ring upon the right marriage finger indicates spiritual initiation. The following descriptions of rings pertain to *the right marriage finger:*

A *gold ring* indicates spiritual initiation and soul-grace.
A *diamond ring* indicates that one is being initiated into the logos of the higher self and into the eternal medallion surrounding the higher self.

Chapter 13

ETHERIC-ANATOMY SYMBOLS
Part III

I give thanks for a new tomorrow provided by the angel
who stimulates my soul's pattern and plan.

HEART

In dream symbols of etheric anatomy *the heart is the initiatory organ of love.* During the night's sleep the heart is sometimes perceived as having many corridors or portals. This indicates that one is undergoing the heart initiation, or the weighing of the many facets of love. When *the heart is seen shaded or in darkness,* the Guardian Angel is showing one that he has misdirected his love or in some manner has abused it.

To dream of *pain in the heart* indicates that one is involved in emotional struggle so that he may open the corridors of the heart. To feel pain in a dream indicates that one must alert himself to physical danger in health. *To be aware of the heart as an organ of the physical body* in the night indicates that one should search his physical tensions and relate himself to his karma as to love or his gratitude-attitudes toward love.

In dreams during initiation an initiate may be taken back to a time in which he was *the victim of heart sacrifice* as practiced by the Inca Indians and relive the terror of his experience. It is necessary in such dreams that one retain a cool detachment toward such reincarnation recollections so that he may recover the essence of the meaning of the era being shown to him. Often after such dreaming one awakens with rapid heartbeat.

In one instance noted in a dream interpreted by the author, a certain initiate was *shot in the heart* by a fellow disciple. This dream drama at the time was given to the initiate to warn him that a fellow initiate was to be used as a karmic pawn endangering his spiritual life. It is grace when one has a dream of forewarning regarding obstacles being placed on the path of evolvement.

HIPS

The hips, the second axis polarity of the body, are the symbol of poise, equanimity, and are the symbol of the sexual and personal will.

To dream that one is being *touched on the hips or thighs* – as in the story of Jacob wrestling with the dweller, or his initiatory contestant – is the symbol that one is being tried for higher degrees of genesis and should be prepared for the coming genesis initiatory trials.

To feel that *the hips are balanced,* and that one is rhythmically proportioned through the structure of his hips, indicates that one has come into a degree of self control. (The center of self-control is at the base of the spine.) Through effortless movement in walking, one comes to understand the etheric forces and currents. Etheric or free vitality walking during the day is the result of the etheric release received in night-flight action.

To receive *a blow on the hips* in a dream indicates that one must prepare to face obstacles of an ancestral or family-genesis nature. He should also be alerted that he fall not into the pit of a sex trial.

To see one wearing *a drape around his hips,* similar to Jesus' drape in His crucifixion, is a symbol of renunciation, sacrifice, suffering, pain, humility.

To dream of any sort of wearing apparel of ancient times, such as *a chastity belt,* indicates that one is in danger of amoral action in sex. The higher side of such a dream if the belt is worn by a woman indicates that she has worn a chastity belt in a former life. In dreams any *restraining fabric placed upon the hips* of a man or woman is a symbol that one is being taught to raise the primitive fire of the will at the base of the spine and the pelvic center into the spiritual fire or akasia.

INTESTINES

To see any portion of *the intestinal tract in a dream* symbolizes that one must be alert to relinquishing and eliminating.

To see *the rectal area* in a dream indicates that one is undergoing an initiation to overcome false pride and lust.

To dream of *a bowel movement* indicates that one has need to search his conscience as to guilt, and also that he should learn to eliminate soiled thoughts and attitudes toward the natural functions in life.

KIDNEYS

To dream of *the kidneys* means that one is being asked by his soul to research himself as to his personal will. He is also being shown the importance of self-control and self-reliance.

To dream of *the kidneys being active, or voiding,* indicates that one is eliminating impurities of the will, or releasing some emotional stigmas.

KNEES

If *one falls to his knees* in a dream and bruises them, it is a harsh reminder that he should pray more and observe reverent meditation.

If one is *kneeling in awe or reverence,* he has attained adoration and devotion to God.

If one should be *kneeling on stones,* it is a symbol that he has accepted a certain penalty, or is making penance and therefore rectification for some imbalance in his temperament, will and emotions.

Should one be struck *a sharp blow to the knees,* this is a symbol that he is being told by the higher worlds to come down to the level of surrender, to give up his self-will and to let God's Will be done.

If one is *kneeling in mud* or if he is *scrubbing a floor* on his knees, it is a symbol that he is learning humility.

If one is *genuflecting in a place of worship,* it is a symbol that he has the need to recognize mediation through the Holy Presences of heaven.

If one is *curtsying* to a person in the physical world, it is a symbol that he is acknowledging that the person has an evolvement more advanced than his own, and henceforth should accept without question the spiritual ambassadorship of that one.

If one is *kneeling on stairs or a prie-dieu,* he has begun to ascend the ladder of illumination through obedience and reverence.

If one is *praying on his knees,* it is the symbol that he is experiencing fourth-dimensional prayer in the devotional cloisters of heaven.

If one dreams that he is *praying in a church or a temple* in the physical world, it is the symbol that he is working that more reverence be expressed in physical places of religion and of worship.

If one is *praying on his knees with others,* it is the symbol of mediative prayer.

A person with knees drawn inward touching one another, commonly called *knock-knee,* is the symbol of seeing a person who has inner emotional timidity and outer emotional aggression; also the symbol of a retreatist temperament.

A person with knees moving outward, commonly called *bow-leg,* is the symbol that the one seen has psychic healing perception based upon ancient primal powers.

To dream of *knees that are straight,* in the line with the ankles and the hips, is the symbol of a balanced alignment between the first and second axis polarities of the body; the person seen in the dream is inclined to be less yielding to the wills of others.

When the soul of a person seeks to direct him toward a spiritual life rather than a religious life, *the Religious Dweller* of the former faith or vortice-pool of worship comes forth to telepathically challenge the person through the level of his reverence and prayer – the knees. In this, the person may be literally thrown to his knees or suffer physical injury to one or both knees so that the disciple-to be may search his intent and dedication.

Should a disciple receive *a slight or major blow or accident to the knees*, it is an indication that he should immediately enter into prayer and continue to *"pray without ceasing"* until that which is seeking to be said to him reveals itself. Such an incident is an alert from soul prompting and grace.

If a disciple is sincere in his dedication to a new vortice pool or place of spiritual instruction, and truly desires a higher degree of evolvement to be found in the vortice-pool, he should pray deeply and earnestly upon his knees. The following mantramic prayer may be spoken from time to time in prayer on the knees so as to aid the disciple to rededicate to serving in the Light.

Father, let it be Thy Will.
Let the past be resolved.
And *"Let the dead bury their dead."*
And in the name of the Lord Christ,
may I be instructed, guided and
enlightened, so that I may better
seek Thee, discern Thee and serve Thee.

*"Strengthen ye the weak hands, and confirm the feeble knees."
(Isaiah 35:3)* The knees are the surrender portions of the body. Prayer on the knees affects the reverence flame of the heart. The knees are the recipients of all of the fears in the thought and the emotions; thus, feeble knees are caused by the registering of fears in this life and in many other lives. Reverent prayer on the knees is the most direct way to overcome fear on any level. Therefore, if the disciple will pray upon his knees to have his fears removed, he shall be healed of fear.

Extreme weakness of the knees may be due to painful remembrance of shock, grief, loss. Apprehension and insecurity, especially as to physical and material security, cause a hypersensitivity of the knees. Reverent, earnest and sincere prayer reestablishes the rhythm of manifestation and will reaffirm one's faith on all levels.

"O come, let us worship and bow down: let us kneel before the Lord our maker." (Psalm 95:6) Prayer on the knees is the first phase of hierarchy work. When men pray toward the same purpose of good for the many, they have begun their first blending in mediation.

"...he kneeled upon his knees three times a day, and prayed, and gave thanks before his God." (Daniel 6:10) When the disciple or initiate reverently prays three times a day, he expresses the love fiat and seeks to manifest the rhythm of the first three fiats, the Will of God, the Life of the Father and the Light of the Christ.

LARYNX AND DIAPHRAGM

To hear voices of ephemeral beauty during meditation or dreams is to have opened the sound current on the higher aspects of the inner ear. To define the source of the voices heard is spiritual grace. To obey spiritual promptings produces immortal talents. To be subjected to the left-ear psychical nuances through the spoken word in waking or sleeping is tragedy.

Many in the world are victims of subtle inverted speech. The voices of evil play upon a fearful and unreceptive mentality, evoking actions of hatred and hostility.

The *larynx is a vibrational box* or organ of voice; its accompanying organ is the diaphragm. When spiritually used, the larynx is the creative *Hum pulse* or sound current for the higher will for destroying karma. When one unites his higher will with the Will of God, he sounds inwardly the humming, unmanifested arche-typal images into outward, tangible pure forms.

The diaphragm works directly with the larynx. When the dia-phragm is repeatedly agitated sensuously due to the ego's lower will, the larynx produces coarse, raucous and irritating voice tones and sounds. When spiritually used, the diaphragm, seated in the solar plexus crown, is the centralized cross-point through which the finer impulses of the emotions flow. If the emotions are nega-tive, they move into the diaphragm in a contraclockwise manner, and the primitive lunar brain in the gross fire of the lower action of the solar plexus is activated. If the emotions are on a high level, they move into the diaphragm cross-point in a clockwise manner, and the spiritual brain in the crown of the head opens to function.

Disobedience to the established laws of society, disregard for the property and individual rights of others, violation of God's law through willful deviation, ignoring the moral laws as given in the Ten Commandments, ridiculing the ethic established by Jesus, using speech profanely, slandering, gossiping with malice, mak-ing untrue statements, making weak covenants or vowing without intent of fulfillment, enticing others to support one's self-inter-ests, speaking mystically without clarity – all of these keep alive the primitive brain centered in the lower side of the solar plexus.

Pure speech is a manifestation and de-manifestation power. To use speech supported by the movement of diaphragmatic flow is to speak creatively. *Healing begins in praising.* Primitive impulses and irrational instincts are kept alive through self-preservation at the expense of others and through self-aggressive acts enforcing brutal cruelties upon the helpless and the weak.

When the diaphragm's action functions on the plane of self-love, the voice reverberates upon the ear of the hearer with oily nu-ances. The tones of the voice contain irritating magnetisms, and the tonal receptivity of the hearer is offended.

The larynx may be either a vibrating, creative speech organ or a destroying speech organ. If one has moved with the spiritual tides, his voice ceases to resound the primitive tones which create the chaos set up through raucous or ill-timed speaking.

When *speech is ruby-toned,* the larynx and the diaphragm are united in a perfected functioning; honor, justice and integrity en-ter into the voice. The larynx becomes an organ of health to the speaker and an inspiration to the hearer.

When *speech is golden-toned,* the pulsation of the soul at the crown of the head and the radiant point of the diaphragm in the solar plexus become one; soul logos is heard. The speaker inwardly hears soul-tones, and sounds them through his speech to the inner hearing of the enraptured hearer.

The diaphragm is a tonal sounding board gathering the tones of the senses, emotions and thoughts into a central or diamond point working in conjunction with the solar plexus. Until man lives at one with his soul's pulsation, the diaphragm will send the primitive tones of the senses and emotions into the larynx. The voice tones of the speaker will be colored by the soiled magnetisms emanating from the primitive brain.

In the winged creature, or bird, may be found two larynxes, one at each end of the trachea. In man the larynx and the diaphragm, while separately defined, are used as twin devices to produce speech.

The more spiritually perfected a man is, the purer the tones of his voice. One judges pure voice and true voice by how peacefully it falls upon his heart and mind; how it stirs and warms his spirit. As one gains spiritual power, the sounds issuing forth from his larynx will convey spiritual integrity.

Voice volume does not denote spirituality. Pure sounds and pure words flowing from a healthy magnetism, spoken with the desire to enlighten without offense, remain with the hearer. Such voices are heard as confirmers of what one has proven and also of what is desired in the better side of the soul.

The continued use of pure speech as a spiritual hearing instrument, or the hearing of the good and the recording of spiritual words unheard by the selfish, will in time give freedom to the diaphragm; voice volume will be increased by the creative sounder and sender.

To repeatedly dream of hearing *voices with subtle undertones,* or in night-hearing to experience words of insincerity and insinuation, signifies that one is using the lower emotions and the primitive brain rather than his rational or spiritual gleaming brain. After such experiences, one should resolve on awakening to speak with love, to fill his words with emotions free from pressure or force.

An inverted or contraclockwise diaphragmatic action stimulates the negative perception of the primitive brain, and one is subjected to entity visitation. *Subtle voices of derangement and envy* seek to seduce him and cause his spiritual fall. *The voices of discarnate entities* penetrate the sublevel of his hearing. *Satanically inspired voices* also stir doubt of the reality of God. These subtle, destroying voices are more often received by insecure, doubtful and indecisive persons. One who undergoes such initiations fears to release himself to sleep; he becomes unsure of himself and suspicious of others.

During the waking state, *to lend one's ears to falsity, slander or accusation* gives provocation to the primitive brain. When the psychic planes are opened by the zealous, intense or uninstructed, one can be influenced by soiled magnetic voices. Unfortunately, one can come under the magnetic, misdirected wills of self-interested persons in the astral planes and in the physical world – resulting in influence detrimental to the soul and to spiritual health. Through day-and-night initiations the pure in heart become pure hearers. They come to discern the ethic in speech motivated by a selfless will.

When one reverently seeks spiritual instruction, he learns to define the difference between a true teacher and a false teacher. He sees that one who *smacks his lips* to emphasize his words is dogmatic, dependent upon the theories of others rather than upon direct and proven spiritual revelation. He sees the speaker, who would glamorize his listener, as a person in reality pathetically insecure, enthralled by the sound of his *egotistical voice*. He sees *the austere speaker* as a fearful man who would be righteous. He sees the harm done upon the nerve reflexes of the listener by *staccato speakers* who chop their words; he understands them all to have psychical larynx diaphragmatic ineffectuality. He hears *a whining voice* and knows it to be the voice of a weakling and a wheedler who, through repeated pressures and irritations, achieves his ends.

The disciple makes a covenant to harmonize his emotions with love. He dedicates to think on true things, to seek to know true things, and to speak of them with faith, courage. The *"demonstration of the Spirit and of power" (1 Corinthians 2:4)* will enter into his entire being, making his larynx and diaphragm vocal vessels for God.

LEGS

The legs represent the will.

To dream of *a person walking* is the symbol of progress. If *a person is running,* it is the symbol of the need to accelerate one's progress.

An injury to any part of the legs is a symbol that progress is being impeded by outside restraints.

A dream of someone *sitting with legs crossed* is indicative that the one seen is shutting away the sentient fire ordinarily received through the soles of the feet.

If one sees himself with *legs crossed in yoga position,* he is being shown that he is contacting the saintly Bodhisattva levels.

If one sees *a scar or mark on the legs,* it is a symbol that he has a blemish on his will – a blemish which interferes with his progress; also it symbolizes memory of past-life chastisement for lagging.

If one sees *legs very hairy,* it is a symbol that he should avoid a display of primitive emotions.

If one sees *a leg has been amputated,* he is being shown that henceforth he must progress in spite of some added handicap or responsibility.

LIPS

The lips are the portals to the palate or the sense of taste. The lips are also the portals to logos, or sacred speech. When one abuses the sense of taste, his *lips are sensuous, voluptuous.* When one abuses sacred speech, his lips portray cynicism, scepticism.

Caustic speaking produces lips bereft of beauty. When one speaks words of love continually, his lips reveal an inner tenderness and charity toward all men.

To see in a dream *lips curled down at the corners* indicates lack of faith, depression, negativity.

To see *lips uneven and one corner of the lips tilted downward* reveals a person of a satiric nature; also indicates some wry experience may be anticipated by the dreamer.

To see *lips from which moisture or saliva exudes* indicates untamed lust and sensuality.

To see *laughing lips* of merriment shows that one has made contact with Cherubic joy.

To see *lips humming, singing, or whistling* indicates that one should be prepared for unexpected happy and rewarding instruction to come forth.

Quivering lips indicate that one is to experience a rebuff for certain deviation, or that one is preparing to experience the deepest grief of some nature.

To see *bruised lips* indicates that one will be corrected for speaking out of timing or out of turn.

When one sees *hands or fingers placed over the lips* in a dream, it is a symbol that one should keep silent and thus avoid being involved in a situation.

To receive *a chaste kiss* upon the lips, cheek, or forehead in a dream indicates that one is receiving a token of the Holy Spirit. If a kiss is received from a person known to the dreamer, and if there be any lingering sensuality in the kiss, it indicates that one should be alerted to untrained sentiments directed toward him by that person. If one dreams of receiving a chaste kiss from a fellow initiate or one who is approaching initiation, this indicates that the one kissing him is a fellow initiate known to him in the night ministry.

To dream of *kissing a person on the cheek* is the sign that both are on the same Light Stream and that they are doing the same degree of work at night.

When one dreams of *lips of another person* as open as if in pain, he is witnessing suffering and is becoming sensitized to a more tender reaction to pain.

If one's *lips are also open in weeping,* one should be prepared to share grief with another person.

If *the lips give the appearance of food being masticated,* it is the symbol that one is being instructed and alerted to his habits of diet and food and his assimilation of and digesting of spiritual and physical sustenance.

If one sees *streams of light proceeding out of the mouth of a Cherubim Angel* or of any angel, this indicates that the angel is working to de-manifest some seemingly unalterable condition.

LIVER

The liver is the symbol of the emotional will; emotional will initiation. In symbology *the liver is the organ of emotional life.* When one has a dream in which he is shown something relative to the liver, it symbolizes that he should research his emotional will. (see Girdle of Life)

THE LOINS (includes the Thighs, Rectum, Generative Organs, Lower Intestines and Hips)

In the Old and the New Testaments may be found a number of

initiatory experiences relating to the power of generation, propagation and procreation.

"For he [Abraham] *was yet in the loins of his father, when Melchisedec met him." (Hebrews 7:10)* This passage in the New Testament refers to prebirth initiation and catalyst association with Greater Beings. Even as Abraham knew Melchisedec previous to his life as Abraham, so do some highly evolved persons have prebirth knowledge of an association with Greater Beings.

"There were giants in the earth in those days; and also after that, when the sons of God came in unto the daughters of men, and they bare children to them, the same became mighty men which were of old, men of renown." (Genesis 6:4) The *"giants"* in this passage relate to the greater Elect known as the Great Immortals who now dwell in the spiritual worlds. These spiritual Beings with celestial powers were called *"the sons of God"* because they were conscious co-workers with Hierarchy in the beginning of the earth's creation. Such giants or Great Immortals projected themselves etherically into the earth after the Adam humanity had established their acts of generation or propagation. They cohabited with the daughters of men and produced others of the Elect of a slightly less degree in evolvement. Their children were to become mighty men, who had been great in other eternities previous to this earth. (See *"...which were of old, men of renown."*) Such men were to become in later lives the great prototypes, such as Noah and Abraham.

The reference to the *daughters of men being "fair" (Genesis 6:2)* indicates that they were virginal even as Mary was virginal, or that is, of a celestial rather than a terrestrial degree of evolvement.

Celestial evolvement pertains to those who have mastered certain degrees of Hierarchy evolvement in former eternity systems. Terrestrial evolvement pertains to having lived in other eternities similar to the earth.

"And when he [the priest] *hath made her to drink the water, then it shall come to pass, that, if she be defiled, and have done trespass against her husband, that the water that causeth the curse shall enter into her, and become bitter, and her belly shall swell, and her thigh shall rot: and the woman shall be a curse among her people. And if the woman be not defiled, but be clean; then she shall be free, and shall conceive seed." (Numbers 5:27,28)* Numbers, Chapter 5, verses 12-31 are Biblical passages which

portray the work of the priest in tribal-genesis with the Angels of Judgment and the Tribal Propagation Angels. Each sacred taboo contained a degree of cursing. The alignment with the Angels of Judgment and the Tribal Propagation Angels through the sacred taboos gave the priest in tribal-genesis the power of direct cursing. In this, persons who had committed adultery could be made sterile by the cursing of the priest so that they would not pollute the tribe with contaminated offspring. Protective laws through the Judgment Angels exist in some degree in every level of genesis. Where there is profane or lustful action in the generation powers, this is suffered *"unto the third and to the fourth generation." (Exodus 34:7)*

As men evolved through the ages into higher degrees of genesis, the power of cursing changed from the priest to the conscience of the individual. When this occurred, promiscuous and irreverent acts began to manifest sicknesses and painful ailments in the area from the thighs to the hips, or the region of the loins.

"And Jacob was left alone; and there wrestled a man with him until the breaking of the day. And when he saw that he prevailed not against him, he touched the hollow of his thigh and the hollow of Jacob's thigh was out of joint, as he wrestled with him." (Genesis 32:24,25) The *"man"* in this Biblical passage was the tribal-genesis dweller who touched the hollow of Jacob's thigh because the thighs are the initiatory center of the genes, generations and genesis. In Jacob's wrestling with the dweller the initiatory center of the thighs was shifted so that Jacob, in future lives, might embody in a higher degree of genesis. All persons undergo initiations through the area of the loins previous to a higher rise in genesis.

"And he said, thy name shall be called no more Jacob, but Israel: for as a prince hast thou power with God and with men, and hast prevailed." (Genesis 32:28) Jacob, through this dweller initiation and victory, received his sacred, genesis name of *"Israel."* In each transition between geneses a person incorporates a new, sacred name, or new impetus. Having died to his former genesis, he experiences a birth to the next stage of genesis, and thus is given new vowels and consonants in his name to express the coming genesis. Some examples in the Scriptures of name changes preceding a rise in genesis are as follows: Abram to Abraham; Simon to Peter; Saul to Paul. Jacob was called a *"prince,"* meaning an adept of the higher worlds. The man *"blessed him" (Genesis 32:29)* signifies that

Jacob's experience with the tribal-genesis dweller was consummated victoriously. Following this initiation Jacob met Esau, and their meeting was loving and harmonious – revealing that the tribal debts between them were resolved. (Genesis, Chapter 33)

Before Jacob had his encounter with the tribal-genesis dweller, he had begun his release from old tribal claims by detaching himself from the tribal possessivism of Laban, his father-in-law. Jacob received guidance in a dream to leave Laban. (Genesis 31:11-13) Laban also had a dream which withheld him from restraining Jacob. (Genesis 31:24)

Samson's compulsion to mingle his propagation stream with another tribe denotes the period in the Bible when men began to express the racial more than the tribal impetus within tribal-genesis. The marriage of Samson to a Philistine woman profaned his Nazarite vow and invoked upon him the seduction powers of the astral world in the form of Delilah and her people. Samson's great strength was made possible because of his alignment with the Race Guardian Angels. His strength as relating to his hair denotes the etheric and electric vitality of his lesser etheric body. The life of Samson portrays tribal intermarriage, jealousy and conflict. (Judges, Chapters 13 through 16) On learning that his wife had been given to his companion or friend (Judges 14:20), Samson's jealousy set up a series of initiatory trials. The loss of his etheric vitality through sexual indulgence with Delilah sealed him away from his communion with the Race Guardian Angels. The betrayal by Delilah, the loss of his hair and sight, and his slavery, all portray the initiate's sexual trial and exposure to dangers from the seductive levels of the astral world. In the time of Samson, intermarriage of persons of different tribes offended the tribal protective taboos and therefore produced insecurity and jealousy. When there is degeneration of love's action, there is the loss of the etheric strength and of the vision or perspective. The Samson trial or initiation is recapitulated in some manner by each disciple in his approach toward greater powers, as it is necessary for the disciple to overcome any remaining or adhering fleshly lust within.

David, in an initiatory trial, offended both the purification laws of generation and the Life Fiat in that he coveted the wife of Uriah and was responsible for the death of Uriah so that he might take unto himself Bathsheba. The result of his adulterous and murderous acts was the death of the first child from their union, as the law of an eye for an eye, or retribution working with the Tribal Angels of Judgment, condemned David for his inverted acts. When men pervert the generative laws with their lusts and their self-wills, the result is tragedy and death.

Solomon had the power of manifestation; therefore, he had the power to magnify and multiply his possessions on an extravagant scale. His life of polygamy, the acquiring of vast territories and great portions of silver and gold denote manifestation powers. Yet due to his self-indulgence, his taking unto himself the idols of his wives, he shut himself away from the greater initiatory powers. Solomon's life is the example of "so far and no farther," for some persons in the world may attain much wisdom but they lack the living life, or the communion with God, to enable them to use the powers of transubstantiation, or the power to have access to the celestial archetypes correlated to the core of the earth. This power is also known as the power *"to go in and out"* or to reincarnate at will as well as explore the inner planes with freedom.

The loins, being the center for the genes, generation and genesis, are the focal point for four genesis dweller trials: (1) tribal-genesis, (2) family-genesis, (3) self-genesis, and (4) the satanic dweller before attaining higher self-genesis and eventually cosmos-genesis. When a disciple is prepared to rise to a higher degree of evolvement, he undergoes a major initiatory trial within the area of his loins. When a disciple dedicates to live more reverently and to unveil the purified flame of the heart so that the soul may speak, the initiatory process begins. He may experience more than one state of former genesis' action in various manners: (1) through dream experience, (2) through health, (3) through associations in karma, such as persons in his life, (4) or he may be subjected to certain temptations presented to him through amoral and unethical persons.

Pain and suffering are more quickly invoked in *offenses against the generation act* than in any other act in the lives of human beings. The higher the genesis evolvement, the greater is the penalty for an amoral life. Chronic ailments, weaknesses and conditions centered in the thighs, the generative organs, the rectum, or the lower intestines are the result of some unbalanced generative actions of this life and former lives.

LUNGS

The lungs are a symbol of the spirit of life. When one dreams of the lungs, he is being reminded that the Father breathed into him the breath of life. He is also being shown that intolerance and prejudice are a suffocating and congesting influence. Peter *breathed on the sick* to heal them. When one sees the lungs surrounded by light, he has touched the power of the Holy Ghost. He is being shown that there is a sacred breath containing the power of healing and restoring.

NAVEL

To see *the navel* in a dream symbolizes that one is researching old Egyptian secrets pertaining to the care of the dead, and that one is researching the lower solar plexus levels of memories of the darkened side of ritual; also denotes the connective processes between mother and child. The navel is the center of the solar plexus. The solar plexus element is fire. It is the center for the primal brain where one sees instinctively. Negatively, the navel or solar plexus center is the symbol for greed. The positive use for the solar plexus is pure primordial sight, giving healing and vitality to the four bodies.

NECK

To dream of *a swanlike or arched neck* indicates that the person has certain passive tendencies and floats with the current of life rather than swims with it.

In dreams, *a goiter on the neck* is a symbol that one has hidden greed, also excessive envy.

A broken neck is a symbol that one is in danger of losing his mental poise; also means karma of past-life betrayals of the light.

A neck corded with muscles is a symbol of brute force, impenetrableness.

Double chins resting upon the neck symbolize that one has overindulgence to overcome.

To dream of *being guillotined* is a memory of a past life experience; a premonition of being cut off from consciousness.

A touch of force or anger upon the neck is a symbol that one is being subjected to inverted astral attacks.

To be *kissed upon the neck* is a symbol that one as yet has infant desires.

NOSE

All appendages of the body are used as antennas for the senses. The nose is the antenna for the sense of smell. It is an open corridor to the breath of life sent forth from the soul.

When one dreams of *the nose or the nostrils,* he is being shown something related to his life-sustaining attributes.

To be aware of *breathing through the nostrils* in a dream indicates that one is being initiated into the prototypal breath whereby he may learn charity and tolerance for the races; he also may be researching the soul-currents affecting the mind and the body; and also mastering the lunar and solar fire sustaining his ego and soul's action.

In dream symbology *the size and shape of the nose* symbolize ancestral inheritance. If one dreams of *a large and bridged nose,* it indicates that he has touched an ancestral memory revealing mountainous origins. If the nose is *sharply pointed,* it indicates that one has acquisitive ancestral inheritance. If the nose is *retrousse,* it is symbolic of greediness, love of sensuous things; also the symbol of irresponsibility. If *the nostrils are wide, flaring, and show signs of quivering,* they symbolize passion, hatred, force, anarchy. If the nose is *bulbous,* it symbolizes dissipation and vice. If the nose is *classic,* it indicates purity.

To dream of a nose without any distinctive characteristics indicates that one is in some manner overcurious as to the affairs of others.

Should one dream of *surgery to his nose,* it symbolizes that he is undergoing a correction for inquisitiveness, curiosity, intrusiveness.

When one dreams that he has suffered *a broken nose,* it is a warning that he has crossed the boundaries of safety in his desire to know more than he is capable of assimilating.

To dream of *a growth on the nose* symbolizes that one has assumed self-appointed honors which he has yet to earn.

When one dreams of smelling *a repugnant odor,* it is the symbol of scandal with unpleasant results.

When one dreams that he smells *a sweet fragrance* or pleasant perfume, it is a symbol that he has touched the Holy Presences of heaven and is being healed through the ministering fragrances of the saints.

When one smells *a sensuous perfume* in a dream, it is a symbol that he is being astrally exposed to adulterous levels of sensuality, or he may have opened one side of the *pituitary portal* of psychic sensitivity.

When one experiences constellation grace, or *an etheric touch, to the left nostril,* his Guardian Angel is warning him that his intuitional sense of direction is faulty. He is being advised by his Guardian Angel to analyze the prudence of his thought, motive and action.

When one receives the constellation *etheric touch to the right nostril*, he is being told by his Guardian Angel to go ahead; this is a "green light" signal from the higher worlds.

When one has *intense itching of the nostrils*, giving off *a feeling of pleasant anticipation at the lower tip of his nose,* he is being alerted as to an approaching event which in some manner has an important bearing upon his spiritual life.

When *both nostrils receive constellation ecstasy* simultaneously from the Guardian Angel, it is the symbol confirming an approaching blessing.

When one has a tendency to be timorous or subjective, his *left nostril opening* is smaller than *the right nostril opening.* When one has *a larger right nostril opening,* he is more positive as to his will and initiative.

OVARIES (same as Gonads)

PALATE, TASTE BUDS, SALIVA

Each organ and member of the physical body has an etheric counterpart. In dream symbols one may research the etheric counterpart of an organ or member of the physical body and thus learn the spiritual, emotional, mental and physical relationships to instruction, initiation and progress in evolvement.

The etheric structure permeating and encasing the brain enables one to use the vortices of light surrounding his mental atoms to think etherically while sleeping, and to see with clarity the cause of deviation from health in emotions, mind and body.

The physical palate has a hard threshold close to the lips. The soft palate lies in the rear of the cathedral-like arch of the mouth. When the etheric counterparts of the hard and soft palates work in unison, one has selective taste buds or right choice of foods; this maintains the physical chemistry of the body. When the etheric palates are separated in their functions, the result is lack of discrimination in choice of foods, or one has an excessive desire for rich and stimulating foods.

One can disorient the etheric palate by over-mental stimulation, or too intense concentration on some unpleasant emotion during consumption of food.

The etheric-palate functions become faulty when one is exposed during a meal to fearful incidents, to unpleasant scenes, or to irreverent conversation.

Holy gratitude for food, reverence in preparation of food, sacredness in consumption of food maintain the balance in the etheric palate.

In dreams *the palate is an initiatory symbol of the Holy Agape or supper with the Lord.* It is also a symbol for the lid upon the ark of the covenant. If the disciple has failed to understand the sacrament in the breaking of bread, his irreverent acts violating this sacrament will be disclosed to him.

Unmastered *gluttony* causes excess in drink, in smoking, in food, in conversation, in sex, in zeal, in works. If the conscience discloses the cause of gluttony, one is corrected through remorse or repentance initiations. When one has earned healing for gluttony, his Guardian Angel reverses the currents of the taste buds working with the saliva and palate, and one is then repelled by the taste and odor of alcohol; tobacco becomes over-irritating to the lungs and throat; foods excessively craved become nauseating. When one experiences the etheric repellings in the palate, the taste buds and the salivary glands, this is grace – and correction is imminent.

If one has retained gluttony in his nature, through initiatory dreams he is shown the penalty – *a famine*; or he sees that a fast is required of him, either through moderation in choice of foods or through an enforced removal of food caused by illness in the physical body.

PANCREAS

When one sees *the pancreas* in a vision or a dream, he is being reminded that he is one of twelve zodiacal prototypes. His soul is asking him to incorporate into his nature and temperament something of the eleven other prototypes existing in the world. When one dreams of the pancreas repeatedly, he is undergoing what is called *the shewbread initiation.* (see Girdle of Life)

SHINS

The shins are the telepathic receivers of new environments. *A sensitivity of the shins* denotes a fear of new environments or places. If one will contemplate the far-reaching results of healing mediation and its beneficial compensations, and blend with the sustaining helps in both the visible and the invisible worlds, he will welcome new environments as being part of his circumference and action in Light.

When the disciple dreams at night of walking in *pure or clear water to the level of the shins,* it is indicative that he is being prepared and insulated against negation, environmental telepathies of both the physical and psychical worlds. Should the water in the dream be *muddy or cloudy*, it is an apprehension warning from his Guardian Angel that the initiate is approaching some unpleasant experience which will stir him emotionally and confuse him mentally. A warning from the Guardian Angel will modify the impact of the experience and also will enable the initiate to discern what is speaking to him in his present phase of evolvement.

Pain in the shins denotes the disciple's unwillingness to face new environments.

SHOULDERS

Shoulders appearing in a dream symbolize that one is researching the first or highest axis portal of the body.

To see *shoulders broad and substantial* indicates that one is capable of carrying a karmic load.

To see *a hunchback* is a symbol that one has abused psychic will in a former life; in its higher aspect it is the symbol that one has been martyred through some form of inquisition brutality.

To see *sloping shoulders* is a symbol that one would prefer to have others assume his responsibilities.

Hopeless appearing, *drooping, tired shoulders* denote that one is overburdened.

To carry *a yoke on one's shoulders* is a symbol that one has denied himself and taken up his cross.

To be *touched upon the left shoulder* is a symbol of being directed negatively by a subtle force.

To be *touched on the right shoulder* is a symbol that one is being directed to the right-hand path.

To have the feeling that someone of a loving nature has placed his *arm around the shoulders* is a symbol that one will be upheld and supported in his efforts.

SINUSES

The sinuses consist of eight cavities in proximity to the indestructible atom in the center of the forehead. The word "sinus" is closely related to sinuous, meaning serpentine-like.

To dream of *weakness of the sinuses or pain* in this area indicates that one is observing the sinus function etherically, or that he is being alerted to the danger of astral pressure upon the sinuses. All horizontal portions of the body are subjected to gravity initiation. To suffer continually from sinus pressure indicates that one is in some manner exposed to astral horizontal bombardments, and thus defenseless against the harsh ebb and flow of sub-sensory movement.

In physical anatomy the sinuses are defined as air cavities in the skull opening into nasal cavities. In etheric anatomy experienced during dreams, the initiate learns that the eight sinus cavities are horizontal orbs and astral defenders of the body. When the etheric envelopes supporting the sinuses are weighted down by sub-sensory energies of the astral world, the result is ineffective mental action and irritation in the physical sinus.

The sinuses work with serpentine action to relieve the electrically charged fluids supporting the tissues of the brain. The sinuses correlate physically and directly to the lower intestinal tract.

When the sinuses are etherically weakened and uninsulated, the heavier gravity and atmospheric pressures fall heavily upon them, distorting their action.

Initiation through atmosphere and gravity is experienced in physical life and also in dreams. While dreaming, the initiate learns how to transpose into light the physical sub-energies pressuring the sinuses.

As one grows older, the astrally stimulated vitalities supporting the sinus action are lessened. The sinuses begin to be laden with the electrical aspect of gravity. The sinus etheric cavities in proximity to the temples and the ears begin to droop downward. The etheric energies supporting the sinuses are more fully exposed to the indestructible atom in the center of the brow. In later life, soul-action memory, imaging and visualizing become more sensitive in the highly evolved person. In the less evolved, the lining membrane of the sinuses suffers partial physical prolapsis. This accentuates an egotistical recollection instinct. Memory is then centered upon ancestral happenings, rather than spiritual events. For the highly evolved, the diminution of gravity electricity weighing upon the sinuses is a blessing; for the less evolved, it is limited action causing self-concern to the aged.

When dreaming of *researching the sinuses*, one often feels he is flowing upon a river winding beneath a castle (the brain); that all is secret, silent. To open the meaning of the etheric sinus sacred atmosphere supporting the sacred or golden fluid of the brain is to be washed in the celestial fluid of illuminative purification.

SPLEEN

The spleen works with the solar or sun energies as a light and vitality bringer to the lesser etheric body. When *the spleen is felt or seen* in a dream, it is indicative that one is in need of revitalization in the lesser etheric body. The spleen, on the left and vulnerable side of the body, can be also an open portal to the principalities and powers of the dark. During night-flight, invisible healing helpers work to insulate the left-side portal of the lesser etheric body so as to prevent psychical intrusion from the living and from the dead. When *the spleen is seen in pure light* in a dream, it indicates that one has earned the grace of insulation and protection. (See Girdle of Life)

STOMACH

To dream of *the stomach* symbolizes that one has a strong desire to be mothered, or has need to find security through the mother-principle. To see *the stomach encased in a blue, white or rosy light* indicates that one is assimilating his lessons, and that he is acquiring the quality of tenderness.

TEETH

To dream of a person with *sharpened or filed teeth* indicates that the person has a cannibalistic temperament, in that he is a vampirist, a destroyer of souls; he is abnormally overpossessive. This symbol also indicates that one is to be exposed to an amoral or degenerate person.

To dream of *large and well-formed teeth* is the symbol of hospitality.

To dream of protruding upper teeth or *"buckteeth"* indicates that the person has squirrel-like hoarding tendencies.

To dream of *losing one's own teeth* indicates that one is to die to himself. To see *another person losing teeth* is a symbol of approaching death for the one seen, or a relative of the one seen.

To dream of *several teeth missing* indicates that one has lost his vitality reserve through carelessness or poor stewardship.

To dream of *losing one tooth* means a death; the end of a situation.

To dream of *having a tooth pulled* indicates that one must undergo a form of painful sacrifice. *Extracting teeth* represents a death or a birth.

False teeth or dentures seen in a dream are a symbol that the one being seen does not have the sense of letting go or releasing.

To dream of *chewing or masticating food* with one's own teeth indicates that one is learning the art of assimilation.

To dream of being in the dentist's chair and *having teeth filled* is a symbol of karma being partly relieved or resolved.

To dream of a person with *the upper teeth being small and immature* – each tooth shaped evenly – is a symbol of a vampire-like person, or one who takes the vitality of others; a psychic drainer.

To dream of *a toothbrush* indicates that one should begin a cleansing of his speaking; a cleansing initiation.

THALAMUS

The archetypal meaning of *thalamus* in a dream may be interpreted as *the divine thalamus,* the great nerve station through which the Father principle makes union with the Divine-Mother principle in the skull of man.

The symbol more often identifying the divine thalamus is *the scarab of Egypt.* The lower part of the scarab represents the lower and higher unconscious; the feminine aspect of the Divine Mother. The lower subconscious represents *kali,* or the dark side of the feminine principle. The higher unconscious represents the Divine-Mother principle. The Father principle working through the upper portion of the scarab symbol represents pure spirit.

When one dreams of *a scarab*, he is being trained during dreams to balance the low and high of spiritual powers.

The thalamus-scarab symbol experienced in dreams will produce in the daytime life manifestations of spiritual balance through physical works or creations.

TOES (see Hands, Fingers; also Feet)

TONGUE

The tongue is the symbol of the two-edged sword; the symbol of logos; the symbol of the Spirit of Truth. When one has *an unruly tongue*, he dreams of the astral clamors and babel. He is warned that he is wasting his words. In the daytime life he will find that his words will either be unheeded or not believed. When one has been *indiscreet in conversation,* during sleep he is warned by his Guardian Angel to guard his words and to treasure creative speech. Through the creative word he learns to speak and hear his sacred name in the inner planes of the dream world. He learns also to speak certain key words of power, that he may reach into higher degrees of light within the night. The tongue is the organ of speech, and the means of communication in the physical world. When the tongue becomes an instrument for logos, it becomes a spring of healing waters, for the word of love is the healing word.

In James, Chapter 3, verses 3 through 11, one may learn from the apostle James of initiation through the tongue.

In night or sleep, if one dreams of a certain concentrated form of *speech instruction*, in speech or conversation, he is being initiated into speech through the spirit of the Holy Ghost, as one cannot be an instrument for the Holy Ghost until he uses his tongue in speech undefiled.

The thyroid gland is the center for the planetary logos of Mercury which rays its energy into the tongue. When there is an adverse Mercury, a retrograde Mercury, or Mars and Mercury are alien to one another, one is inclined to speak with sarcasm, bitterness, cynicism, malice. During planetary negative periods, bitter and doubtful thoughts may move into the tongue and the hearer is wounded, offended and repelled. Also one may be too talkative or prone to gossip in negative or retrograde Mercury periods.

When *the tongue is used for flattery,* the hearer is receiving an insult, as he has given his time and his listening to a liar and a cheat.

True words on the tongue, when heard by a liar, are offensive — agitating the conscience of a liar.

One should seek to record *words heard during a dream,* and the meaningful nuances sounding through the words.

When one is undergoing dark trials in the subtle regions of the astral world, he often hears *words colored by sneering, scoffing or scorn.* These trials seek to produce self-doubt in the initiate. If he

refuses to give up egotistical self-praise, he will invite the satanic
scorn-trials both in the subtle worlds and in the outer world from
persons he contacts in his daily life.

To be *glib with the tongue,* or impulsive in speaking, or to promise
something one knows deeply in his heart he can never fulfill, is to set
up an inverted action diverting one into loss of time and energy.

The disciple learns to use the organ of the tongue as an instrument of truth. In the higher initiations, he is shown *the spiritual
fire residing at the root of his tongue,* correlating to the pineal
gland and the higher aspect of the will.

The initiate seeks to *praise* true things, good things, clean things,
beautiful things.

In initiation the initiate makes a covenant and a dedication to
calm the waters of agitation through fearless speech. He learns to
abhor a divided tongue or over-mystical conversation. He is taught
the lesson of brevity. Through daily contacts with others, he is
shown that any word he might utter containing shallowness, irresponsibility, exaggeration, or fantasy will be met with some coarse
rebuff, as there is no greater reproving to a spiritual seeker than
reproof for wrong speech and wrongly timed speech.

The logos of the higher worlds is free to the initiate when he
once opens the door to the power of words stemming from the
power to will a word through speech into action.

In higher initiations, a taciturn initiate is taught a freeing logos.
An incessant conversationalist is brought face to face with the
necessity for brevity. The initiate is shown that a person who
mumbles his words is unsure of the truth in his words, and that a
person who speaks to excite through words is an exploiter.

The initiate becomes aware of his tongue as an organ of spiritual
power when he learns how to defend those who are inarticulate, or
absent and cannot speak for themselves. He learns to defend a fellow
initiate through speech, to speak for a cause in right timing. When he
finally has perfected a speech of holiness, he will speak for God, and
the Spirit of Truth will enter into him, healing, manifesting.

The Recording Angels and the Guardian Angels, with the Planetary Logos Angels, send their ideas and their impulses through
the will, memory and imagination of the initiate. When the tongue
becomes a spiritual organ, the initiate will speak for God, and the
Holy Ghost will use him.

TONSILS

To see *the tonsils* in a dream is symbolic of astral influence through thought and speech. When *the arch of the throat supporting the tonsils is illumined,* this means that one has the power to *"go in and out"* of the spiritual worlds with protection.

In the negative, the tonsils are the psychical repository of astral poisons.

UTERUS or WOMB

The uterus is the symbol of the birth matrix. To research in dreams the symbol of the womb is to unite with the mother principle and to gauge one's own attitude toward conception in the womb. The womb is a receptacle of receiving, as is the heart, and correlates to the heart. To dream of *being surgically operated upon* and *in danger of losing the womb* reveals that one has a fear of mutilation. The loss in womb power in a woman indicates that one has in some manner in a former life failed to respond completely to giving through birth.

Each organ of the body is the exact duplicate of an etheric organ in the etheric body. If physical surgery is performed on any organ, the etheric organ will remain intact and thereby keep the etheric equilibrium of the flow between all organs. Thus, if spiritual attitude is reverent toward the giving of life through the womb, one does not disconnect himself from the sacred aspect of giving life as symbolized by the womb.

Dream experience is one-third research or evaluation into one's own nature, also one-third instruction as to the mind, and one-third participation as to serving the light in the night. In research one sees himself as he is. Through dream instruction one is told how he may correct or bring balance to his life. Through actual participation or experience in dreams one retains the power of the action manifested in dreams and reproduces it in the outer or physical world.

In both man and woman *the genital organs* are used in dreams as symbols of one's own attitude toward chastity and non-chastity. *The most sacred gift of physical-plane life given of God is the use of sex.* When the sexual nature is abused or profaned or impure, it is out-pictured in the night by quelle or the subconscious.

In the spiritual life, *instruction in dreams begins with one's attitude toward sex.* If there is any particle of lust in one's nature, he is confronted with his *lustful tendencies* in dream experience. This occurs in the chimera and grotesque astral level of action in dreams, wherein distortions in his own nature are recapitulated, magnified. One awakens from lust-research dreams with a feeling of a sense of unworthiness. In time, he determines to use his body as a vessel of purity and love. In the physical or waking world, it is often the case that one appearing to have a chaste or controlled sexual life must yet understand his own inhibited, thwarted or stifled sex in his biological flow of life. More often, sexual prudery has been caused by former life non-giving.

The quelle monitor action of the night, or the higher unconscious, seeks to teach one of the sacredness of all functions of the body.

The quelle censor action of the lower subconscious in the night reveals one's karmic and also unknowing frailties through dream. The quelle mentor or the higher unconscious side of quelle shows the one dreaming how to correct and to accept life in its higher aspect of reverence and love.

Will man ever cease to use the function of dreaming? The answer is *No;* the function of dreaming is vital and necessary to the state of waking consciousness. The true and right attitude toward dreaming produces an unceasing, vital interflow necessary to the spiritual survival of the ego, the body, the emotions, the mind and the spirit. In dreams and dream guidance and instruction may be found the creative, vital, communicable flow of God speaking in all actions, human and divine.

WAIST

Symbols seen *below the waist* relate to earth and earth passions, and earth zeals of the will.

Symbols seen *above the waist* are spiritually creative and sacred.

When a Master is seen standing on the earth, and his full body is disclosed, he is an earth Master still connected with his gravity atoms.

When a Master is seen from the waist or heart upward, he is a Great Immortal released from the wheel of incarnation.

PHYSICAL-AILMENT SYMBOLS

ANEMIA – Memory of unhappiness in marriage.
ARTHRITIS – Repression.
CANCER – Derangement of sacred cell centered in the sacred atom of the heart.
CEREBRAL HEMORRHAGE – Too heavy conscience.

CONSTIPATION – Lack of cooperation.
DIABETES – Shutting away the remembrance of the soul's power.
EYESIGHT, FAULTY – Self-centered.
  Blindness – many lives of willful prejudice.
  Cataracts and tumors of the eye – a desire to have, out of
    timing.
FEVERS – Fear, haste, impatience.
GALL STONES – Unwilling sacrifice.
GOITER – Greed.
HEARING, FAULTY – Stubborn, noncomplying.
  Deafness – misdirected attachments; shutting away soul's
    guidance.
HIGH BLOOD PRESSURE – Lack of self control; pressure from
  outer persons.
JAUNDICE – Desire frustration.
LIVER CONDITIONS – Emotional frustration.
KIDNEY CONDITIONS – Lack of sharing; over-self-willful.
LEUKEMIA – Fear of relatives and close blood relationships.
LUNGS (Chronic disease of) – Race prejudice, lack of charity,
  intolerance, fear of association with others.
  Pneumonia – lack of assimilating of race pictures.
MARROW-OF-THE-BONE SICKNESSES – Karma heavier
  than usual due to intermarriage blood tie beyond the third
  generation.
MUCOUS IN BODY – Unresolved compulsions.
ORGANS, DEFORMED – One is out of alignment.
RECTAL CONDITIONS – Pride.
SINUS – Complacency and egoist pride.
SPLEEN (Sicknesses of the) – Detachment from the Image of the
  Father.
TUBERCULOSIS – Desire for freedom from race; overcoming
  racial aversions.
TUMORS – False sense of self-importance; going beyond one-
  self; overambitious.
TYPHOID FEVER – Old malignant condition of karma dissolved
  by fire of the body.

Chapter 14

FOOD SYMBOLS

*There is more to a day's ending than setting the clock and
drawing the curtains. There is the going forth into the soul's
Light-time and the joy of return to soul life, to soul peace.*

Food seen in dreams and visions can apply to many aspects of initiation. *The most important meaning of food pertains to the food of the sacrament of the Lord's Table.* Food as a symbol in dreams sometimes means that a lesson is being offered as spiritual food.

To eat food in a dream denotes one of the following: (1) spiritual nourishment; (2) training of the palate; (3) a need for certain nutriments within the food eaten in the waking state; (4) evaluation as to greed or gluttony; (5) a symbol to determine location and placement in former lives. Example: One seeing a tropical fruit in a dream would indicate that a former-life locale is being revealed; a tropical fruit, such as a papaya, would denote that one has made contact with a Lemurian memory, papaya being a Lemurian fruit.

> *Food, Warm* – to baby; to comfort.
> *Food, Hot* – overaggressive learning.
> *Foods, Sweet* – indulgences; obesity lusts for food.
> *Food, Unseasoned* – nonsensical ideas.
> *Food, Spilled* – unable to digest lessons.
> *Food, Cooking* – preparing for the sacrament.
> *Cooking bread* – preparing for the sacrament bread.
> *Food, Unable to prepare* – acknowledging oneself to be
> inadequate.

ARTICHOKES – An ordinary happening; a rose-shaped vegetable with thorns meaning discipline on mundane levels.

ASPARAGUS – Cleansing and healing of the kidneys.

AVOCADO – Healing oil of the spirit. *Avocado Tree* – the healer with anointing grace. The avocado is the feminine fruit of the East. Pomegranate is the masculine fruit of the East. The avocado relates to the Mary principle. Its oily texture signifies the oil of healing peace through tender, anointing love. The pomegranate is a passion fruit. It relates to the passion of the pain of the cross and the power of blood sacrifice of our Lord.

BEANS – All beans contain mineral fire necessary for steady memory and mind. Beans seen or eaten in a dream indicate that the etheric body is in need of mineral fire.

BEETS – Indicates need of iron.

BEVERAGES
> *Coffee* – hospitality; energizer; stimulator; to produce active thoughts; stimulates pituitary gland and adrenal gland; a psychic food.
> *Milk* – (see Milk) to receive of the lesser mysteries; also a strength token from Divine Mother.
> *Tea, cup of* – symbol of gossip; symbol of healing of separateness. A teapot is also a symbol of gossip.

BREAD – The sacrament of the Lord's body.
> *Gingerbread* – indulgence.
> *All sweet breads* – indulgence.

BUTTER – Cream of effort or rewards.
> *Too much butter* – indulgence.

CABBAGE – Need of calcium.

CAKE – Indulgence.
> *Wedding cake* – the initiation of the bride and the bridegroom through the Christ.

CARROTS – Need of vitamin A, also mineral ether.

CAULIFLOWER – An ordinary or mundane blossoming.

CHARD – Vital need of vitamin A.

CHEESE – The rewards of effort.

CHOCOLATE – Indulgence.

COCONUT – Primitive.

CORN – To reap a harvest; the inner ear to be opened; a certain level of feeling that can be used by the Father in guidance.
>   *Ears of corn* – new projects and persons; clairaudience.
>   *Seed corn (planting)* – starting new harvest.

CREAM – Indulgence.

CUCUMBER – Memory of Egyptian luxury in eating.

DUCK – Astral floater, migrator.

EGGS – Fertility; pregnancy; the great cosmic egg or new beginning in creation.

ENDIVE – Healing helps for the etheric matrix of the eyes.

FISH – Symbol of a Christ initiate.

FRUITS – Fruits grafted by man, such as the grapefruit and nectarine, are used as symbols in dreams to indicate that one has removed himself from the first source of original ideas, and is being mentally divided by counter idea-streams. Fruit may also be used as an allegorical symbol of temptation, or the eating of forbidden fruit and the gaining of forbidden knowledge. Ripe fruits on a tree symbolize grace. Green fruits symbolize grace to be earned. Dried fruits indicate condensed solar etheric sugar aiding blood and digestion.

>   *Apples* – gravity.
>   *Apricots* – a symbol of the first fruits, giving certain blessings, in the month of the summer solstice.
>   *Bananas* – symbol of the inner core being investigated.
>   *Blackberries* – symbol of an astringent.
>   *Blueberries* – symbol of spiritual manna; a Lemurian fruit.
>   *Cantaloupes* – lunar fire.
>   *Cherries* – symbol of happiness.
>   *Cranberries* – symbol of bitter herbs; sacrifice.
>   *Currants* – English red currants – need of vitamin C for over-carbohydrate eaters.
>   *Gooseberries* – symbol of a silly desire.
>   *Grapefruit* – symbol of a hybrid, or not being wholly rewarded.
>   *Grapes* – symbol of the harvest; of a redeeming sacrament.
>   *Honeydew Melon* – symbol of rewards.
>   *Huckleberries* – symbol of efforts and rewards.
>   *Lemons* – astringent and healing.

Loganberries – rewards.

Olives – symbol of Gethsemane.

Oranges – symbol of golden-fleece initiation, or gaining the prize of the soul.

Papaya – mending of the uterus etheric matrix; cleansing astral poisons.

Peaches – grace; a domestic token of grace.

Persimmons – symbol of autumn cleansing and rewards.

Pineapple – symbol of the crown of health.

Plums – symbol of joy in a ripe state; memory of an Eastern life.

Pomegranate – (see Avocado).

Prunes – symbol of frugality; a frugal table.

Raspberries – a balancer for protein indulgence.

Strawberries – a morning touch of night dew or a blessing.

Tangerines – a saucy child stimulating the old folks.

Tomatoes – a nectar for the lazy.

Vineyard – the symbol of germinal life, or expanding life in all substances.

Watermelon – humanity; the moon's fairest planting.

GRAINS – In the study of grains while dreaming, one learns of the Agrarian Angels, of the mineral fire within the grain, and of the storing-up principle in Nature and man.

The type of grain indicates locale or placement pertaining to past lives, or may signify location and placement in the present polarity action. To see or eat *barley and rye* in a dream signifies the Arabic, Syrian and Hebrew countries. Ireland and Scotland may be identified by the symbols of *rye and oats*. *Rice* would indicate China, India or any East Asian country. *Wheat* in a dream or vision symbolizes a Western country where wheat is predominant as a source of bread.

To be *harvesting grain* indicates that one is ready to labor in season. To *sow grains* means that one is a selfless server; however, this does not indicate that one will reap the harvest.

To eat of *fresh-baked bread* in a dream is a symbol of spiritual nourishment from the Lord's Table, blessed by His Son; it is also the sign of being fed in right timing, and of benefiting by one's labors and efforts.

To *pound or tread grain* indicates that one is being asked to serve in lowly tasks, that others may eat.

To see many *sacks or bags of grain* means that one is advised to be frugal, to store up against an approaching famine.

To see *grain in a field in flower* indicates that one is ready for a harvest of grace.

To see *an ear of corn* indicates that one is developing inner hearing.

To eat of any *dried beans*, such as lentils, indicates that one is facing a hardship period, and must rely upon food containing a high percentage of mineral fire to sustain the physical body.

Eating *leftover food* in a dream means one is being nourished by leftover ideas from old or antiquated religions.

Barley – to heal etheric matrix of the lungs.
Bread (see Bread) – to accept sacrament; comfort.
Buckwheat – to reap the good.
Cornmeal – to work with diligence; African memories.
Lentils – to fast.
Oatmeal – to be sturdy.
Soy Beans – survival.
Tapioca – to depend upon non-substance.
Wheat germ – to unite with the Angels of Planting.
Wheat flour – to be hospitable.

HERBS AND SEASONINGS (as symbols in dreams and for the etheric palate in health)

All health begins in the etheric body. Every organ and every cell of the physical body has its superior overlord or an etheric counterpart. In dreams one is shown the food, herb or seasoning needed to protect and to seal away any weakened processes of the physical body. If an organ is etherically weak or weakened by psychic drainage, the corresponding physical organ becomes weak or impaired. Thus, illness occurs in the physical body.

In dreams one should alert himself to these suggestive symbolic helps, that the etheric body may be recharged and stimulated by the God-given variety of helps to be gathered from the plant world.

All herbs work with etheric energies of the lower etheric body. Herbal helps – when taken with the idea that they are etheric helps to strengthen, nourish and balance the physical body – should be used in moderation with reverence.

When one is fully aware that true chemistry begins in the spiritual realm of healing, the Great Physician will send His angels to guide him as to the herb containing the essence for his renewing life-vitality.

When one receives the guidance to develop his selective palate, he will understand that the angels can guide him in dreams to a godly dispensary offering vigor and health.

All herbs and seeds are expanders of the selective palate. In the refinement and sensitivity developed in the spiritual life, one must give heed to the selective palate guiding him to the true and pure resources of life-giving vitalities supporting his spiritual life.

Allspice – preservative for the body of the dead and for the stomach of the living.

Anise – healing for the saliva.

Arnica – for fear centered in the emotions, affecting the muscles.

Basil – for psychic protection against the dark; an herb for overcoming negativity and the subtle dark.

Bay Leaf – a blessing from the saints.

Caraway – a healer of the etheric processes of the saliva in the mouth and the digestive processes in the etheric mold of the stomach; a cleanser of the intestinal canals. The vibration in a caraway seed removes the psychic toxins in the blood, veins and system supporting the abdominal region.

Cardamom – for healing of heart or love offenses; also healing of heart ventricles.

Cayenne – to set free etheric processes of calcium, healing the root pigments of the hair, and also the fingernails and toenails, that magnetism may flow freely from the hands; affects the etheric matrix of the thyroid gland, giving resonance and expansion to the sound of speech, also a tonic for the lower etheric body, circulating the energy canals of the lower etheric body. Cayenne is a solar food. Next to honey, it gives more support to the lower etheric body than any other food.

Chamomile – for the angel healing; healing of the eyes; for healing peace.

Chicory – to heal the etheric matrix over the kidneys, over the liver.

Cinnamon – for the healing of the lower mind, and slowing down the psychic energies of the lower mind; to overcome psychism.

Cloves – for neutralizing harsh speech or to speak true; healing of the throat etheric atom; service.

Cumin – for lapses and procrastination; for weakness of the pancreas.

Dill – for soothing a harsh will; for hospitality; settling the stomach.

Dulce – for the healing of fear and emotional timidity, affecting the etheric adrenal gland.

Fennel – for peace and for purity, affecting glandular cleansing.

Garlic – to exorcise dark spirits; sealing away the solar plexus.

Ginger (fresh) – for extending feminine reverence; healing of ovaries and womb.

Honey – for healing of the etheric body; strengthens the solar energy within the lower etheric body.

Horseradish – etheric pituitary matrix; to relax and expand.

Iodine – for the etheric vitality in the glands and lymph system.

Kelp – for the healing of impotence; for the etheric healing of sperm and ovum.

Lemon – etheric cleanser of the blood; de-personalizer of the ego.

Licorice – Egyptian memory; for circulation; for the nostrils.

Mace – for the spinal etheric nerve currents.

Marjoram – for healing of thyroid weaknesses; to overcome ego-pride and egotism.

Mint – for the healing of the undisciplined; mint is the healer of the etheric esophagus.

Mullein – for the solar plexus healing.

Mustard – to overcome moon-tide weakness occurring during the dark of the moon; the mustard-seed allegory.

Myrrh – for healing of outrage, of rectal weaknesses; to develop detachment.

Nutmeg – for overcoming material arrogance and to open the pineal gland; on the physical plane, should be used in moderation.

Oregano – for healing the etheric supports of the muscular system.

Paprika – for the etheric spinal nerves or nadis energy canals; to stimulate and to cleanse.

Parsley – pituitary etheric encasement; to balance the overflow of emotional depressions; also to set up etheric circulation in the kidneys.

Pepper (black) – to recharge.

Peppermint – to neutralize.

Pimiento – palate stimulator; brain feeder.

Rosemary – for the etheric brain; for illumination; to build reverence.

Sage – for wisdom to overcome suppression and chronic diseases such as arthritis, diseases of the bones and of the liver; to enforce will power.

Salt – for attracting the saints and their protection during the full and new moon; to heal the etheric matrix of the kidneys; to cleanse, purify and to protect from the dark.

Sauce, Hot – over-intellectualized attitudes toward instruction, desiring stimulation rather than wisdom; a desire to cover up an unreal situation; satisfying the sentient palate.

Spice – for courage supports, affecting the etheric centers of the ears, sinuses and the eyes.

Tarragon – intestines; for the healing of the etheric cambric covering, supporting the intestinal vitality.

Thyme – for the thymus gland and protection for the solar plexus.

Valerian – against psychic astral chimeras; healing for nerves and spleen.

Vinegar – to gain alkalinity balance and to gain control of energy processes in the digestive system.

Wintergreen – for charity, tolerance and for the insulating of the etheric matrix of the lungs.

HONEY – (see Herbs)

KALE – Vital need of vitamin A and calcium.

LEEKS – To be cleansed.

LENTILS – To receive prophetic powers from dreams; a Daniel initiation.

LETTUCE – To be tactful and intuitive.

MACARONI – To watch gross appetites.

MEAT – Animal sacrifice; research into killing as a sin; also means study of more advanced spiritual instruction.

MILK – Spiritual truths in their first phases.

MOLASSES – To be stuck in error.

MUSHROOMS – A psychic symbol of lower astral growth; psychic exposure to dangers for the dreamer.
  Poisonous mushroom – symbol of negation growth.

NOODLES – Chinese memory.

NUTS – All nuts contain etheric mineral fire healing to the mind. Nuts in a dream symbolize mineral fire needed for bones, cells, brain.
  Almonds – purest mineral fire; solar influences.
  Hickory – heavy mineral fire ruled by the planet Saturn.
  Macadamia – lunar etheric mineral fire.
  Pecans – heavier mineral fire ruled by Venus.
  Walnuts – relaxing mineral fire ruled by Jupiter.

OKRA – To be cleansed.

ONIONS – Tears.

OYSTERS – Symbol of retreatist in search of the pearl of his soul.

PAPAYA (see Fruits) – Papaya seeds symbolize mending of the stomach etheric matrix and upper intestine.

PARSNIPS – Discipline and sacrifice to overcome inflexibility.

PEAS – To open a secret.

PORK – Symbol of greed.

POTATOES – To be impoverished; also symbol of the need of earth minerals.
  Small potato – demotion of ego.
  Big potato – desire for authority.

POULTRY – Domestic; family-atom.
  Chicken – a young woman.
   Hen – old meddling woman.
  Rooster crowing – betrayer of the Lord.

PUMPKIN – Symbol of autumn.

RADISHES – To be cleansed.

RICE – To remember China.
    Wild rice – to recover Western Indian memory.

RUTABAGA – To struggle.

SQUASH – To grow with the moon.

SPAGHETTI – To indulge sentient appetite.

SPICE – (see Herbs)

SPINACH – To seek obedience.

STRING BEANS – To climb or to shape.

SUGAR – Indulgence.

SWEET POTATOES – To satisfy home supports.

TURKEY – Symbol of the autumn.

TURNIPS – To discipline.

VANILLA – Indulgence.

VINEGAR (see Herbs) – To cleanse.

WATERCRESS – To cleanse the ether in the blood.

YAMS – To protect.

YEAST – To expand faith, mind and powers.

ZUCCHINI – To unite with lunar ethers.

ALLEGORIES USED BY THE PLANETARY ANGELS

The *vineyard* is the symbol of germinal life, or expanding life in all substances.

The *hedge* is the symbol of the time factor through which man creates. The hedge imposes certain restraints by the law of cause and effect, a law put upon each man-made thing.

The *tower* symbol is the overlook, or foresight-wisdom given to those who will receive it; thus, they are in advance of other men in evolvement, earning authority.

The *wine press* is the symbol of extracting the essence from substances or circumstances; blessing when there is sorrow, or grace when one makes an effort; the reaping as a result of action. In spite of man's abuses of the law of God, he still receives grace *if or when* he makes the effort to tread the wine press; he shall reap the fruits thereof.

When the vineyard was planted, God had established the germinal life for the earth.

When the hedge was built, He established laws to protect man from self-destruction.

When the tower was created, He gave to man a way that he might rise, overcome.

When the wine press was set into action, He showed man the fruits of the harvest provided by self-effort.

Chapter 15

GEOMETRICAL, ALPHABETICAL
AND NUMERICAL SYMBOLS

The day's sunset is the star rise of my soul. O souls who work as I work, let us respond to the call and the music with joy.

Since the beginning of man's entry into the gravity world, geometric symbology has been throughout the aeons and the ages the means of his recovering his memory of the heavenly states within the heaven worlds.

When a person fails to understand the hidden meaning within symbols experienced in dream, meditation and spiritual telepathy, he is blind and deaf to what the soul is saying or seeking to interpret to him. Geometrical symbols experienced in dream, meditation and spiritual telepathy are in alignment with the Cherubim World, as all geometrical symbols are received through the help of the Cherubim Angels.

To better understand symbols as part of the soul's vocabulary, one should familiarize himself with the following outline which contains major root or key symbols.

Geometrical symbols are being used constantly by the soul, the higher self and the powers of Mediation. To open and disclose the etheric code within dream, meditation and spiritual telepathic experiences, one should look for the identifying pattern and form of the symbol. For example, if a tree is seen in a dream, the tree fulfills the symbol of the vertical line.

The telepathic instruction through such a symbol would relate to one's necessity to make pure alignment so as to think vertically and to use the will selflessly. The tree would also indicate one is entering into a discipline to achieve a passionless life, as the tree symbolizes passionless life – that is, the stilling of the sentient atoms.

All geometrical symbols are under command of the Cherubim Angels who initiate man into the mathematical processes in the use of mind plasmas or akasia.

The Seraphim Angels initiate man into techniques of light, whereby he comes in contact with the archetypal ideas as given by the Christ Mind.

The Seraphim Angels lead the mind of man into the six dimensions or the door to the Third Heaven, where he is then initiated by the Archangels into the archetypal light and the archetones under command of the Holy Ghost.

INVERTED TRIANGLE – Secrecy; dark; left-hand path; perverted; mystery; feminine principle; mystic nature.

TRIANGLE OR TRIAD – Transcendental consciousness; pure consciousness; perfected action; mediation.

CROSS – Initiatory trial; renunciation; assuming a burden; mastery of the cosmic forces.

SIX-POINTED STAR – Matter and spirit blended; marriage of emotion and thought; blended masculine and feminine polarity; power of transubstantiation.

CIRCLE – Physical sun; individual or ego; the soul; protection; the eternal. Three circles relate to three phases of understanding coming to balance.

CIRCLE WITH DOT IN CENTER – The eternal self; the Christ within; invisible sun; Celestial Angels' help; Archangel protection.

HORIZONTAL BAR – Magnetic currents of astral world; astral construction; emotional indecision; opposition from persons; animal kingdom.

SQUARE – Karma; abstract world; foundation; four bodies; obstacles; four dimensions or planes.

SQUARE WITH DOT IN CENTER – Release from karma.

FIVE-POINTED STAR – The holy stigmata communicableness between disciples; raising of the senses; telepathy; the command center between the eyebrows.

SPIRAL – Love; releasing from the lower bodies into the higher consciousness; a phoenix initiation; freedom from karma.

EIGHT-POINTED STAR – Jesus.

RECTANGLE – The form of man; the initiation through forms and objects; the door; a new experience; meeting the Master.

VERTICAL LINE – Alignment; the will; oneness; vertical thinking; discipline.

CRESCENT MOON – One week's time; lesser etheric body; feminine polarity; initiation into manifestation.

A TRIANGLE ABOVE AN INVERTED TRIANGLE – Manifestation; dimensional alignment; command of the elementals; knowledge of Nature forces; communion with Angel Kingdoms; power to etherically enter the interior of the earth.

ALPHABETICAL AND NUMERICAL SYMBOLS

All letters and numbers have a positive and negative potential in energy. If a person is highly evolved, he uses the higher values and the higher degrees of the letters and numbers. When a person is of lesser degrees of evolvement, he expresses the negative tone-value in the vowels and consonants.

All vowels contain spiritual potentials. All consonants contain physical-action energies. In dream symbols having numbers or letters, the vowels are A E I O U Y.

In dreaming of numbers, one should add the numbers. For example, to see the number 356 in a dream – 3 plus 5 plus 6 equals a total of 14. Fourteen is ruled by Neptune. The number 14 can also mean a period of 14 days.

One should gauge what is being said in a numerical dream by weighing the accompanying symbols connected with the numbers. Should he add the numbers 1 and 4, this would indicate the fifth month, or May, or may indicate the fifth day of the week, Friday.

A 1 Will, the higher will, Spirit
B 2 Analysis, separation, judge, benevolent
C 3 Trinity, consciousness, Light, wisdom, the soul, Guardian Angels
D 4 Karma, sacrifice, the builder, Cherubim
E 5 Mind, science, transition

F 6 Service, affection, love, healing, purity
G 7 Initiation, the key, spiritual ritual, Recording Angels
H 8 Mastery of astral, protection in dreams
I 9 Archangels, religious authority
J 1 Action, self-will
K 2 Sharing, exploring, pioneering
L 3 Love consciousness, naivete, timidity
M 4 Home, house, manager
N 5 Nervous, uncertainty, negative, tension
O 6 Sex, desire for love, courtship
P 7 Intuition, partners, legality, surgery
Q 8 Inner or unknown knowledge relating to the astral and psychic pressures received from the *eighth sphere*
R 9 Force, pressure, stubbornness, tradition, karma of family, lung condition
S 1 Beginning, dissolving, entrance
T 2 Trial, truth, trust, trick, indecision
U 3 Surrender, passivity, releasing
V 4 Conclusion of things material, accomplishment
W 5 Victory in mind, scientific mind
X 6 The unusual, the disturber, sexual subtlety, subtle telepathy
Y 7 Covenant, intuition in things to come, unusual dreams
Z 8 Evil, darker force, the withdrawing force, subtle electricity

DYNAMIC NUMBERS

10 – Hierarchy energies
11 – Physical mastery
12 – Discipleship
13 – Invisible disciple; the angels; saintly powers
14 – Neptune; imaginative powers
17 – Terrestrial-initiate
19 – The power of physical and spiritual manifestation
20 – Moon-initiate; mystical powers
21 – Sun-initiate
22 – Spiritual mastery
32 – Initiate
33 – Higher initiate

NEGATION OR SUBTLE NUMBERS

These numbers are the karmic determiners.
15 – Psychic negation
16 – Makes an electrical body for evil negations
18 – Sub-elemental magic
30 – Judas Ray; betrayal

THE NUMERICAL TONES THROUGH THE SOLAR SYSTEM

10 – Saturn
11 – Uranus
12 – Mercury
13 – Sun
14 – Neptune
15 – Venus
16 – Mars
17 – Earth
18 – Pluto
19 – Jupiter
20 – Moon
21 – Invisible Sun

Chapter 16

MISCELLANEOUS SYMBOLS

Tonight, with the help of my angel, I shall count my blessings, and tomorrow my works will be anointed. May my Guardian Angel of tomorrow go with me into the market place, and may I know his presence in my prayers.

ABACUS – The Recording Angel.

AIR – To dream of clear or pure air indicates that one has reached a level of releasing to things spiritual; means freedom, hope. To experience *breathlessness* in dreams indicates that one has stayed overtime in the inner planes.

AIRPLANE – The higher etheric body.

AMULET – Protection. Also, an amulet received in a dream can be an actual gift from the Master. The amulet need not be reproduced in the physical world, as it has been set into action on the etheric planes, thus affording unusual protection against the forces of the dark.

ANTIQUE – An outmoded condition or relationship; also can be an object to open reincarnation memory.

ATHLETIC SYMBOLS

Archery – determination.
Badminton – study in intrigue and repartee.
Baseball – the ritual of moralistic law.
Basketball – a sexual evaluation.
Games with guns – violent tendencies.
Games of war – researching one's militancy.
Gliding in the air – night-flight techniques.
Golf – the game of self-evaluation.

Hide and seek – self-delusion.

Hopscotch – childlike attitude toward the game of life.

Horseback riding – to unite with the animal kingdom for progress.

Hunting – ruthless nature revealed.

Ice skating – warning to take advantage of timing due to grace.

Jousting – a memory of medieval attitudes and actions.

Jujitsu – an Asian memory of aggressive attitudes.

Karate – a discipline of the will and the use of the akasic fluid in the body as used against the dark.

Parachute jumping – return to the physical earth after night-flight.

Pole vaulting – to rise over an obstacle.

Pool – a game of kinetic power techniques.

Running – will.

Scuba diving – research into the astral labyrinths.

Skeet shooting – symbol of atavistic inclination to kill or destroy.

Skiing – skills in night-flight.

Soccer – a Western Indian Atlantean memory.

Swimming – effort.

Tennis – to combat the adversary.

BABY – Represents one's spiritual age; also represents need to express tenderness; *birth of a baby* means birth to the higher self. *Delivery of a baby* means to be a midwife to the birth of the higher self of another person. To dream of *accepting an infant* means that one is accepting the birth to the higher self. To *refuse to take an infant* to raise in a dream means that one is resisting birth to the higher self, and therefore is denying the responsibility of the spiritual life.

BAIT – A snare or test. If the bait is on a hook as for catching a fish, it indicates that one must prepare to meet the great Fisherman (Jesus).

BAKER – Indicates a person who is a mediator for the bread of God, or one who prepares and offers the sacrament.

BALL – To learn to play the game. To overcome competitiveness. The use of the will with ethic.

BAREFOOT – Humility.

BASIL – An herb for overcoming negativity and the subtle dark.

BATTLE – Indicates that one is being conditioned in the use of his will. To be involved in a battle of war indicates that one is in the midst of karma relating to the masses.

BELT – Desire to be supported. Fancy or jewel-like belt – girdle of life; grace; protection.

BIBLE, OLD, FALLING APART – Religious or sacred concepts need mending, new supports.

BICYCLE – Use of the lesser will. Traveling on a bicycle in a dream means one is researching his level of human progress.

BIT, HORSE'S – Discipline; one is warned to guard his tongue.

BOOK, OPEN – Akasic record; soul's record; contact with the Recording Angel. *Large room filled with books* means research of the akasic records during sleep.

BOULDER – Inert mass of energy; a source of energy; spiritual potentials yet untapped; the unmanifest. If in one's path, means a karmic obstacle to overcome.

BOWKNOT – Mastery of electric and magnetic currents; symbol of yang and yin or male-female polarity – left side, feminine; right side, masculine; also, will initiation. *When tied,* means protection; *when loosed,* means one has forfeited his protection. In the positive, when tied means operating on duality level; when string is pulled, one has acquired androgynity.

BOWL – Baptismal font; the begging bowl; grace; purification; receptacle of one's love; hospitality; a mother symbol; a womb symbol of security and protection.

BOX
>   *Square* – to be confined or enclosed or imprisoned; karma.
>   *Rectangle* – a coffin or death.
>   *Round* – womb.

BREAD – Life substance; sacrament. If given by a person, this is the bread of life as a healing agent.

BRIDGE – Bridge over chaos; passageway to the Master; overcoming the astral abyss.

BRIDGE (card game) – Persuasion forces; use of cunning mind.

BROKEN CUP – A disciple's fall, or failure to be a disciple of the Master.

BROKEN DOLL – Means one has lost his illusions; also is preparing to research and reevaluate his ideals; he is being told that his idol worship is finished.

BROKEN STICK – A person with a brittle nature; inflexible; broken by life or karma.

BROKEN VASE – Indicates one has damaged his etheric body and is in danger of intrusion from the dark.

BUBBLE – Astral delusions stemming from an infatuated heart, self-love, emptiness. *Faces seen in a bubble* are astral entities floating around a person with mediumistic tendencies.

BUILDING, MARBLE – A symbol of Venus initiation. *Star above Hall of Wisdom* indicates a Venus light supporting the Hall of Wisdom.

BUILDING, UNFINISHED – Something yet to be resolved.

BULB – Eternal life; immortality. A flowered bulb indicates spring.

BUTTON – Safety; protection.

BUY – A lesson in exchange of energies.

CACTUS – A miracle.

CANDELABRA, CRYSTAL, OR GLASS – Higher astral world insulation.
> *Seven candlesticks* – initiation into the seven astral planes and the use of the will; to rise above the astral into the Spheres of Light or Second Heaven.

CANDY – Indulgence; need of discipline.

CANE OR REED – Discipline. *Bamboo cane* means the presence of the Master or Bodhisattvas. The Master is near. Be prepared for initiation.

CAR – Higher etheric body. Any vehicle means higher etheric body. *An old car* means antiquated ideas. *Old woman tries to get into dreamer's car* – old woman represents the past. If refused as a passenger, one has passed the test and has overcome the burden of the karmic past.

CARDBOARD – Unsubstantial, uncertain ground.

CARDS – Psychic and magical forces.

CARRIAGE – Indicates spiritual transportation earned from past-life grace.

CASH REGISTER – Learning the law of stewardship or of selling all to meet the Master.

CASKET – A symbol of death to the old life. A *jewelled casket* indicates grace.

CAULDRON – A melting pot of purification; martyrdom past-life memory.

CAVE – Womb; the heart portal; also the initiate's inward home. Touching the archives. *Whirling cave* means contact with the great sound current and heavenly planes.

CHAIR – Support. *Teacher in a chair* means he has passed away or he will pass away. *Person in a chair* means not using his will.

CHALICE – Soul; sacrament under Christ; heart symbol initiation.

CHAMOMILE – For healing peace.

CHARIOT – Levitation powers under Elijah's blessing.

CHESS – The royal ethic; rules for the royal path.

CHILDREN – To dream of children repeatedly is a sign that one has begun his night serving and is meeting probationers to the Path while in sleep.

CLOCK – Timing; also Recording Angel reminder. Hands on the clock identifying time are revealing the timing of an event. The hands pointing to three o'clock relate to a third day, a third week, a third month or a third year, etc.

CLOTH – *Yards of cloth* indicate the silver cord. *Odds and ends of cloth* indicate that one must mend the silver cord and the etheric body.

CLOTHING

> *Bridal gown* (a woman clothed in) – initiation of the feminine polarity being united with the masculine polarity to become a bride of Christ.

Coat – protection and insulation.

    Fur coat (frayed) – abuse of conversation or logos.

    Fur coat (in hot weather) – out of season; impractical; lesser etheric body too highly charged; psychic drainage.

    Fur coat (old) – symbol of outmoded or worn-out religious or political ideas.

    Great coat– traditional; on the defense against new ideas.

Clothing, brown – over-materialistic.

Earrings, diamond – grace in hearing true; inner hearing.

Garment, striped – change or transition of a spiritual nature.

White or gray garment – indecisiveness due to karma.

Garment bag – physical body.

Gloves – service; warning to be tactful.

White gloves – clean, pure hands.

Handkerchief – healing; magnetic vehicle for healing the impossibles.

    White handkerchief – spiritual dreamer will have small miracles of healing.

Hat – a teacher.

    Black hat – a dark guru.

    Lace hat – a teacher of spirituality.

    Chef's white hat – a teacher of diet and health.

Jacket, covered with stones of many colors – higher astral or emotional body; a Joseph's coat.

Necklace – a symbol of spiritual royalty; also a symbol of rare spiritual powers.

Nightgown – higher etheric garment.

Robe, bath – warning of physical weakness or health.

    Monk's or nun's robe – memory of a monastery life.

Sandal – indicates willingness as a disciple. If worn with difficulty or hesitancy, indicates reluctant feet, or some conflict in clarification.

Shoes, white (see Feet) – spiritual, pure intent of dedication. To lose shoes in a dream is a warning to be careful of losing the spiritual path and the resulting progress.

Slippers, pink satin – pure love; true devotional progress.

Socks – world progress on physical plane.

    Indigo socks – telepathy from the Masters, assuring the disciple of his progress.

> *Stockings, gray* – depressed thoughts due to non-use of will.
> *Stole* – a mantle; protection.
> *Suit, dark blue* – Saturn-ruled; means a slowdown in evolvement and more discipline; with odors, means the physical body needs purification.
> *Sweater* – lesser etheric-body protection.
> *White sweater* – spiritual insulation.
> *Vest, white* – a spiritual breastplate; a shield of insulation.
> *Uniform, white* – an invisible helper or healer of the night.
> *Soldier's uniform* – a Mars Angel assisting a person who is in danger.

CLOWN – To be confronted by a clown in a dream indicates that one feels himself to be a figure of self-pity. The Cherubim Angels use the symbol of a clown also to tell the dreamer that he is refusing to face reality. To play that one is a clown in a dream indicates that one feels he has been duped or made ridiculous.

COFFIN (bare or wooden) – Means death to the little self; also fear of physical death.

COINS, GOLD – The soul's effulgence in the higher etheric body.

COINS, SILVER – The moon's power; lesser etheric body; the law of earning and spending; worldly affairs; negative Judas-mind current.

COLLEGE – Dreams of college or university mean the night schools in the Second Heaven or Spheres of Light, or initiation levels of dreams; also Hall of Learning in First Heaven.

COLUMN – Uprightness; an upright condition or person; wisdom; a support; also a Master in the Hall of Learning; an incorruptible initiate; a teacher, a guru or Master.

CONCH SHELL – Inner hearing; the eternal sound current.

CORD – The *Brahmin cord* worn by Brahmins; a tie between persons on the path. If the *cord is untied*, it indicates probation; *worn as a necklace*, indicates full sainthood. If *held in the left hand*, indicates punishment; *in the right hand*, the beginning of will initiation. If *worn around the waist*, indicates monastic repression.

COUCH – The lesser etheric body in sleep.

CRATE – A study of form, or research into *maya* (matter) and the causes within form.

CROSS, GOLDEN – Indicates soul power through renunciation. *Cross seen in fire* indicates a fiery trial to consume the negatives of sensuality. *Golgotha cross* means sacrifice and resurrection. *The Cross of Jesus crucified* reveals a soul contact with the crucified Jesus, giving resurrection power.

CROSS ON A HUMAN FORM – Indicates a saint. Cross seen in light means sacrifice glorified.

CUP OF TEA – Symbol of gossip.

CUP OF WATER – Discipleship; called by Christ.

CURTAIN
>*Lace curtain* – etheric body; the Divine Mother symbol of protection.
>*Pink curtain* – emotional initiation; an emotional veil over one's eyes; a mystic mind veiling away reality.
>*Stage curtain* – a new action or drama in life.

DANCE – Inner night emotion evaluation of the rhythmic tides of one's sexual life; also a lesson in the necessity to observe rhythms in spiritual life.

DESERT – For the erasement of egotism, one is facing one of the greater polarity initiations of which there are four: desert, ocean, mountain, city.

DESK – Contact with the Recording Angels.

DICE – A fate action in use of kinetic energies; a belief in fatalism; a warning against gambling away one's destiny.

DOOR – Jesus; opportunity to serve the love fiat.
>*Golden door* – inner-plane instruction.

DRUGS – Satanic deviators; unreality; seeking escape way from reality; a warning in dream to master one's desire for intoxication or excitation.

DWARF – A by-product of sub-genesis caused by many lives of deviation. A dwarf is the result of karma made through an over-exalted opinion of oneself. To see one in a dream is the symbol that one is being thrust backward in the genesis scale.

EARTH – *Freshly plowed*, indicates that one is working with Nature to fructify the earth. *Eroded earth or soil* indicates that one has sown his seed on sterile ground. *Wet earth or mud* indicates that one must extricate himself from an unsavory situation in health, in mind, in morals. Earth is the symbol of the earth mother or Nature, an aspect of the Divine Mother.

EARTHQUAKE – The Holy Ghost; a warning that one's world will be turned over, and that one's former conceptual bliss has come to an end; also to be shaken free from evil or weakness.

ELEVATOR – Night-flight. To dream that one is *going downward into the earth in an elevator,* and knows not to open the door because strange creatures are standing outside, indicates that one is in danger of being exposed to frightening elements in the astral world; also indicates that one is passively giving freedom to the overflow of the subconscious mind. If *the elevator is rising,* it indicates that one is ascending into the higher planes of consciousness during the night's instruction.

EMBROIDERY – One is sewing or creating the tapestry of his spiritual garment.

FACES – *Angelic*, a study of the angels; *astral*, exposure to the existing subtleties of earthbound entities; also research into the elemental planes of the astral world, viewing the sub-born or astral forms never having birth in the physical world. To see *the divine countenances* in the dream is to unite with the Bodhisattva instruction and to become aware of heavenly countenances and presences. One must have moved over the tumults of the astral world to unite with the holy countenances.

FAN – To be cleansed, to sift, to purge and to cool off a heated emotional or mental atmosphere.

FEATHER, WHITE – Sacrifice. *Feather with blood at its tip* indicates martyrdom. *Feather on a quill* represents the Recording Angel who is telling the dreamer to write what he sees and hears in Holy-Spirit experience.

FENCE – Protection, insulation; also signifying one's limitation within a confinement area. *White*, protection; *old*, abuse of privilege; *brick,* materialistic protection; *wooden*, protection by Nature.

FERRY – Crossing over from materiality into the spiritual or from the physical into the inner planes. Also preparation for the last journey in the physical life into death.

FIRE – Purification, initiation. If controlled, one is protected during cleansing. If out of control, one is being warned of violent results due to hatred. Also indicates sickness with fever.

FIREWORKS – Symbol of ignited ideas.

FLAIL – Self-persecution or being persecuted for carrying the light. Sadistic, satanic contact.

FOREST – The maze of oneself; also contacting a Rishi instruction from a forest guru or Master – one is being told that he is entering into a form of retreat consciousness.

FOUNTAIN – Woman Master.

FUNERAL – Preparation to gauge death as a necessity; also instruction to fortify one against the fear of death. In some instances, dreaming of a funeral can be prophetic, preparing one for his own passing and can also be a sign that one is learning of death rituals and their meaning as an aid to the soul in the state of death.

GLASS – Insulation from lower astral world. When one is encased in glass, he is insulated from lower astral currents. Window or glass indicates protection; also, witnessing and receiving astral-plane knowledge without karmic consequence.
> *Broken glass* – the end. Magnifying glass means stepping out of the lower mind; breaking out of the boundaries of the lower mind and the magnified senses.
> *Glass receptacle* – *"a cup of cold water in my name."* One is receiving grace from beyond the planes of the astral world.

GLIDER – Effortless night-flight by a trained initiate.

GOLD – Spiritual power; spiritual reserves; reward from the level of the soul.

GRASS, GREEN – Healing pastures, peace; dry means rejection, also a dead life force.

GREASE ON THE FLOOR – Soiled and uncertain foundation; warning to control careless emotions. Too much *oil on the skin* means parasitical and sensual nature. Person with *over-greasy complexion* indicates hostile atavistic person.

HAILSTONES – Fearful karmic situation to be thawed out and resolved.

HAIR – Virility. If *luxurious*, indicates good health of lesser etheric body. If *dry, oily, coarse, over-thick*, indicates malformation of the lesser etheric body. *Dry hair* indicates over-timidity and hypersensitivity. *Oily hair* indicates stubbornness. *Coarse, thick hair* indicates hostility and aggressiveness. Color of hair in a dream signifies the degree of genesis. *Titian hair* indicates astral tendencies in a racially aware person. *Blonde hair*, appearing on a woman to male dreamer, indicates the temptress. *Blonde hair* seen on a male by a woman dreamer indicates a messenger from God. *Brown, black or auburn hair* seen in a dream relates to the following: *brown*, self-genesis; *black*, tribal-genesis; *auburn*, higher self-genesis. *Luxuriant hair on the skin* seen in a dream indicates tribal-genesis tendencies in the person seen. *Weird hairstyles* are seen on astral forms in the night, such as wild, uncombed tresses. *Orange colored hair* is an astral elemental color. *Matted hair* is indicative of laziness, unreliability. *Hair braided in many braids* indicates overzealousness. Angelic hair is seen always as filled with pranic light. To dream of seeing *the hair of an angel luminous in light* is to receive a blessing of vitality.

HAMMER – *A carpenter's hammer* represents Joseph, the father of Jesus. *A household hammer* represents the need to correct a neglected family situation. In a dream, to be *using a hammer for pounding* – as on an anvil – is to be shaping and molding one's own aggressiveness into pliability.

HEDGE – Protection; if one is inside the hedge it means negative limitation.

HILL – The high place of exaltation; indicates a necessity to climb and to make an effort on the path.

HINGE – To understand the cause upholding and supporting one's instruction.

HOOFS – Symbol of Satan, a satanic force or one having mesmeric powers.

HOOP – *A hoop of fire* indicates a challenge affording danger; a trial by fire. *A metal hoop* indicates that one is to be hemmed in and disciplined.

HORN – *Conch sound* indicates summoning of the Host. *A horn overflowing* indicates bountifulness. If empty, one must yet earn to secure prosperity.

HOSPITAL – Research in the night in the precincts of healing. Indicates that one is preparing to be a night server or healer in the night. Can also be prophetic symbol relating to one's own need to care for the body.

HOTEL – A symbol of transit or temporary state of consciousness; indicates that one feels disoriented and displaced.

HOUSE – A house with a pleasant domestic aura or atmosphere as seen in a dream indicates spiritual approval of one's own effort to make life pleasant for others. Also a mark of grace and assurance that one is to bring his personal house into order. A house in which more than one person is seen to be living indicates that one is gauging or weighing his relationships in the family-atom with which he is affiliated in the physical world. A house experienced in a dream having *one or more floors* relates to the bodies of the person dreaming. For example, *the basement* represents the subconscious mind. *Downstairs* dreams always relate to old karma of tribal or family-genesis. *The first floor* relates to one's everyday contacts in the physical world; also, to one's outer or objective consciousness life, and of his way of thinking on the physical plane. *The second floor* relates to one's individuality or ego, as one thinks himself to be; relates also to one's secret vanities and use of the will. *The third floor* relates to the mind and its functioning as a vehicle of higher consciousness. *The attic* relates to one's pride and also to hidden resources yet to be seen, stemming from the soul-powers. To repeatedly be in a *house familiar to oneself* and to dream over and over of this same house indicates that one is researching his own emotions and desires, or that he is seeking to find his real self which inhabits the habitation of the soul.

To dream of a house produces nostalgia in the waking consciousness. To long to know oneself and to yearn to unite with the real, one dreams over and over of *a house having rooms yet undefined and unexplored*. In such dreams one is aware that these rooms exist and is always seeking to find the door or entry whereby he may go in and dwell, and thus expand himself.

A house of several floors requiring an elevator can also mean that one is exploring the many mansions of heaven or planes in the First Heaven and Second Heaven. In such dreams one is usually accompanied by a presence which may be an angel, a night server or a Master. In some instances one may be accompanied by more than one presence, especially if he is going into higher reaches of the building. This is indeed a grace blessing in night flight.

A house can also represent the four bodies: the physical, the etheric, the emotional and the mental. *Balconies* mean regions above the astral world; overlook onto dramas of initiation. *Balconies or mezzanines* represent specialized instruction in the night in which one acquires spiritual techniques, skills and gifts that he may extend the time limit of his instruction; that he may become a mediator in the physical world; and that he may go in and out with freedom in the First Heaven and the Second Heaven. He must have extremely loosened vehicles while in the waking state to master these spiritual techniques. In time, such initiates are free to go in and out of the body in the waking state. Extended time freedom in night-flight comes only to him who has received these specialized skills under the direction of a Master.

To be in a house of God or church duplicated in a night vision or dream shows the one dreaming that he is visiting the Second-Heaven or Hall-of-Wisdom precincts called Shambala. One researches his own worship in the great Hall of Sacraments where all religions are interfused and blended. In Second-Heaven night initiation one learns what the true sacrament is and also learns that worship on earth is but a shadow of the true body of worship in heaven. While traveling at night to the Second-Heaven Hall of Sacraments, one learns that all religions are interconnected necessary bodies, that men may keep their soul covenants with God.

A basement represents the subconscious mind; residual karma yet to be resolved. One goes into a basement in the night's sleep preparing himself to meet old karma in the outer or external life. He also learns something of his own faults or guilts in basement-like planes in the night. The arid vaults of the subconscious are opened to him, that he may condition himself for the painful processes exacted in the resolving of karma. Any dark secret place giving off atmospheres of revulsion, of pain and of suffocation experienced during dreams relates to one's unwillingness to come out of the dark of the hidden side of his nature.

To dream of the *rooftop of a house* and *jumping off the roof* indicates that one is returning to the physical body too abruptly. To feel that one has been in a state of falling just previous to awakening from the state of sleep always indicates that one is in need of training so that he may have an effortless return to the physical body on awakening. To feel that one is severely shaken up or in a trembling state before awakening is caused by a sudden return to the physical body. The silver cord being over-taut causes a severe yank or jerk to the physical body.

The color of a house is important in a dream. *A pink house* indicates love and protection in the domestic scene of the waking consciousness. *A white house* indicates stability, public recognition, purity in the outlook of home environments. *A brown house* represents material prosperity; *a red house,* danger; *blue house*, mental security; *unpainted house,* neglect of stewardship. A stone house indicates that one is secure in his trust. *A brick house* denotes that one is a steward or shepherd of his physical and domestic life. *A trailer house* symbolizes that one is living as an air plant with no roots emotionally or mentally.

Subdivision of houses indicates that one has a lack of home consciousness and that the family-atom security is being filtered out.

A porch of a house in a dream means a temporary plateau, giving a new overlook; also indicates an invitation to enter in and to explore. To be in *an entryway before the main door* of the house means that one has yet to be accepted as a disciple. Dream of a person coming up to a porch means a new or unexpected event in the life of the person coming toward the porch. *A house afire* means consummation, purification, renunciation.

The chimney of the house indicates the soul of the house. *The hearth* in the house indicates the Guardian Angel watching over the house. *A fire on the hearth* indicates that the life in the body, or the house, is functioning as a living force. *The window* in the house in a dream indicates that one has limited vision influenced and controlled by domestic situations. Seeing through a window in a dream identifies the one seeing as having a beginning of reality. *A house without windows* indicates that one is self-engrossed, seeing materialistically only within the physical planes.

HOUSEHOLD SYMBOLS

Bathroom – indicates that one is in a state of cleansing and eliminating.

Bedroom – a conjugal scene related to one's sex attitudes; also a scene of retirement from clamors of the day. Childhood bedrooms remembered – a desire to return to security. Bedrooms disordered indicate emotional irresponsibility. Bedrooms fragrant, clean, orderly, indicate one's attitude is balanced as to life, death and birth.

Bed pillow – symbol of security, support; if over-soft, symbol of sensuality.

Broom – a new lease on life.

Chimes on door – be prepared to meet the special guest, or the Christ. In the negative, be prepared for a message of death.

Cooking vessel – warning to watch diet and health.

Dining room – a symbol of hospitality, of family-atom association; also of the Lord's Supper.

Dinner bell – indicates timing to be corrected in domestic life.

Duster – refusing to accept surface evidence as being true.

Linen – sheets, pillowcases, quilts – all indicate that one is preparing for comfort, covering. When clean, indicates purity. When soiled, indicates sickness.

Living room – indicates a special place for mingling with loved persons.

Mop – to meet issues with force and industry.

Parlor – a symbol of prestige, appearance, a front put on to deceive or to delude.

Phonograph – symbol of banked recordings or telepathic directives waiting to flow into the outer mind.

Radio – symbol of the heart center, of being receptive.

Refrigerator – a reminder to keep on ice or to remain cool or to not be impulsive.

Silverware – symbol of etiquette, refinement, luxury.

Telephone – an alert to be ready for conversation with the inner planes; also a symbol of telepathy.

Television – instruction from the Master.

Wallpaper – covering. Type and pattern indicate one's reflection of ego; also reveals hidden desires.

Washing machine – to give someone else a job of cleaning up one's affairs.

HOVEL – A symbol of spiritual poverty. A warning that one should open his faith to purity of the body, of the emotions, the heart and mind. A fear symbol denoting that one has not spent his grace wisely. Any form of *soil, filth, or disorder* seen in a house while dreaming is a reminder that one must come into discipline on all levels.

HYPNOSIS – One can be hypnotized during sleep when his karma leads him to certain regions of the astral world. Here he meets the left-hand path gurus who work under Satan's direction. Love of self, abuse of spiritual power will draw one into the satanic caverns of the lower astral world. The dark gurus or shadowed brothers use the hypnotic, mesmeric powers to transpose the will of an egotistical person into a powerful self-deception of self-sufficiency. Egomaniacs upsetting the world have subordinated themselves to the hypnotic, subtle directions of the astral underworld. The allegorical story of Faust selling his soul to Mephistopheles is a true allegory based upon man's desire to become greater than God.

Hypnotism on the physical planes has negative results in dream life and in the state of dreaming. To submit to hypnosis on the physical plane is to subvert oneself and disconnect him from his own symbolic dream flow. One subjected to hypnosis in the waking state comes under the dream symbols of the one giving the commands and suggestions through hypnosis. Such persons dream in disorganized symbolic sense. No relief, therefore, is given to them in the state of sleep. Mixed dream symbols induced by human rather than soul commands produce incoherent thought patterns for the day. True and clear dream symbols produce a mind and thought action supported by pure and true willing. Hypnosis either in dreams or waking upsets the pure flow in dream symbology. The high suggestibles received through mantrams and meditative alliances do not intrude upon the will of one dreaming. Through the speaking of mantrams one can clear the field for sleep, that he may enter into the most deep sleep or the fourth dream veil where he experiences the greater dimensional consciousness. An ordered sleep experience produces an ordered outer life.

Every person is sacred to God. One should go into sleep knowing that he is a necessary particle of consciousness making up the supreme consciousness. It is necessary for God that each particle of consciousness shall be a free, uninhibited consciousness. As each day's waking consciousness should add to one's superconscious state, so also must the night's sleep provide addition to learning, knowing and being.

> *When night skills and day skills are even, one is no longer driven. He is free to dwell within eternal light, made equal in day and night.*
> *Let no man take thy will or twist thy consciousness. Magnify thy mind through the inward sight fixed on God. And thou shalt have dreams of peace, of joy, of realization. Thy virtues are counted in the night, that thy works of the day may give a way to fulfillment in the light.*

ICE – A frozen condition, limitation. In a dream to see *ice on a growing thing,* such as a tree or plant, indicates that the substance of life is not being used freely. To be in a place of ice *surrounded by ice* indicates that one has to thaw out his emotions. *Walking on ice* indicates that one has slowed down his progress. The dreamer must be prepared to thaw out and let the Son of Life warm him, that he may flow into the one life.

ICE CREAM – A symbol of indulgence, of wanting all things pleasurable. Ice cream is used in dream symbols by the Masters to warn the disciple that he is yielding too often to the sensual nature.

IDIOT – A symbol that one is on the borderline of doing or becoming imbalanced. A warning to keep one's mind and will fixed on God.

IMBECILE – A misshapen karmic result caused by wrong willing and rebellion. In the lower astral planes in dream life one often sees *misshapen and malformed persons* to warn him that powers of the mind, when abused, produce distortion and deformity.

JESTER (see Clown) – Also relates to one who has cultivated wit, so as to distract others from knowing of his own bewilderment and suffering. In a dream a jester means that one must alert himself and become less artificial in his thinking.

KEY – In meditation and in dreams when one sees a key, it is a sign that he has reached the threshold of the door. If he will make the effort, he will find the door containing the lock. A key can also mean that one has found the cause and the answer to his problem. The key is a symbol very often used by the Master to signify that the disciple is ready.

    Keys – to see a bunch of keys indicates that one is opening more than one dimension simultaneously. He should be prepared for many initiatory trials in the offing. Through such initiations one opens vistas to greater knowledge. Keys also represent the opening of the mysteries.

KILL – To dream of killing, proof of latent hostile and aggressive tendencies dangerous to the outer peace.

KNIGHT, WHITE – A protector or a Guardian Being over an initiate.
    Knights – karmic powers on the chessboard of life.

LADDER – Spiritual ascension to the higher worlds; also represents the kundalini.

LEASH – To dream that one is restrained by a physical person, or that one's freedom is threatened.

LEERING – If in a dream one is being leered at or mocked in the night and made to feel that he is subjected to satanic humiliation, one should look in his environment as to his guilt-laden associations.

LIGHTHOUSE – A lighthouse or a tower in a vision indicates that one has contacted a Most High Saint's protection. One of these Saints is Saint Barbara.

LIGHTNING – Indicates instant karma or retribution for wrong acts of the past. To dream of *thunderstorms and lightning* indicates that one is to be faced with uncontrollable situations created by karmic tension. To feel that one is *being driven by a storm*, he is being shown by the heavenly dream monitors that the storms of the senses are being intensified so that he may become aware of the Presence of God and His protection.

LOCK – Symbol of making all secure. To experience a dream panic, thinking the *lock has failed* to be fixed, shows the one dreaming that he has neglected the spiritual aspect of his nature providing protection. To feel that the *lock has been turned by a key* in a dream indicates that one is being assured that he is protected. To dream of *burglars breaking a lock* indicates that one is being shown he has failed to use ordinary precautions against the forces of the dark. These precautions are prayer, reliance on God, good stewardship.

To encounter *a thief opening the lock* indicates that one must watch his own lack of responsibility. The thief is in reality his own lower nature seeking to steal from him his true higher attributes protecting the house of his spirit.

LURING – If in a dream one is being led or lured off the path of morality and spirituality, the Divine Mother is warning him that challenges are to come regarding sex and possessiveness.

MACABRE – A macabre symbol or death visage indicates that one has fallen victim to his fears and that he should pray to overcome superstition, unnecessary doubt and dread. Macabre symbols are used by the Death Angels to warn of loss, death and disaster.

MALLET – Symbol that karma is ready to be invoked; some discipline to rectify the karma is being required of the disciple. To dream of *the mallet or iron hammer of Thor* indicates that the world is to be given a purging, a lesson, in some great catastrophe such as tidal waves, volcanic eruptions, floods, plagues. As men come now to the end of the kali-yuga materialistic age, the hammer or mallet of Thor will be seen in dreams by those who are attuned to the world-soul action.

MARRIAGE – Indicates that one is being initiated that he may unite with his higher self. *To meet the bridegroom* in the night indicates that one is under Christ Jesus' blessing. To *be a bride* in the night is to make union with the higher self. The marriage symbol in a dream is the most powerful symbol of all symbols, for it is an assurance that one has truly entered the path or the walk in light. *To refuse marriage* in the night, to have *torn or soiled veil or garments,* to be in *a disheveled atmosphere* indicates that one is profaning his soul powers and delaying the marriage or union with God. As long as one is in an earth body, his dreams will seek to lead him through the many doors and corridors of initiation. The marriage symbology defines one's state of evolvement and attitude toward the spiritual life. *Birth, death and marriage* – these three symbols are used over and over in the initiate's life to define his placement in the divine plan of his soul's progression.

MASTER – To dream of *a man's voice* or of *a man helping one* in a unique and significant way should alert one that he is under the direction of a Master. However, the dreamer should ask that such voices of the night be voices of light under the Christ. An initiate knows his Master's voice and remembers it in the night.

MATTRESS – *Lying on a mattress* in the night indicates that one still has some attachment mentally to his lesser etheric body and physical body in the night and is thinking of himself as physical rather than spiritual. Lower-grade dream symbols in which one thinks himself to be totally physical, not recognizing that he has a finer body, occur in the dreams of the uninitiated. One will in time come to know that he has other bodies besides the physical, gravity body of the earth. Some persons are similar to children who hold onto a blanket as a symbol of protection in the night. These hold onto their physical, fixed symbols of assurance. Thus their dreams are filled more with *materialistically oriented symbols.* The finer the body in dream experience, the more sensitive, ethical and beautiful are the dream symbols experienced in the night.

MAZE – A labyrinth in the astral planes. If one is emotionally disorganized in daytime action, he finds himself in the *astral labyrinth.* He faces the *chimera mirrors or mirages* of astral repetition. Symbols are distorted in unequal magnification. One awakens from such dreams exhausted, feeling a sense of futility. To dream that one is *trying to catch a train,* or *packing a suitcase,* and is never able to catch the train, or he is running to catch the train as it is leaving – this is a labyrinth astral dream caused by emotional disorganization.

MENDING OR DARNING – Mending or darning a garment or any physical object indicates that one is agreeing to set out on the task of retracing his steps. The garment or object in the dream used as a symbol holds the code key to what one is mending. If he is *repairing a piece of wearing apparel,* it indicates that he is working to revitalize one of his bodies or vehicles. If he is *darning his socks,* it means that he must mend his will actions. If he is *repairing something in a house or a building,* it indicates that he is overhauling his outer world appearances and personality.

MIRROR – One encounters the mirrors in the Hall of Judgment in dreams. Here he sees himself as he appears to others. In deeper aspects of initiation these mirrors in the Hall of Judgment will reveal to him the erroneous side of his karmic soul-record. In the night one becomes his own judge and jury in the Hall of Judgment. However, even though he is not aware of this, he is always accompanied by his Recording Angel who permits him to see only that which is related to his lesson in the present time. Before one can obtain the soul power of dream cognizance, he must enter into the mirrored recesses in the Hall of Judgment. Sometimes one is exposed here to a chain of former lives, that he may incorporate their meaning into his mind in the life of the present. The Hall of Judgment is located in the Hall of Learning. One is cleansed when he accepts what the mirrors reveal to him. From this comes wisdom to forbear and to forgive.

MISSILE – Leaving the body at night.

MONK – Symbol of renunciation or adoration. *A monk robed in brown* seen in a dream indicates division in spiritual groups, societies or fraternities. *The brown monk* is a cowled, divisive, astral agent, appearing only when a group is ready to be initiated and sifted. *A monk in white* indicates a White Brother. The White Brothers work with the risen and the unrisen dead. The monk's habit or robe in earth was inspired by the robes of the White Brotherhood. A monk's habit in earth is a duplicate of those worn by the White Brothers in the First Heaven. *A blue habit or monk's robe minus a cowl* indicates a brother of the Illuminati Cloisters. These Cloisters are under the direction and influence of St. Luke, the apostle. One sees a monk in a dream in a blue habit when he has come under the Illuminati monitors. Thereafter he will begin a true work of creation for

God. All blue-robed Illuminati Brothers have been artisans or creators in the earth. They inspire men in earth to create and to serve God.

When one sees himself as *a monk or a nun* in dream experience, it means that he has had a cloistered life in a former life. After this dream-vision one can enter into depths of self-understanding as to why he has healthy or unhealthy attitudes toward religion, sex, or sharing. If he has failed to fulfill his vows, he will be rebellious in one of these areas. If he has been truly devout, he will unite with these powers in the present life.

MOTOR – To see a motor in a dream indicates that one is uniting with the functions of his heart. If *the motor is in need of repairs,* he is being guided to watch his affections, his love and his forgiving. To contact *the motor mechanics of the heartbeat* in sleep will accelerate one's night rise and unite him with the greater motor or the audible hum of the life current supporting all life in this world and in all worlds.

MOUNTAIN – Primitive energy; unused energy which one is to take into himself and master; potential spiritual power to be manifested; also indicating a climb or rise or effort to be made in attaining spiritual powers. To see *the Himalayas* in the night, or *a snow covered mountain* indicates that one is communing with the great Masters overdwelling the creative mentality and soul powers of man. *Skiing* on a mountain indicates that one is learning the techniques of in-and-out consciousness or night-flight procedures.

MUD – Slander, scandal, persecution; to be mired is to be in a karmic situation of soil and unhappiness. Also, a scandal with an unpleasant outcome.

NAIL – Symbol of Jesus crucified.

NEEDLE – Symbol of eyebrow center. To go through *the eye of a needle* in a dream indicates that one has successfully released himself from the physical body to night-flight. To dream of the *needle as sharp and piercing* indicates that one should guard his tongue and his words; also, mend his ways.

NEGRO MAN – For a Caucasian to dream of a black man, it means a complete change of environment, business, residence, or a change of conditions.

NEGRO WOMAN – When a Caucasian dreams of a black woman, it means a key to complete change of attitudes.

NETTLE – A bitter lesson.

NEWSPAPER – Some form of public attention to be focused upon the dreamer, or the dreamer should alert himself to an event of public concern. A newspaper is always used as a means of prophesying in dreams. One should ask that his Guardian Angel read to him what has flashed across the screen of his dream consciousness.

ODORS – Odors and fragrances are important in dreams. Distasteful odors represent discarnate spirits, satanic wavelengths, unpleasant or evil manipulative powers of the dark. Pleasant fragrances are received in dreams through the higher aspect of smelling. To contact saintly presences in the night is to be healed and to be made well in the etheric body, and thus receive a happiness blessing in consciousness. (see Flower Symbols)

OIL – *Pure oil* indicates that one should be grateful for the oil of anointing. *Crude oil* indicates that one has researched the inner layers of the earth. In dreams the initiate learns that oil is the liquid breath and prana for the mighty atom centered in the core of the earth.

OIL WELL – Indicates that one is to tap the resources of the earth for his own personal use. This is not a prophecy, however, that one will discover an oil well; merely that he will receive assurance of the supporting substances of the earth.

PADLOCK – Symbol of reinforcement, security, of safety against the brigands of the dark.

PARTY – A conclave of initiates met in the night to exchange spiritual vitalities. A time of joy and holy recognition of co-atom persons mingled together. A celebration or a festival of exalted personages. *A raucous party with sexual influences* indicates that one is pandering his soul powers through the use of his lower senses. *A carnival* indicates that one is selling his spiritual powers to the unappreciative, and is being told that he should not give his pearl of wisdom to the swine-consciousness of callous-minded persons.

PATCHING – One is reminded in this dream that he cannot put a new piece of cloth on an old garment or use old practices and formulas for a new situation. This dream symbol can also be telling the dreamer that he should patch up or reconcile himself with those whom he has offended.

PEN – Indicates that one is receiving the indented record of his past incarnations; also it is a promise of creative talent in writing. One is being reminded that the written word can be received by some initiates more powerfully than the spoken word, while some can only learn through the spoken word. When one in his evolvement combines the wisdom aspect of the written with the spoken word proceeding out of the Holy Ghost, he becomes an epistle-apostle for God.

PERFUME, FLORAL – To soften the psychic pressure on the pituitary gland and open the pineal gland, and thus gain spiritual sight.

PERFUME SCENTS

Jasmine – a scent given by the risen dead to awaken nostalgic memories of the good; a token from the Beloved.

Lavender – a saint's healing for peace.

Rose – a healing for emotional instability, and to open the heart center.

Saintly scents and fragrances, such as carnation, magnolia, pine, arbutus, violet, wildflower and honeysuckle are Deva-Angel helps sent by the saints.

All flowers with *obnoxious scents* experienced in dreams are astral destroyers of peace, reminding one of his own inertia and danger of soul-decay.

Perfume, musk – to attract astral forces; psychic expansion; sensuality.

PINS – *A pin or brooch* indicates that one has received a protective gift or talisman of reverence; admiration from a loving source, spiritual or physical. *Ordinary pin* means to make secure.

PLAY – A play represents a former-life record in which one, as the main actor, is acting out a former life in the Hall of Archives where one encounters certain aspects of his akasic records. The Hall of Archives is located in the Hall of Learning. The greater Hall of Archives is located in the Hall of

Wisdom where one sees portrayed the dramas of the great civilizations and sees the part he has played in these eras of the past.

PLUMBING – A symbol of the collective subconscious mind functioning in a family unit or family-atom. Also indicates one's subconscious mind and is a symbol correlating to the physical body. The one dreaming is being alerted to the kidney system and elimination functions of the body.

POLICEMAN – A protective angel representing the law and Will of God. To see a policeman in a dream or to encounter the help of one is grace. To be *chased by a policeman* as a lawbreaker, one is being reminded that he has offended the laws of God and must expect some confrontation with his physical karma and its payment in his physical life. If one *receives a ticket* from a policeman in the night, the payment of karma is close by and inevitable.

POOL – A birth matrix or font of birth. All souls enter into the birth matrix before returning to the earth to reincarnate. The birth matrix pool is a deep indigo color and can be seen in the night when one is observing the processes of his soul's return to earth. Also, an angelic healing pool in which angel vibrancies purify and cauterize wounds of karma shading away the soul's light. To experience being *immersed in a pool for baptism* is a symbol of being received by the Christ, as Jesus was received and penetrated by the Christ when He was baptized by John the Baptist. To see a *pool of slimy, stagnant water* in a dream indicates that one is in a state of soiled passion and sorrow. One must move over the astral slime in his sensuality to avoid such dreams.

PREGNANCY – To feel that one is *pregnant with child* indicates that one is preparing to give birth to a new self or the real self. *To fear the state of pregnancy* in a dream indicates that one is irresponsible as to spiritual life and the consequential disciplines.

PRONE TO FALL – Means to be knocked down by one's rebellious will. Over-egotism invites discipline from the higher worlds. When one finds himself in a dream *flat on his back like a beetle,* unable to turn over, he must alert himself that he has come under the supervision of the Chastising Angels that he may deflate his egotism and correct his unruly will. *To feel helpless and futile* in a dream is a warning that one must see God as the Supreme.

PUMP – Indicates that one is uniting with world pulsation or the great hum, and that the pulse points in the body, the energy etheric canals in his etheric body, and the astral currents are being regenerated.

PURSE – A symbol of grace. To *lose one's purse,* to be seeing a *thief taking one's purse* in a dream is to be shown that one is gambling or flirting with his grace and is in danger of losing his grace. One reunites himself with his grace and thus avoids such frightening dreams by keeping alive continually a flow of gratitude and gratefulness for God and His blessings and creation.

RAINBOW – Indicative of saintly protection during night-flight and during daytime action. To see a rainbow is to know that one is a protégé of the saints.

RAKE – Stewardship, harvest time.

ROCK OR STONE – Latent strength as to small matters; a memory of the ancient retribution laws of stoning. Also a symbol that one is in danger of stumbling against a stone, or some issue that is painful. *Rock house, rock castle or rock building* represents primal reliance upon etheric laws.

ROD – Symbol of discipline, the spine, and the power to measure and to gauge. Also, the symbol of an upright will.

ROOF – Symbolic of the mind, of covering for one's mental body. If in good repair, indicates mental stability. *If in need of repair,* indicates one should enter into the calm of his omniscient mind or mind in Christ. A roof is also a symbol for the Father who is the covering for all – both the physical father and the Father Divine.

ROPE – Symbol of the silver cord; also, in some instances can be revealing the processes of kundalini power. A rope can indicate a means and a way of escape.

ROSEMARY – A peace offering.

RUG – Symbol of one's lower etheric body. *To be seated on a rug,* one is experiencing former-life memory methods of meditation. *To be kneeling on a rug* reveals that one has had a contact with Islam practices in a former life. *To slip or fall upon a rug* is a warning that one should watch his moods and temperaments regarding habit slavery of the body. *To see a rug as a wall hanging* in a dream is a warning that one must be alert, that he become not a victim to "skinners," or those who would abuse his confidence. *To see a prayer rug on a wall* is to be communing with a mandala outpicturing his soul communion and union with the Master.

SALAMANDER – Represents a fire hazard. A salamander seen by a night dreamer indicates that the dreamer will be protected by the Salamander Angels who are the angel guardians over fire in the earth.

SAND – Futility. *A sand mountain* indicates one's own doing is in danger of engulfing him; dreams placed in unreality; unlasting situations; a smothering situation; a symbol of time. *Sandy soil under home* – *"house built on sand cannot stand."* *Sand storm*, trouble and tribulation. *Sandy path*, the beginning of a new phase. *Waves breaking over sand*, astral currents. *Quicksand*, warning of danger through engulfment in a situation. *Walking in deep sand*, futility.

SAW – Symbol of the great Carpenters, Jesus and Joseph. A symbol of one of the apostles who was sawed in half by infidels. Also a symbol of one learning the art of the mastery of spiritual building. Its negative aspect is to be divided or cut in two; temptation. *A dark red saw* means to eliminate aggression. *A deep blue saw* means to eliminate mental confusion. Also can be used as a prophetic symbol of amputation or surgery.

SCALES – To be weighed by the Recording Angels as to one's karma or grace. A symbol of justice rendered in the Hall of Judgment.

SCARAB – The symbol of quelle balance, or the Mother and Father principles united at the base of the skull.

SCEPTER – A wand of royalty, spiritual and physical. A prestige symbol. Glamor dreams sometimes place the dreamer in the situation of one in power or authority. These egotistical reflections in dreams occur just before a humility demotion-cycle is to begin in the spiritual life.

SCHOOL – Hall of Learning, university of the night. A reminder that one should apply himself to instruction in both day and night. The two facets of instruction – obedience and discipline – are necessary in both the world of waking and of dreaming.
School grounds being torn up – eliminating devitalizing old thought patterns, so that one may attain a new attitude toward spiritual instruction.

SCREEN – *Screen of a window* indicates that one is being protected from astral intrusion. *Screen of a television* shows that one is making contact with archetypal projected instruction. One method used in contemplation by certain initiates is to visualize a screen between the eyebrows, permitting the projected thoughts, ideas and pictographs from the Masters to appear.

SCROLL – Reading of the grace records. Could be the records of the world soul or the record of one's own life. *A scroll seen in the light* indicates that one is to become a creator united with the grace records of mankind. To tap the Scrolls of Light is to contact the archetypal worlds.

SEWING – Night Ministry industry. To mend the garments of ether. To be *making a garment* shows that one is building his spiritual garment during initiatory processes in sleep.

SHELVES – Plateaus or levels of consciousness in the astral planes. Also a symbol of support for the akasic records to be seen in the fourth plane of the astral world. *Old shelves* indicate the catacombs or method of burial for the early Christians.

SHEPHERD'S CROOK OR STAFF – Indicates that one has come under the guidance of Jesus.

SHIPS – Symbol of a sanctuary or an environment as a means to the spiritual way of life; also a way of passage over the astral world into the spiritual life. *Captain of the ship* can indicate an angel or a Master who is the protecting and directing power leading one over the astral tumults, that he may enter into the spiritual precincts of higher instruction. *Old ship or boat* in a dream means outgrown or outmoded methods of reaching God. *A sinking ship* means that one has reached the end.

SKELETON – Research of origins and of death.

SKI LIFT – A symbol of gaining a certain momentum for night-flight and serving.

SKULL – Death.

SKY, CLEAR BLUE – Clarity of mind. A blessing from heaven. A symbol of levitation and night-flight.

SKYLINE OF VAST CITY – Night travel. Dreamer is incorporating content of a certain city, getting ready to help people in that city. It is the greatest goal in night-flight to heal a city.

SLATE – The akasic record.

SLEEPING PILLS – To dream of a person taking sleeping pills means the person seen in the dream will not face things; he is an escapist.

SNOW – Frozen energy or matter. An impasse. Death. An end of fruitfulness. *Snow on a mountain* indicates contact with the Himalayan Masters.

SOAP – To cleanse. The need for cleansing.

STAGE – Initiation to new spiritual powers and spiritual expression; to appear before others as a spiritual representative; to be used by the higher worlds as an actor on the stage of life. Its lower aspect is when a chimera action is expressed on the stage in that one is a *bad actor and is mixed up,* and is playing out a negative act in the play of life or living. *Seeing a play on a stage* means that one should alert himself to what the play is stating as to his own karma and its pattern. Also, one can gather important clues to former lives' experiences. One should search for the dream code revealing what the lives were.

STAIR – To rise to higher levels of consciousness. To climb through one's own will toward the light. *To climb a stair on the left side of a building* indicates that one is in danger of entering the left-hand path. *To climb a stair on the right side of a building* indicates that one is entering into initiatory powers of the right-hand path. *To walk upon a central staircase* indicates that one has entered the path of the Masters. This is the golden middle leading the initiate directly to the Christ.

STAR – One is being shown his eternal origins and uniting with his own direct star. *A five-pointed star* indicates the command center between the eyebrows.

STEPS – *Three steps* indicate that one is being initiated into the three greater initiations: spirit, soul and mind.

STORM – Cosmic forces taking over one's life, exacting penalties and corrections. *A storm at sea* indicates that one has opened an astral current out of timing and is in danger physically.

STRING – One should be alert to tie up all loose issues or to keep one's word.

SUN – Communing with the Christ. Researching the inner core of the earth.

SWAMP – Reveals that one is caught in a slimy, stagnating, astral action. Also indicates the atavistic guilt collected in the lower subconscious. *To see a swamp in a dream with trees cut down in the swamp* indicates blood guilt or remembrance of taking of life in a former life.

SWEATER – Symbol of the spiritual garment or the ephod breastplate.

SWORD OR KNIFE – In dream indicates the tongue wounding in speaking. *Held upright by hand* indicates the Spirit of Truth sword. *Sword piercing the earth* represents war. A sword in water represents instability. *A fiery sword* indicates the fiery trial or the consuming of evil.

TABLE, RECTANGLE, WITH WHITE CLOTH – The body or form of the Lord; an agape or feast of love in the night with the Christ.

TABLE, ROUND – The combining of disciples together; being instructed in the higher worlds; sacred intimacy; instruction at night.

TABLE, SQUARE – Personal and family karma.

TABLECLOTH – If soiled, means desecration of the sanctuary; pure white, means sanctification under Christ.

TAU – Cross of Egypt. Indicates old Egyptian powers.

TEACHER – *In a chair with feet off the floor* means the teacher is getting ready to leave the earth world. *Teacher in a vision with feet above ground* indicates an inner-plane teacher. *Guru or Master seated in lotus position* indicates one who has yoga levitation powers. *A Master seated in a cave* indicates a new prophetic message. *Many Bodhisattvas seated in caves* tells the dreamer that he is seeing the Saint-Bodhisattvas who control and maintain the initiatory trials on the path.

TEAPOT – Gossip.

TELEPHONE – Symbol of telepathy; telepathic communication. To dream of a *telephone ringing* – a warning being sealed into one.

TEMPTRESS – When a man dreams of a temptress or *a prostitute*, he is being warned that he will be tempted in the waking state as to any remaining lust in his nature.

THEATER –To dream of a theater or the gallery of a theater means that one is being an observer in this night of dreaming.

THISTLE – Guidance to hold firm in time of indecision.

THREAD – Symbol of one's night industry in mending or weaving the tapestry of divinity. Also denotes one's being led by a clue to a meaning sought for.

THUNDER – Symbol of retribution or reaction due to one's hasty or rash actions.

TOBACCO – Psychic dust thrown into the eyes of one seeking psychic excitation. *To be smoking* indicates that one is indulging his senses through the use of psychic, mesmeric powers. Tobacco in the waking state produces an overcharged psychic mind.

TOWER – Symbol of overlook, or foresight-wisdom given to those who will receive it; thus they become higher than other men in evolvement, earning authority. A teacher's or Master's insight.

TRAIN – Night-flight. To be frustrated in *catching a train* indicates that one is in need of clearing his thoughts before sleep by the use of mantrams. All transit dreams relate to techniques in night-flight.

Train traveling – setting out in a great railroad station means that one is getting ready for a deeper extension of night travel, and therefore is tuning in to the resources of the powerhouse. *The station agents* are the angels, and *the ticket seller* for the trip is the angel who decides how long one may stay and how far he may travel in his night-flight. *The baggage master checking one's baggage* indicates that one must leave his earthly cares of the day in the hands of the angel at night, that he may travel light and free.

TRUCK – Symbol of a person who must relate himself to the common-sense practicals of earth necessities. If one is *traveling in a truck*, he is going by slow freight in his spiritual progress.

TRUNK – Family memories. *A trunk lost en route* on a trip in a dream indicates that one has lost touch with his former-life memories or grace supporting his belief in his fellow man. *A trunk in an attic* indicates inheritance from one's family or from a relative. *A trunk in a closet* indicates that one is ashamed of a relative or his relatives.

TUNNEL – Moving out of gravity through the help of the silver cord. In night-flight, all experience this tunnel and come to the end of this tunnel where there is light and sound and joy.

UMBRELLA – Instruction under a true Master or guru. When *the umbrella is open,* it is a sign of protection from a teacher; one is ready to come under his teacher. When *the umbrella is closed,* one is still a probationer and unaware of the Master's presence.

> *Black umbrella* – a black or astral guru mesmerizing the mental faculties of the one dreaming.
> *Golden, opened, upside-down umbrella* – fair weather and plenty of supply.

VACUUM CLEANER – Cleansing of a family-atom.

VASE – Symbol of quelle or the lower and higher subconscious. *Broken vase* – an injury or damage to the flow between subconscious and the objective mind. Symbol of the womb or the human birth matrix. The feminine principle. *If flowers appear in the vase*, it is the symbol of fertility. *If the vase is of plain glass*, it is indicative of sterility or being unable to conceive.

VEHICLE, MOVING – Night-flight body.

VEIL – Symbol of the Divine-Mother veil of forgiveness that she places over her recalcitrant children. Also a symbol of the dream veils of which there are seven: the first or lowest being the grotesque; the second, the fantasy veil; the third, the wish veil; the fourth being the akasic record veil; the fifth, initiatory observing and participating veil; the sixth, the veil of bliss, prophecy; the seventh, spiritual illumination, initiation through the saints.

VINEYARD – The sacrament. *Workers in the vineyard* indicate those who are initiates and disciples, night servers and healing helpers of the night.

WALKING – An act of the will.

WALL

Green wall – higher astral world; chlorophyll energy region of the astral world. Healing of astral sicknesses caused by unknowing use of psychic energy.

Stone wall – indicates a fortress against negation.

A hedge of vines or plants indicates that one has a cultivated and insulated environment necessary to his present state of evolvement.

WATCH – Timing. A reminder that one should come into timing. Time hands on a watch pointing to a certain hour indicate a period or time important to the dreamer. Any number can signify either a day, a week, a month or a year.

WATER SYMBOLS – Water is the symbol of emotional initiation and astral initiation. Bathing, falling into water, etc.

Black water – ominous, guilt, death.

Brown water – deception.

Cascade of water – spiritual power.

Clear water – purification.

Cup of water in saucer, spilled – lack of poise; failure as a disciple.

Cup of water – to be the Master's disciple.

Dark water, mud in basement – encountering karmic pictures in the lower subconscious; guilt on subconscious level; a dry soul-time, a low tide of the soul.

Lake – blending emotions.

Muddy water – involvement, scandal.

Ocean – to learn the origins of life.

Pitcher of water – purification sacrament; hospitality.

Pool of clear water – the First Heaven; a birth matrix.

Pool, small, rectangular – purification of physical body.

Riding or moving over water – protection in night-flight over the astral planes; sign of victory over the astral.

River – humanity.

Rough water – storm of the senses, warning of adversary action, and of karmic debts to be met.

Small boat in distance – the disciple is to meet the Master.

Stream of water – one's conscious flow of life moving to the ocean of all life.

Walking on water – miracles; levitation; astral projection.

Water to armpits – healing of the body.

Water under house –- an unresolved emotional family-atom condition underminging the security of persons in the family.

WHEEL – *The wheel of karma* or the magnet of equation drawing man back to birth that he may resolve his faulty or unjust actions. Also the symbol of the chakras. *The number one chakra* in the etheric body begins at the end of the spine, and contains the curled kundalini fire waiting to rise to the crown of the head, that one may be spiritually illumined. Its negative aspect is lust. The sense correlating to this wheel is the sense of smell. *The second wheel or chakra* is located along the spinal etheric canal directly above the pelvic bone. Its function is to keep alive the sexual propagation impulse in the biological life. This works through the gonad and ovary systems of men and women. One purifies this wheel or chakra by drawing up the life force centered therein to the heart, which develops an *ojas* or great spiritual strength in creations. The negative aspect of this chakra is anger. The sense correlating to it is taste; its element is water. *The third wheel or chakra* relates to the area between the navel and just below the heart. This is the center of the solar plexus and pertains to seeing or vision due to the sun's fire gathered in this area or chakra. The negative aspect of this center is greed, ambition. The element is fire;

the sense correlating to it is sight. *The fourth chakra* is centered in the heart. This is the center of touching or of empathy generated by selfless love. Its negative aspect is delusion. Its element is air; the sense correlating to it is touch. *The fifth wheel or chakra* is centered in the center of the neck just below the hollow of the throat. This is the great Nadam center where the Hum of the Divine may be contacted. This wheel is the wheel of logos. To speak a mantra, such as *So Hum*, opens this chakra. As the sacred Hum is uttered one frees himself from karma. The element correlating to this chakra is ether. The sense correlating to it is hearing. The negative aspect is envy, pride. *The sixth chakra* situated between the eyebrows is the command center where one combines with audible sound current and supreme consciousness. Superconsciousness mind is freed through this command center. The element correlating to this center is the moon and sun androgynous fiery akasia working with the pranic life currents. When one opens this chakra, he overcomes the dualistic aspects of his nature and makes union with the Supreme One. The negative aspect of this chakra is hypnotic suggestion or abuse of willing. In its highest aspect one uses the higher extrasensory perception. *The seventh chakra* is the wheel or center of the great AUM, or the thousand-petaled lotus. This is also the bliss center of supreme blessings. Its element is pure spirit. Its center is the pineal gland. The sense correlating to this is prescience or Christ consciousness. Its negative aspect is atheism. In the great AUM chakra residing over the soul's pulsation centered over the crown of the head, one makes union through his higher self with the Supreme One or God.

WHIP – A symbol of Satan; also, of the flail used by the Pharaohs. In a dream *a flail* indicates that one is to come under the heavier side of his karma.

WIND – *Wind on the desert* represents chastisement during initiation. *Wind on a mountain top* indicates a cleansing set into action by the Master. *Wind as in a storm* indicates mass cleansing of astral currents or soiled guilts. *The Seraphim wind* which bloweth as it listeth, or as Spirit wills it, produces the holy cleansing in one's spiritual life. One hears the Seraphim wind through the audible sound current between the eyebrows in either sleeping or waking. This becomes a music flooding one's being with a divine ecstasy and expectancy of rightness and well-being.

Wind, cold – an ominous symbol of death to one's desires or wishes which have no support from the true law of being. Also, *a cold-wind experience during meditation* indicates that an unrisen dead or earthbound entity is near. True presence from heavenly reaches is determined by warmth, glowing emanations, joyousness.

WINDOW – Protection from astral forces.

WINE PRESS – Reaping as a result of action good or bad. Also a symbol of preparing the new wine for the sacrament.

WORMS – A symbol of observing a balance of Nature through bacterial life.

WRITING – Contact with one's Recording Angel.

YAWNING – Constant yawning reveals that one has used up a surplus of energy in the lesser etheric body and needs to use pranic breaths to recharge the etheric body. This is done by infants and children automatically. As one evolves spiritually, he learns to recharge the etheric body through pranic breaths. In the night universities one learns to use the techniques of cosmic prana that he may always have a reserve of energy regulated to his need in the use of magnetic association. All healers to be successful must be initiated into the use of recharging the etheric body through cosmic pranic-breath rechargings.

YOUNG BOY– To dream of a young boy indicates that one has contacted Krishna, who will teach him to be a fisherman of the souls of men. In this dream he is seen near an ocean. One may also encounter the boy Jesus in a similar dream. From such a dream one knows that he is under the care and direction of the Christ. He is also opening what is called in the Rishi teachings the *Buddhi,* which is centered directly over the seventh chakra. The Buddhi principle provides one with divine intuition, the higher discrimination. To unite with Buddhi is to have at hand always the answer to the question one is asked regarding spiritual life and law.

Chapter 17

THE INITIATE

May all of the prayers spoken on this night combine for
the Glory of God. May holy mediation produce the miracle
needed for the helps on the coming day.

The Will of God seeks to move man into a greater dimensional capacity. Resisting God short-circuits or blasphemes the Holy Ghost. Holy Ghost is the urgent archetonal sounding agent of God moving upon the mind, emotions and soul of man as a mighty upper-thrusting wind.

The higher orders of intelligence, seen and unseen, work mediatively to encourage men to look beyond the senses, beyond space, beyond time, and beyond one's own limiting perspective. Holy Ghost inspires man to unhook himself from the limiting frustrations of sense report.

Courage of a very unique and special kind is needed to move beyond the chimera of the lesser sense report into spiritual report or confirmation. Courage plus self-modesty are the two most valued attributes of the spiritual initiate.

Holy Ghost sounds the tone that men be stirred in acceptable times. Under the Will of God, man responds and moves. Christ reveals, when man matures. Charity under the Christ sees man yet in the state of maturing, rising, ascending. All shall rise under Him who came to lift men and to bring the Light.

Holy Ghost as a Being and Comforter is known by the Father and Jesus as "the Spirit of Truth." Holy Ghost, working with the Alpha Hum and Omega Tones of the earth, animates all life with the Word or Spirit of Truth.

Holy Ghost as the Spirit of Truth is in command of equation.

His auric vibrational tone sounds can erase or manifest. The Will of God uses the Holy-Ghost sounding to renew men and to decrease men.

In the present time, the sounding of the Holy Ghost is producing a new charisma in the world. Man exists in a state of chaos, that he may open the eternal atoms of his higher mind, and thus stand more upright for God.

Spiritually sensitive souls are aware of the Holy-Ghost action, and respond according to their spiritual aptitudes. Negative persons respond with irritation, dissolution, rebellion.

The Holy-Ghost tone will cease not until all are rectified under the Will of God. When Holy Ghost works with the resurgence tones of man's renewal, one may be said to fall into the hands of the living God. This is why it is stated in scripture, *"It is a fearful thing to fall into the hands of the living God." (Hebrews 10:31)*

It is terrifying to behold brash men made gentle through cleansing and correction. It is indeed awesome to behold men caught into forces superior to their own willing and self-desiring.

The meek will be blessed in the Omega periods of Holy Ghost sounding, for they shall flow with the currents of regeneration with joy, and their souls shall sing with the musics of creation. While the tides of dissolution are at their height, into the hearts of the meek or good shall come the tones of joy united with the acceptable time of God's perfect wonder and creation.

THE TRINITY

> *Go ye therefore, and teach all nations, baptizing them in the name of the Father, and of the Son, and of the Holy Ghost.* -St. Matthew 28:19

There are infinite aspects of the trinity. All true trinity functions express the universal principles of the Will, the Word and the Law of God.

Our Father in Heaven, His Son, Christ Jesus, and the Holy Ghost are Omniscient Mediators under God. These three work in triad action: the Father as the Imager and Life Principle; the Son, or Jesus, as the Love Principle; and the Holy Ghost as the Power under the Spirit of God. Through the conjoining of their eternal atoms, the Father, the Son and the Holy Ghost work as one. This law is true in all mediation, affecting dream states and waking states.

God manifests His Spirit through innumerable forms. All persons and Beings have individual identities. All Beings and persons having life are individual expressions of light.

All Beings, when blended, work in triad action to accomplish a particular thing for God. Elohim Hierarchy, the Father and the angels worked together to create the forms of men in the beginning of this eternity system. They still work to shape and form man, that man may become a perfect prototype in the earth.

THE DIVINE TRIADS ARE:

COSMOS TRINITY: God, Christ, Holy Spirit.
COSMIC TRINITY: Father, Son, Holy Ghost.
HUMAN SPIRIT TRINITY: Jesus, Holy Ghost, Soul of Man.
ELOHIM TRINITY: God, Father, Hierarchy.
HOLY FAMILY TRINITY: Jesus, Mary, Joseph.
ANGELIC TRINITY: Archangels, Seraphim, Cherubim.
MANIFESTATION TRINITY: Father, Christ, Jesus.
TRINITY OF TIMING: Father, Ancient of Days, Melchisedec.
MAN'S TRINITY OF CREATION: Spirit, Soul, Mind.
ETERNAL ATOMS TRINITY: Eternal Sustaining Atom, Indestructible Atom, Sacred Heart Atom.
FAMILY-ATOM TRINITY: Father, Mother, Child.
MORTAL TRINITY: Birth, Life, Death.

MAN'S TRINITY OF CREATION: SPIRIT, SOUL, MIND

The spirit of man ceases not to manifest spiritually. The soul of man ceases not to live eternally. The mind of man – from morn to night, from birth to death, and death to birth – continues to create for God. Regardless of divisions or separations, deaths, trials, sicknesses, sloth, defeats or fears, creation persists; for spirit is the life in creation – and the life of spirit knoweth not death nor defeat. The spirit of man is of Eternal Spirit. Eternal Spirit in man is eternal creation. When man creates for himself, he is in reality serving God, and his creating will eventually lead him to the One or God who creates through him. The soul steadfastly projects the unmanifested creation into the mind of man. When one is ready, he manifests the unmanifested into the receptive minds of other men in the world. So does the Spirit of God in man make Himself known to the knowing of man.

THE PHOENIX FIRE AND THE SELF-GENESIS MIND

The Lords of Mind working with the higher mentality of men are called Seraphim. To be initiated under Seraphim is to prepare for illumination under Christ.

The Seraphim-Angel overlords, perceiving the initiatory trials of the higher mental initiate, come forth to aid and to counsel one who has mastered the lower phases of sentient thought.

There are eras or periods of enlightenment for advanced egos in the world. During these times, the Seraphim Lords of the mind work with certain egos, that they may give to mankind advanced ideas. These ideas stem directly from the *greater archetypes* and are the salvation for mankind. Only men having selfless desire to instrumentalize themselves as servers for God may sustain this very special apprenticeship.

During the self-genesis era now beginning for mankind, egos spiritually advanced in previous incarnations are as a holy nucleus clustered into a highly charged electrical atmosphere. Though separated by continents, they are mentally responsive and morally responsible to one another; through telepathic communion, their Elect-rapport supports the ethic of man's divinity.

The Seraphim Angelic overlords seek in this age to quicken a heretofore unused mental capacity in mankind so that men exposed to the new science of physical energies will absorb and apply avidly the greater mental ideas accompanying the use of the solar, lunar, oceanic, arctic and interspace dynamics.

Men now on the threshold of a great epoch of manifestation, will undergo a period of confusion and emotional twilight. The accelerated increase of interiorization will cloud and obscure certain instinctual supports formerly suitable for the just past and dying era. New and extended faculties of the mind, moving upon the emotions of the masses of men, will incite to wars and revolutions on all levels – wars to obliterate obsolete habits, emotions and thoughts.

In this chaotic atmosphere, the Seraphim Angels are accompanied by the Warrior Guardian Angels who electrify men to rise and to resist their stifling stagnations. The mores of the ages will crumble; men will awaken from their sleep to see with new perceptions into a golden promise of a life fulfilled.

The Seraphim come to say to men: "Arise; be born to the might of creation in thy mind. Behold Hierarchy in thy thought. Come out of the mire of darkness; come into the light of thy mind."

Higher self-genesis ideas will come to the masses in the Aquarian Age, and will begin to manifest outwardly in the year of 2568. Higher self-genesis ideas are presently being expressed by the initiates under Seraphim. Their light, known as the Phoenix fire of heaven, quickens the mentality impulses of everyone attracted to them. They are the Initiators or *Maha-Matras* of their age – known in heaven as "the twinkling-of-the-eye Initiators." Blessed is he who has been called to instruction under the Phoenix fire.

HEALING INITIATORY HELPS FROM THE MASTERS

Innumerable healing helps are given to all spiritual initiates during specific stages of initiation. An initiate recognizing the floundering dangers and crucial stages experienced by a fellow initiate sends forth a soul cry upon the etheric light waves. The Master closest to the destiny of the initiate responds; miracles of illumination and strengths occur.

An initiate's call for another initiate is never refused. The Master responds. To ask of the Masters is to receive. Initiatory healing helps entering into the life of the receiving initiate set up a reciprocity action. The one being initiated becomes the receptacle for blessings spreading as a reciprocal network unto those in his path of association. All persons important to the progress and advancement of the initiate are touched and blessed by the receiving. This produces a banked repository of blessings, which are activated as an intense holy concern for the welfare and good of the one being initiated, and in turn returning to the one who has sent forth the call for help. All are blessed.

The initiate calling for help, knowing well the stewardship of initiatory strengths and powers, understands that for every call sent forth the cordon of light supporting mediation is made more luminous, more efficacious – and thus requires of him a positive step forward in dedication. His concern for his fellow initiate has opened a wider range of demand and of action. Therefore, with each process of birth to the spiritual realities, he must make himself more worthy to serve and to mediatively heal. With each manifestation over weakness, he sees that his divine obligation to the Master and to God is a necessity to continue in his search for the real, to press on and pursue the spiritual life above all.

The asking initiate knows the ethical healing approach to help

his fellow initiate is to call on the powers of mediation, as personal involvement in a fellow initiate's fiery trial offends the spiritual law of necessary individual experience. A disciple becoming
personally overinvolved finds himself sealed away from the zone
area of the initiatory process. His call may be heard, but his own
reciprocity blessing will be short-circuited if he seeks to enter into
an over-personalized participation in a fellow disciple's birth to
additional light.

The positive attitude of unanxious thankfulness and gratitude
will give help rather than hindrance to the one experiencing the
wonderful helps and love of the Master during initiation.

In co-atom association initiation with a fellow initiate, healing
mediation under the Master is a unique experience for both initiates. Something is accomplished beyond reciprocity blessing.
However, in the individual as well as in co-atom initiation, the
ethic of mediation is by necessity impersonal.

THE PROMISE OF SLEEP

To keep the rhythmic flow of dream instruction, healing and
initiation alive and meaningful in the waking state, one should
keep a dream diary to flow out and cleanse the subconscious. A
dream diary discloses the action of the subconscious, assisting the
psyche or soul power to make clearer the etheric codes and symbols in dreams.

One may obtain dream cognizance through night initiation, and
thus master the mentation power necessary to understand and utilize the intelligence contacted in dreams. Upon arising one should
meditate and contemplate, that he may actualize and formulate
the energies within the symbology dramas in dreams.

*If one dreams of a person in distress, he should pray for that
person for five days on arising.*

The progressive stages of dreams are revealed when one keeps a
dream diary. These are: (1) the latent and unmastered sexual impulses; (2) money stewardship; (3) personal relationships and
motives; (4) the use of etheric powers; (5) karmic nuances from
past lives; (6) contact with the Divine companions, angels, Presences and Masters; (7) the parabolic dramas containing the dream
codes. Thus, the dream flow of the code symbols becomes intelligible, opening the recollection of night serving – and with this
will come the power of healing in the night and in the day.

To live a whole life, one must come out of his sleep apathies in the daytime and in the night, and recognize that he is a conscious entity in all states, all planes and all actions; that he is limitless as a soul, and universal as a cosmic spirit. The more one knows of his dreams, the more he will know of himself as a consciousness spirit in the Will of God.

To know dreams as a reality is to be proportioned as a whole consciousness being. One no longer is dependent upon the sundown of his subconscious; but he is always in the state of the sunrising of his spirit – observing, seeing, knowing, becoming.

To benefit from the night's progress in dreams, one should have an ephemeris by his bedside so that he can determine the sign of thc zodiac in which the moon is active. One should note in his dream diary the position of the moon when a dream occurs. This will enable him to keep his dream diary current with the cosmic, progressive flow of sleep. Everyone is tested and shaped emotionally, mentally and spiritually by the planetary and lunar action of the night.

A pre-sleep mantram* should be spoken before sleep so as to obtain the highest benefits of the dream experience. A pre-sleep mantram acts as a protective seed mantra falling into the subconscious, giving a high suggestible reinforcement. This enables the sleeper to receive intuition, mentation and healing. When a pre-sleep mantram is spoken, the Guardian Angel and Recording Angel working with the dreamer in the night protect the one dreaming, and give to him a wider research in dreams and a longer extension of time through which he may penetrate the world of sleep harmlessly and spiritually.

One should never feel that he is separated from the greater Intelligences and intelligence provided by God when he does not recall his dreams. There are periods when one fails to remember his dreams because of externalized ultra-involvement on the physical planes.

The Recording Angel sees to it that all dreams are registered and retained in quelle. Negative dream memories are retained in the lower subconscious portion of quelle. Grace dreams are retained in the higher unconscious portion of quelle. The Recording Angel assists each person to have access to certain memory resources in dreams.

A greater percentage of dread and apprehension thought to come from the instinctual side of one's nature comes, in reality, as a warning from one's Recording Angel. Also, hope and faith stem from reassurances gathered from the Recording Angel during dream experience in the night.

The wise dreamer is rocked in the cradle of wisdom. It is he who dares to make his dreams into flesh and to manifest as a creator within the Will of God.

Watch your dreams, and become aware. Watch your dreams, and become a full craftsman. Watch your dreams, and speak with an open tongue, that you may overcome your fears of death and of life.

Dream-knowing is to be immortal. Dream-understanding is to be free. Enter sleep always with cares emptied out, with trust, with expectancy of the wonders of the night and the glories of sleep, and keep always nigh to the pillow of your sleep the expectancy of a good tomorrow provided by the angels of God who watch over the soul in sleep and in waking.

THE END

----

*Further information regarding pre-sleep mantrams may be obtained from:
    Ann Ree Colton Foundation of Niscience, Inc.
    Post Office Box 2057
    Glendale, California, 91209
    Telephone: (818) 244-0113
    Fax: (818) 244-3913

GLOSSARY

AKASIA – The pure, vitalized, supernal spiritual life-substance used by consciousness. The akasic light is soul-light. The color of akasia is indigo blue and is seen often in visions during meditation. Ether is the coagulating life substance. Prana is the energizing life substance in ether. Akasia is a light *consciousness* animating substance. Akasia substance is used in the highest form of spiritual telepathy. The more highly evolved one is, the more akasia he has in his mental and soul-light. One breathes in pranic energy to renew life force. One meditates to increase akasic light in his mind.

AKASIC RECORDS – Records of former lives.

ARCHETONE – The Word under command of the Holy Spirit used in conjunction with all great archetypes. When the archetone sounds, the archetype comes alive with whatever compulsion is ripe or ready to be manifested. Thus an archetype remains dormant until the archetone sounds. The Holy Ghost working with the Will of God sounds the archetone, that the great ideas or new impulse for man may enter the world or fall into the mind of man in timing to the Will of God.

ARCHETYPE – Original or divine blueprint for the mind and life processes in the earth. The greater archetypes work first as the unmanifest or as the Word yet to be made flesh. These spiritual, creative, divine archetypal compulsions move in tides into the world through the minds of men. In each great archetype is an archetone. The Holy Spirit sounds within the archetone when the divine Word is ready to enter into the mind and life of man.

ARCHETYPES, GREATER – Concern the greater life-waves directing and changing reincarnation tidal flow; also, determine the timing of the appearance of new ideas in the receptive minds of the Elect or Adepts in preparation for new eras in time and evolvement.

ASTRAL – Star or planetary reflections. The astral is a unique, unceasing, fermenting, mirroring and moving action producing in man a state of emotion, mood and inductive feeling and thinking.

ASTRAL BODY – Emotional body.

ASTRAL WORLD – The astral world is supported by the magnetic belt around the earth. The higher astral world is the First Heaven. The lower astral world relates to man's subconscious mind in death and in life. The grotesque level of the astral world reflects the sin-body of the earth. The four lower planes of the astral world are the recipients of the lower vibrations and energies of the planetary light. This sub-planetary energy produces a chimera mirage-like effect upon the emotions of man in life and in death, producing glamor and mesmeric effects upon the lower mind and senses of man. The astral world in the Bible is called "the serpent." Man commands the astral world by the use of his higher will and higher mind.

AURA – The energy field around the body.

BUDDHI – Buddhi is an ignited and illuminative understanding which produces mentation or interpretation of dreams and visions. Buddhi also pertains to the informing principle, igniting the mind with prophecy.

CENTER Q – Same as quelle.

CHAKRAS – The seven soul-vortices located over the spinal canals of the etheric body.

CO-ATOM – To be co-atom to any person, one must be on the same wavelength of energy emanating from a sacred atom, as to be co-atom to Jesus one must have an open circuit in his own heart's sacred atom to the heart of Jesus. To be co-atom to a teacher or a Master, one must have a wavelength open circuit or a degree of light in his mental atoms to the mental atoms of his teacher or Master. In this way he is telepathically communicable to the mind and thoughts of his Master and teacher, and thus receives a continued flow of instruction. One can develop his own capacity in co-atom association through meditation and through thoughts of oneness with all life as given of God. When two persons have instant recognition of one another, and absolute congeniality, they are co-atom to one another. This can only occur when one has been with the other person in many lives where relationships have proved to be harmonious. When God prepares to use a person for a greater work, He first sends to the one chosen a teacher or Master; secondly, He sends to him a co-atom person in the world, that the work may be consummated and fulfilled.

COSMOS-GENESIS – After man has reached the perfected self-genesis stage of evolvement, he will become a cosmos-genesis man. His emotional body will be fully developed and he will be at one with the love atoms of Jesus, the Lord of Love. All great Bodhisattvas of the East had reached full development of their emotional bodies, and thus gave to man the bhakti love instruction. John the Beloved, the disciple of Jesus, had a perfected emotional body and therefore was the closest disciple to the heart of Jesus.

EFFLUVIA – An intelligible, animating, reflecting side of ether through which one is informed. Seership would be impossible without the effluvia chemical action in ether. Effluvia reflects what is, and is an instrument for all pictorial life, living and dead. Clairsentient psychics are familiar with effluvia's chameleon-like and versatile action. Everything a man touches leaves a revealing effluvia through which a psychic may extend his senses to gain knowledge of persons or objects. Effluvia is not a permanent substance, lasting only from sundown to sundown. Ether remains in environments; however, with time the effluvia is withdrawn. One therefore can be aware of ether imprints long after a person has ceased to inhabit an environment. But if effluvia is absent, he cannot penetrate the most intimate details concerning a person or an environment.

EGO – The higher individuality supported by the higher thoughts of past lives and of the present life.

EGOTISTICAL SHELL – Condensed electrified ether covering the ego, causing one to be bound into the lower mind supporting self-aggression and assertiveness. This shell must be dissolved through meditation and spiritual works, that the higher ego may come into its own, and the soul be given its fullest expression. One cannot be free from his heavier karma until he has dissolved his egotistical shell.

EIGHTH SPHERE – The great abyss where Satan and his dark angels hold reign. One must cross over the third abyss or eighth sphere when he is being initiated into the higher mind.

EMOTIONAL BODY – The emotional body and the astral body are one and the same. In the less evolved, the emotions work primitively. The emotional body is an ovoid sphere of feeling. The shape of the emotional body determines that every positive or negative feeling shall return to the one who feels it, also that the desires of a person shall inevitably be manifested. The emotional body and the astral core work as hand in glove. The astral fiery core keeps alive and supports the feelings within the emotions and desires.

ENTITY – An earthbound-dead person lingering in the lower astral planes.

ETERNITY SYSTEM – Any system having a sun, earth and planets. There are countless eternity systems in the universe. All are born and die as man is born and dies.

ETHER – The life substance supporting all life, called "prana" in the East, and called by some "bioplasma" in the West. Ether is a coagulating semi-gelatile and semi-fluid substance. Ether is quasi-tangible. It can be photographed. Ether supports electric and magnetic action and other forms of energy yet to be discovered by man.

ETHERIC BODY – The double of the physical body. It is made of ether and prana. Its life substance is supported by the sun. The lower aspect of the etheric body supports the life in the physical body and the life of the lower mind. The higher aspect of the etheric body supports the spiritual and higher mental life. The higher etheric body survives death. The lower etheric body dissolves with the physical body.

FAMILY-ATOM – An etheric encasement psychically charged. Father, mother and children in a family-atom are held together by the psychical charge or lines of force which have attracted them to one another. The low charge of psychic energy in a family-atom keeps alive the soul-debts memory between persons born in the family. The combined soul-grace of the persons born in the family-atom is watched over by a family-atom Guardian Angel. If grace is abundant, all souls in a family-atom progress. If the family-atom is heavily laden with karma, the result is suffering and sacrifice, that all may eventually evolve in a cluster of human souls.

FAMILY-ATOM DWELLER – The condensed negative shadow-body of family karma challenging the souls encased in a family-atom. The sins of the fathers are visited upon the children through the family-dweller action.

FAMILY-GENESIS – Persons dependent upon ancestral myth inheritance as expressed through a mother and father in a family-atom. Family-genesis impulses seek to build a society patterned after ancestral heritage. From the family-atom compulsion comes the building of churches, the building of societies and education.

GOOD BROTHER – There are three hundred Good Brothers working at all times in the earth. Their mission is to appear as a means of help and succor when all else seems impossible. In their physical memories, the Good Brothers rarely know they are Good Brothers; in their etheric memories they know, and are compelled to act during crisis periods. In time of trouble, they smooth the way and move on, asking nothing by way of reward.

GURU – Teacher.

HALL OF LEARNING – Located in the seventh plane of the First Heaven. All initiation in the Hall of Learning is preparation to serve as a night healer and a daytime initiate. Dream research of the night is under the supervision of the great Masters and pure gurus in the Hall of Learning. All spiritual aspirants are initiated in this precinct of heaven, that they may render a knowing service in the world.

HALL OF WISDOM – See Heaven, Second.

HEAVEN, FIRST – The First Heaven is the higher astral world. Each of the planes of the astral world contains seven regions. The lowest, or Plane 1, is the Grotesque plane. Plane 2 is Fantasy. Plane 3 is Wish. On the fourth plane of the astral world, the action of the First Heaven begins. Here one reads his akasic records and hears the audible sound or music of the cosmos. On the fifth plane of the astral world, one unites with the Masters, the Saints, and begins his night instruction and night-ministry work. On the sixth plane of the astral world, one enters into the prophetic side of dreams. On the seventh plane of the astral world, one contacts the great Bodhisattvas who prepare him for initiation into the Second Heaven.

HEAVEN, SECOND – The greater cloisters of heaven where one meets the Most High Saints, the Illuminati and the Great Masters, and receives instruction in the Hall of Wisdom or Shambala. Adepts are initiated in dreams through the seven planetary Logoi or the Archangels over the seven planets. These prepare the adept to make union with the Third Heaven.

HEAVEN, THIRD – The Third Heaven is the homeplace of Jesus and His apostles. Here, the initiate and adept receive the power of archetypal light directly through the assistance of the Christ Spirit overdwelling Jesus.

HIERARCH – The Elohim, the host or the zodiacal Overlords assisting this earth or eternity system in its development. Hierarchy uses the power of imaging or making. Sending their rays into the sun and the earth, they assist the Father and the Christ in the creation of mankind. Each Hierarch Overlord is a zodiacal prototype or blueprint for man, such as Aries, Taurus, etc.

HUMAN-GENESIS – Same as family-genesis.

INITIATE – An ego who has followed a spiritual path in previous lives and is in a state of being initiated into greater illumination and spiritual power in this life, that he might better serve the world.

KARMA – The law of cause and effect or sowing and reaping.

LIGHT-STREAMS – The stepped-down rays from Hierarchy working with the planets.

LOGOS – The audible sound of the Holy Ghost speaking through inspiration, illumination and revelation. The center of logos is between the eyebrows.

LUNAR BRAIN – The abdominal, automatic, primitive brain supporting the instinctual life. The center of clairsentience situated in the solar plexus.

LUNAR PSYCHIC – One who is engrossed psychically with his emotions and sees all through emotions and feelings. He is dependent upon the astral lunar reflective light for his psychic powers. The lower lunar psychic is unable to interpret what he sees. The higher lunar psychic sees in part.

MANTRAM – The sounding of word-combinings to dissolve karma, tension and fear. A mantram contains molecular energy particles of light. A mantram spoken with love and absolute belief is a freeing way.

MAHA-MATRA – Meaning Master-woman under the Divine Mother.

MAYA – The changing world of gravity energy producing change, creating the illusion in man that earth life is all.

MEDIATION – Mediation is the most unselfish and unclaiming means of spiritual serving through which one remains impersonally involved with the karma of those whom he would heal or help.

MEDIATOR – One who makes himself a divine artery or channel for the light. A mediator asks for no rewards for his mediative prayers and suggestible helps. He only asks to remain a perfect instrument, that the power and Will of God may flow through him – supporting, healing and lifting. When the mediator is sincere and wholly dedicated, he is free from the karma of those whom he would heal and help. He avoids boastfulness of his healing works. He asks no personal or physical rewards for his healing helps, knowing himself to be but a channel through whom God sends and heals. The highest technique used by a mediator is his use of Angel-to-Angel Mantrams; for he knows, on his releasing the one whom he would help to the angels' suggestible helps, that the angel taking charge of the one to be healed knows with an exact and precise wisdom what can be done and what will be done. Thus, in the angelic mediative helps miracles occur – as it is left to God to reveal to the angels what is the right and just way for the healing to come.

MENTAL BODY – A composite field of light. The higher mind expresses itself in the mental body through three mental atoms. The lower aspect of the mental body, called the lesser mind, is dependent upon the psychic energy coils of force inherited from past lives, from ancestral mental habits. The lower mind serves the physical senses, using instincts from tribal-genesis memory and ancestral memory. It is the work of all spiritual aspirants to still the more atavistic aspects of the lower mind or lesser mind and make of it a complementing additive partner to the higher self and the higher mind. The higher mind seeks to clear the field, that it may come forth as a supernal instrument in creation. In all selfless works of creation, the higher mind is in command.

MENTATION – Mentation is a knowing dimensional-consciousness. Mentation is a divine gift earned through the soul's action in past lives. All souls having attained realization of God make union with one another through the power of divine mentation.

Mentation is cognitive union with the first principles centered in the Will of God, the Life of God, the Light of God, the Love of God. Mentation is the gift of understanding accompanied by a pictured fourth and fifth dimensional vision. Through mentation, one absorbs the wisdom of God, and manifests it into human and personal clarity. Mentation through dreams quickens spiritual power in the soul, producing spiritual action on the physical planes. Having mentation, dreams are realized in a pure or supreme-consciousness state. Retention of pure and true dreams with soul-inferences is a mentation action producing bliss feelings, peace, acceptance of all happenings in the physical world. The spiritual art of concentration, contemplation and meditation leads one to mentation, whereby he is at home in all worlds. Apprehension is absent from mentation, for in mentation one functions through the mind of God. In mentation there is neither fear nor frustration.

NADAM – Sounding the Name of God.

NADIS POINTS or **CANALS** – Seventy-two thousand energy stations in the lesser etheric body.

NEUTRAL FIELD – A non-decisive mental atmosphere inviting entity possession. A neutral field is the product of many lives. One builds a neutral mental field by refusing to participate in the responsible issues of life. A neutral-field mind is described in the Bible as being "lukewarm." It is said that persons having such minds are "spewed out" and of little use to God. Mediumistic powers in the hands of a neutral-field person are sometimes pure, sometimes impure, as both the dark and the light can be housed at one time in a neutral-field mind.

OJAS – The sacred life-force centered in the sexual drives to be raised to the heart center through sacred thinking during the sexual act, thereby healing and eliminating lust.

PRANA – Life-force energy. Prana is the higher energy level of ether working simultaneously with the molding and shaping action of the effluvia in the ether. The energy in high prana has yet to be analyzed by science. One contacts prana through breathing. Prana life-force may be unlocked and freed into the etheric body through cosmic exercises, yoga, breathing, speaking of mantrams.

PRO-GENESIS – When men have become like Jesus, as promised in I John 3:1-3, they will be pro-genesis men with cosmic powers of manifestation. They will do all things, as did Jesus. Following pro-genesis will be all-genesis in which all mankind will be at one with our Father which art in heaven. And finally, men will become the sons of light with hierarchy powers. This period is called one-genesis.

QUELLE – The subconscious seated at the base of the skull. Quelle also has a higher aspect, called the higher unconscious.

RISHIS – Ancient sages, wise men and teachers of the East.

SELF-GENESIS – The individualistic person concerned with his own evolvement. In lesser self-genesis he is engrossed with his own self-interest; in higher self-genesis he recognizes the right of every man to become an identity and to relate himself to the Cause of his being, or God.

SOLAR INITIATE – He is united to the informing principle. In his psi powers he is a scientist working with the Spirit of Truth.

SOLAR PSYCHIC – Same as solar initiate.

SOUL-MEDALLION – A pulsating vortex of supernal light in constant movement around the head of man, keeping alive his soul impulses and mental creative compulsions. The soul's medallion works in conjunction with the heartbeat in expansion and contraction. In the uttermost upper point of the soul's medallion directly above the skull is a pulsating vibratory action. This pulsating action becomes the heartbeat for the spiritual body after death. The soul's medallion records on its outer rim man's negative actions. This is called the vibratory hum. The vibratory hum of the soul's medallion is reflected into the lesser mind. Each time a person meditates he must clear the field of the vibratory hum and slow it down.

TRIBAL-GENESIS – Nomadic segments or clusters of people who have interlocking blood ties sealed into tribal encasements. Dependent upon primitive etheric laws, tribal-genesis persons live close to the tribal consciousness and taboos of their forefathers.

WORLD SOUL – The combined lower and higher subconscious impulses of all sentient and consciousness life of the earth united with the love of God, under command of Him who is the Regent of all souls of the earth – Jesus.

In Memoriam

Ann Ree Colton's transition from the physical body occurred on June 28, 1984 in Glendale, California, due to complications she suffered following a stroke at the age of 85. Born in Atlanta, Georgia on August 17, 1898, a new moon day, Ann Ree's passing also occurred on a new moon day. Her soul dance in life bore testimony to her perfect union with the sacred cycles and providence of God.

Four days following her passing, Ann Ree's body was anointed by three beloved students in preparation for cremation. During the anointing, the three students saw tears fall from Ann Ree's eyes. Ann Ree's ashes are interred under the right foot of a sculpture of Mary, in Mary's Garden, on the grounds of the Niscience Foundation in Glendale, California, which she founded in 1953. The bronze plaque marking the site is engraved with the phrase Ann Ree always used to close her letters: "You are loved."

Ann Ree served as a teacher of the higher life for over sixty years. As "prophet for the Archangels," it was her soul's covenant in this life to articulate the "new wine" in Christ. She was the author and co-author of twenty-three books on spiritual subjects. Her spiritual aptitudes were many. She was a prophet, clairvoyant, cosmos disciple, spiritual teacher, healer, author, lecturer, counselor, creative artisan, as well as an adept, articulate in the inner mysteries.

Ann Ree's teachings and life exemplify the versatile gifts available to the spiritual initiate under the Christ. Her legacy includes not only the memory of her magnificently gracious spirit, her personal spiritual attainments, books and creations, but a path or method, known as the System of Niscience, through which sincere seekers may also recover and increase the treasures of their souls.

History, Aims and Ideals
of the Ann Ree Colton Foundation of Niscience

The Ann Ree Colton Foundation of Niscience (pronounced NISH-ence), founded in 1953 by Ann Ree Colton and Jonathan Murro, is a non-profit religious and educational foundation which is supported by tithes, offerings and gifts from Niscience members and friends. The Niscience headquarters is located in Glendale, California. Various Niscience satellite units are located throughout the United States and abroad.

Niscience, a word which means *knowing*, adheres to the principles supporting all pure teachings founded upon truth, and it also presents many new facets of truth. Niscience is an initiatory school, as well as a deeply spiritual system of study, worship, creativity, research, healing and teaching based upon the teachings and ethics of Jesus, the Bible, and other sacred scriptures. The Foundation seeks to impart religious, philosophic, scientific, and spiritual truths, that its members may be inspired to study and create through the divine ideals given by the Christ.

The Niscience life is an affirmative life producing peace and spiritual understanding with a focus on world mediation. Niscience approaches current issues of global concern, such as the ecological crisis facing our planet, through education and the mediative application of prayer, fasting, creative movement, and ritual.

The purpose of the Foundation is to establish and sponsor devotional chapels and research units and to bring together religion, philosophy, science, and the creative arts – thereby furthering man's creation through his innate love, reverence and devotion to God. The credo of Niscience is "to inspire others, to create, and to serve God."

The vitality of the Foundation is sustained by the theme of participation; each member, if he/she so desires, is given the opportunity to express his or her creative potential. Many come to Niscience unaware of their hidden aptitudes and talents. Through the application of the System of Niscience their lives are soon transformed through self-discovery. Based upon an organized daily rhythm of meditation and prayer, the System provides its adherents with a modulated, disciplined pattern of living. A monthly "White Paper" study program, prepared by the Founders, is available to anyone interested in learning more about the System.

Membership is open to all who would devote themselves to a spiritual life based upon practicality and ethic, the cornerstones of the Niscience teaching.

Weekly unit meetings are held throughout the United States and several other nations. Units conducted by Niscience members provide the following services: sharing in contemplation and meditation, research into spiritual subjects as related to serving in the world, and training in the art of creative logos or speaking. A list of unit locations is available upon request.

Annual Conclaves are held at various locations and timings throughout the year. For more information on the Conclaves, or the books, lessons, tapes, classes, or worship services of the Foundation please call or write:

Ann Ree Colton Foundation of Niscience, Inc.
P.O. Box 2057 (for mail inquiries)
336 West Colorado Street (for visitors)
Glendale, California 91209
Telephone: (818) 244-0113
Fax: (818) 244-3913

Index

It is suggested that readers familiarize themselves with the research format utilized in this index. Many symbols have been classified as subheadings under their various subject categories. For example, under the heading of "household symbols" are listed references to attic, basement, chair, table, etc. Other broad index classifications containing many subheadings include: ailments; anatomy, etheric; Angels; animals; athletic symbols; birds; colors; fish; flowers; food; fruits; geometrical symbols; insects; jewels; jewelry; music; nuts; trees; vegetables; and water symbols.

Other Books by Ann Ree Colton

DRAUGHTS OF REMEMBRANCE
An extraordinary book on the subject of reincarnation.

ETHICAL ESP
An important book defining the difference between lower and higher ESP.

ISLANDS OF LIGHT
A book of initiation with an underlying prophetic theme.

KUNDALINI WEST
Knowledge of the kundalini and the chakras for the Western initiate.

MEN IN WHITE APPAREL
A book of vital revelations about death and life after death.

MY SON, IKHNATON
The life story of the Egyptian Pharaoh, Ikhnaton, as seen through the akasic records.

PRECEPTS FOR THE YOUNG
Appreciated by the adult...inspiring to the child...and beneficial to the family.

PROPHET FOR THE ARCHANGELS
The life story of Ann Ree Colton.

THE ARCHETYPAL KINGDOM
Knowledge of the three heavens and their work with mankind.

THE HUMAN SPIRIT
A scientific, spiritual and healing book on the creation, purpose and destiny of man.

THE JESUS STORY
A miracle book in timing to the need for miracles.

THE KING
From the personal hieroglyphic journal of Ann Ree Colton.

THE LIVELY ORACLES
A prophetic book on world events.

THE SOUL AND THE ETHIC
A profound book on the soul and on the ethical use of soul power.

THE THIRD MUSIC
A powerful book describing the energy-world of the mind, the soul and the Universe.

THE VENERABLE ONE
An initiatory book for those who love Nature and who would unveil Nature's secrets.

VISION FOR THE FUTURE
A prophetic book to comfort men in a perilous time.

INTERPRETE SUS SUEÑOS
Spanish version of *Watch Your Dreams*.

Books Co-authored by Ann Ree Colton and Jonathan Murro

GALAXY GATE I: THE HOLY UNIVERSE
A remarkable book of spiritual revelations about man, the solar system and the Cosmos.

GALAXY GATE II: THE ANGEL KINGDOM
A book filled with enlightening insights into the world of Holy Mediators between God and mankind.

OWE NO MAN
Scriptural principles of good stewardship and Divine Providence.

PROPHET FOR THE ARCHANGELS
The life story of Ann Ree Colton.

THE ANOINTED
Sacred keys to healing, exorcism and the Divine Marriage.

THE PELICAN AND THE CHELA
A priceless book describing the classic teacher-student relationship.

Books by Jonathan Murro

GOD-REALIZATION JOURNAL
A book opening a new world of understanding related to the Presence of God. *God-Realization Journal* also describes the author's initiatory transition from a devotee to a teacher of the higher life.

THE DIVINE IMAGE
A definitive book related to the Eternal Image of God in man.

THE PATH OF VIRTUE
A comprehensive book that describes the classic route to union with God traveled by all great souls of the East and the West.